KV-051-012

BOTHY

BOTHY

IN SEARCH OF SIMPLE SHELTER

KAT HILL

William Collins
An imprint of HarperCollins*Publishers*
1 London Bridge Street
London SE1 9GF

WilliamCollinsBooks.com

HarperCollins*Publishers*
Macken House
39/40 Mayor Street Upper
Dublin 1
D01 C9W8, Ireland

First published in Great Britain in 2024 by William Collins

1

A catalogue record for this book is available from the British Library

ISBN 978-0-00-861902-2

All images are authors own, except on the following pages: p.3 and p. 48, Images reproduced courtesy of the University of Dundee Archives and the DURC; p.18, Nicholas J. R. White © 2023; p.337 image reproduced with the permission of the Mountain Bothies Association.

Quote from 'Entirely' by Louis MacNeice, with permission from the Estate of Louis MacNeice, p.16; 'The Marriage of Psyche' by Kathleen Raine (Faber and Faber Ltd.), p.141; 'Love Spell' by Kathleen Raine (Faber and Faber Ltd.), p.141; *The Living Mountain* by Nan Shepherd © 2008, 2014. Extract reproduced with permission of the Licensor through PLSclear, Canongate Books Ltd. p.151; Gary Snyder, 'For the Children' extract from *Turtle Island*, copyright ©1974 by Gary Snyder. Reprinted by permission of New Directions Publishing Corp. p.334.

Sandy's Canoe at Peanmeanach © Nicholas J. R. White (endpapers)

Typeset in ITC Garamond LT by Palimpsest Book Production Ltd, Falkirk, Stirlingshire

Printed and Bound in the UK using 100% Renewable Electricity at CPI Group (UK) Ltd

For all those who agree with Callum's rule.

Contents

This map was created by my dad for this book.

PROLOGUE

If you have never been to a bothy, let me tell you what to expect. You will walk there most likely, to a basic cottage in the countryside, having left your car at some far-flung spot in the Scottish Highlands or perhaps near a mountain in Wales. It's almost a given you will have damp socks by the end of the walk, even if it's dry. You will have decided what to bring with you, what to leave at home, and you will live and die by your choices when you get there, regretting that you forgot that packet of food and cheering that you remembered the whisky. You will be on the lookout for signs of activity as you approach to see if anyone is home. You will say you want to meet people and will be happy if you do but may also be quite glad if you have the place to yourself. You will push open the door, holler a greeting, get a reply or not. You will see one, if not all, of the following:

- A stag's skull collected from the surrounding area and placed as a totemic guardian.

- Some candles, tins, books, maps, etc. left by previous visitors.

- A collection of gas canisters, some empty, some full.

- Coal/kindling/firelighters (if you are lucky).

- The bothy book, aka a visitor's register.

You will lay out your kit, light the fire, provided you have enough fuel. You will roll out your sleeping bag on the floor or sleeping platform, ready for when you want to crawl into bed and then you will decide what to do for the night without electricity, running water and a phone signal.

As the light dies you may step outside to stare up at the dark sky and the million stellar worlds above you, lulled to rest by wind or waves or wild sounds of the night.

And you'll find comfort in doing this every time, in similar but different ways, in different places, possibly alongside others doing the same.

A sketch from Corrour bothy book from 1943.

To those for whom the call of the outdoors is strong, few things are more appealing than a hut in the wild, removed from the stresses of modern life. And who among us hasn't talked about the desire to get away from it all? Bothies offer this in spades. They are basic mountain huts that provide shelter for walkers in the Scottish Highlands, Welsh mountains and English peaks free of charge, unbookable, and unlocked for any passer-by. They are simple structures, normally old farming buildings, stalking lodges or crofting cottages that sit in remote places, perhaps by a loch, or at the foot of a Munro. At best, they might have sleeping platforms, a working stove and a compostable toilet, at worst they are a simple room and four walls.

No one quite knows where the word 'bothy' first came

from, but it's probably a corruption of vernacular words for hut, the Irish *bothán* or Scottish Gaelic *bothag* or *bothan*. It might also come from 'booth', whose archaic form meant a temporary dwelling woven from boughs, or from words intertwined with the history of summer shielings.[1] In 1777, naturalist John Lightfoot described how a dairymaid would lay protective rowan above the door of the 'sheal boothy or summer-house' to which she had driven the herds for summertime pasture.[2] By the nineteenth century, bothy cottages referred to the accommodation built for single estate workers, young men, who sang bothy ballads on cold nights. Highland Clearances and changing land use saw many of these abandoned, but bothies have been reclaimed by hikers who roam the hills. The word 'bothy' now signifies not a rural home, but a free shelter from the wind and the rain. Versions of this are found all over the world. Wilderness huts in Scandinavian forests, the *autiotupa* of Finland, *Biwakschachtel* on German mountains, or Adirondack lean-tos in upstate New York. But the most famous incarnations are the bothies of the Scottish Highlands.

It's a rough kind of shelter that the bothy provides but one I have come to love. Four years ago, I didn't know much about bothies, although I was familiar with a few popular-culture references to them. I have a vivid memory of watching the film *Under the Skin* on a cold, dark December evening in my house in Oxford and feeling unsettled, joyless. Partly because of the movie, but also because I knew it was a disconsolate time in my life as my marriage began to fracture. Towards the end of the movie, Scarlett Johansson, playing an alien in human form, shelters in a bothy near Loch Lomond. I watched the scene and vaguely clocked the cabin in the woods, but little could I have guessed that bothies would provide me with a kind of shelter as I navigated the complicated path away from a life that was making me unhappy.

For many years bothies have been providing respite for people. The place of bothies in walking culture was formalised after World War II as more and more people took to the mountains for leisure and for a break from their working lives. The bothy movement grew out of the increasing desire to get out into the hills that characterised parts of the twentieth-century tourism industry. The appeal of Scotland's romantic landscape was already well established, but travel to the glens and mountains was initially the preserve of the rich. As travel became cheaper, it was possible for more people to get away from the grime and noise of the city. Dilapidated, run-down and empty cottages or shooting lodges had long been used for shelter by hikers, but many were falling into ruin. The Mountain Bothies Association (MBA), the charitable organisation that has become the custodian of many bothies, was formed by men and women who wanted to preserve these places for future generations, and in the later 1960s they began to renovate and look after the crumbling buildings.

Tunkseen was Bothy Number 1. In the summer of 1965, as short nights stretched over the dark skies of Galloway in southern Scotland, Bernard Heath and friends gathered at Tunskeen. Bernard, the son of an engineers' tool inspector and a tailor from Yorkshire, loved to roam the mountains with his friend Frank Goodwin, and they often made use of bothies and huts. The old farmhouse, Tunskeen, had fallen into disuse as a home in May 1939 but had been a makeshift shelter for hikers ever since. Wanting to maintain it for those to come, Heath and company made the abandoned home a useable refuge and out of this grew the MBA, Tunskeen its first official project.[3] A few months later forty or so people gathered in the Scout Hut and then in the Town Hall in Dalmellington, paid a 5-shilling sub, and drew up some rules.[4] Thus, the MBA and its code of rules was born, although they were a little more informal at this point. And here Bernard met a woman called Betty (short for Elizabeth) Taylor, starting a love affair that was to last their whole life. She was from a different world, educated at Wycombe Abbey and great-granddaughter of Johnnie Walker, but they shared a love of huts and hiking. Known lovingly as B&B to the bothy world, they married in 1970, and their relationship was always intertwined with the MBA and an enjoyment of outdoor adventures.[5]

There are now around 100 bothies in England, Wales and Scotland made habitable by the MBA, which is staffed by volunteers and funded by members, as well as several non-MBA and unofficial bothies. As an organisation, the MBA formalised what had long been common practice – finding places of shelter for those who wanted to get out into the mountains. From these humble beginnings, bothying has evolved into a favoured pastime for keen walkers in the Highlands and beyond. It's a passionate community that thrives on fellowship, walking, songs and a love of mountains, but also has its fair share of conflicts.

This community is also growing. Bothies used to be a

fairly well-kept secret, but in recent years the passion for bothying has exploded. Guides, blogs and a book known as *The Scottish Bothy Bible,* written by Geoff Allan, have made them more and more accessible, much to the disappointment of some traditionalists.[6] The *Bothy Bible* was published with the OK of the MBA and is a travel guide of sorts for anyone wanting to have a go at bothying, with details of routes, access, water and firewood sources and short histories of each bothy. No longer do you have to plot coordinates on a map, possibly acquired by word of mouth. You can simply put the name of your bothy into a mapping app. They still sit in wild, beautiful, windswept locations surrounded by nature, embedded in landscapes with deep pasts, but modernity increasingly impinges on this wildness and the bothies themselves.

Bothies intrigued me immediately. I wondered what bound this community that cares about and for a particular place, who seem to reject the shackles of modernity for a moment and who are entangled with questions about humanity's relationship to wilderness and the non-human world.

You might like the idea of shelter that the bothy provides or you might not. But we've all needed shelter some time from rain or wind, from the dark, or from stress, from arguments at home, or a job you hate. For me, bothies were intertwined with finding a space for myself again in my life and career. In the small, enclosed comfort they provide, they gave me respite from more than the weather.

I thought, perhaps like a lot of people at 30, that I had it all sorted. Out of the ups and downs of my twenties, I was in a successful permanent academic job as a historian of sixteenth- and seventeenth-century Europe, I was married, I owned a house with a garden, I had and still have a loving family – three wonderful siblings who are always there, and caring, encouraging, gentle parents – and I had a hobby that I adored which took me all over the world to compete. Brazilian jiu-jitsu, by the way, if you are interested.

But then everything went pear-shaped. Things started to crumble as I commuted from Oxford, where we lived, to Norwich, where I worked. Exhausted, uncertain and cramped by the vision of domestic life that stretched before me, cracks appeared. And one day on the train back from Norwich, I decided I couldn't go back to the home I shared with my husband. What followed was a tumultuous decade. It included wonderful things – travelling to amazing cities, martial arts titles around the world, new friends, academic success. But it also was a time of divorce, heartbreak, depression and dislocation. The refuge I sought after I left my husband was into the arms of a narcissistic partner where there was no comfort to be found. I sought rest in being too busy and filling my head with the noise of competing, working and achieving. I sought shelter by running away, and I have moved fourteen times in eight and half years. My respite, too, was hurting myself, and the scars I bear will for ever be pale silver reminders of that time. But with every attempted escape, I failed again and again to break free from a toxic, damaging relationship that broke me down a little bit more each day we were together. All the while I had the nagging, unshakeable, guilty knowledge that the work I was doing and the life I was living were never going to make me happy.

And then I found bothies. As the new decade dawned, I ventured out into the Scottish landscape and sought shelter in four simple walls. Over the coming few years I would go back again and again to places in the mountains and by the coast, and following my nose as a historian, I was delighted to be digging into the archival record. I searched for records, reports, any documentary traces. In simple huts and hideouts, I read about these stories from the past and made my own.

I don't want to give the impression I went on one bothy trip to Scotland, found the wild and it set the world to rights. Life is rarely that neat, and it is unfair to expect that landscapes can suddenly heal us in those dramatic ways that we sometimes demand. But I am also surprised how quickly things can change and how life can shift. We felt that in terrible ways during Covid, when the world shut down and our accustomed methods of moving and making disappeared. But as I started to explore bothies, I found a place to talk about all those things that inspired my mind, a place to know the simple, warm company of people who liked me just as I was, a place to experience things I wanted, and a place to dream about what I might want the world to be like if I could wave a magic wand in a time of environmental crisis. I began to connect the fragments of the life that I desired, mismatched pieces that I had been gathering slowly but had never quite been able to fit together. It wasn't some immediate recovery, but in the small space of the bothy, every time I went, I began to put the bits together again.

Deep down I love bothies because of where they are, and because I wanted to connect with places and with the living world in ways that I couldn't quite remember by the time I was 30. I grew up in Shropshire, always out in fields and climbing trees, but my adult life for so long had been in cities, commuting on trains and pounding streets. Amidst rising dissatisfaction with the demands that academia was putting on me and my purpose in that career, as well as concern about how to respond to the challenges of the Anthropocene, I felt the need to do something 'environmental', though I didn't know what. After all, the stories we tell in the Anthropocene will shape the world to come, and as a historian, I had a sense of duty to engage with our environmental pasts, presents and futures. Somehow, I wanted to help build shared futures, shared stories. I toyed with starting teaching businesses that had something vaguely to do with nature, doing my biology A Level and running from the path I had chosen. In my spare time that didn't exist, I embarked on and completed an MA in Environmental Humanities. Before Covid hit, I was all set to write a field-changing book on Mennonites, non-conformist religious communities going back to early modern Europe but now most commonly associated with rural America. I had a massive grant to do so. But I turned it down.

Instead, I decided I wanted to write a book about bothies and the communities they create, in conversation with the environmental challenges our contemporary world faces. Bothies lured me in, and they are often in undeniably beautiful places. Many people are drawn to them by that sense of wild escape. But wilderness is a controversial ideal in environmentalism, a utopia. No places in the world remain untouched by human impact. Critics of the term argue it promotes an unrealistic idea about visions for the wild, and it places humans outside the natural world, as observers of wilderness. I was intrigued by bothies too because they hint at the conflict between our desire to preserve something isolated and wanting to encourage a love of those places through visiting. It is not lost on me that I raise questions about the commercialisation of the wild, but this is itself a commercial book. Instagram and social media are filled with problematic and overly romantic visions of remoteness, and yet there's no denying that bothies are often in simply stunning places. To be able to hold this truth while not idealising places that are living, working landscapes is important. We need to discuss what this tension means, and how we might usefully engage with the love of wild places, how we go about living with and in nature. The bothy community idealises the wild at times, but it also creates connection in a world that laments the destruction of nature and growing disconnection.

Some people feel that pull of the outdoors keenly amidst the pace of the modern world, and they seek retreat from its noisy demands. I know the apparent simplicity of everything you do in a bothy made me feel at peace. My particular anxiety comes from rejection or silent treatment, the legacy of a destructive relationship, so being out of signal or, indeed, interacting with people who you may never know again feels oddly soothing to me. I remember distinctly how I sought a respite from the stresses of life, as so many bothiers do. That sense of walking away from the world into the wild draws together this community of bothy dwellers. So many of us have felt that instinct to escape from modernity, even if just for a moment. I don't want to idealise the bothy life and the desire for retreat as a solution to all ills. But bothy culture allows us to examine the appeal and value of a simpler way of being, as well as the problems it throws up. It says something about the contemporary world that we want to get away from it, that we feel we gain by losing something, by replacing driving with walking, WhatsApp with talking, even when we indulge in romantic, nostalgic views of a simpler past.

It also might seem a little odd to seek shelter in damp, old cottages. Bothying is quite a peculiar activity, and it draws in particular people, but in that shared oddness is community. The comfort of people and community matters for so many people in these small spaces, as it mattered for me. I remember stopping off once in a café in north Edinburgh, and I noticed the *Bothy Bible* sitting on the side.

'Are you bothy fans?' I asked the young woman behind the counter, who was running her hand under cold water after scalding it making coffee.

She said the book was the owner's, and she'd done a few, with them and with friends. Jura was next on her list, with some hikes thrown in.

We chatted about the pros and cons, the best times of year (she said February/March and October/November, as it was quieter) and what happens when it all goes tits up, as it often does.

'Still, it's great craic!' she said.

I nodded in agreement.

Community is something we all seek but sometimes fail to find, and bothies allow an exploration of what it is that binds people together. Songs, stories and legends grow up around bothies. They are restored by many hands, and some have been renovated in memory of people (Hutchison Memorial Hut in Coire Etchachan was built in honour of Arthur Gilbertson Hutchison who died in a climbing accident in 1949). They become places for fellowship and kindness, with conversations over fires or messages in bothy books. We all crave human connection in some way. We scan social media apps, pack into bars, chatter endlessly, but yet so often feel alone in the emptiness of a blank city. Or maybe that's just me. But out here, in relative isolation, that loneliness seemed to melt away. Wanderers brought together find a sense of community which makes you feel at ease even when you are meeting for the first time. Yet there are also plenty of arguments and conflict too about how to behave, what to bring and what proper bothying looks like. There's a formal MBA code of responsible use but also more informal rules about behaviour – it's debatable whether playing music on your phone is in the spirit of a bothy, for example. Bothies also seem to offer equality of access to the outdoors, as these are free, open spaces, but seen critically, the traditional bothy with its stripped-back outdoor aesthetic can often feel masculine and exclusionary, with an emphasis on macho feats of daring-do. Simply put, more men than women use bothies, certainly when doing it alone. I never felt unwelcome or unsafe, but I sometimes encountered surprised faces if I turned up at a bothy by myself. There are also very few people of colour who use bothies, a problem that extends to access to nature and the outdoor world more broadly. I may be a woman in a masculine world, but I speak as a middle-class white visitor and with all the privilege that brings. Bothying offers only one idea of simple or sustainable living that can reinforce a problematic notion of the wilderness. And the communities who use bothies and the land they sit on often disagree with one another.

These places, the people and the landscape are at the heart of this book. It is their story, not mine really. I move through them and explore, but this experience may be different for you – I hope it is. It would be a boring world if we all did things in the same way. On the journey, you will meet many characters who come and go: my good friends, bothy visitors past and present, animals and birds, the rocks and rivers, and of course the bothies themselves.

These huts reveal the potential and problems that surround humanity's relationship with place and the living world. Bothies are built around a critique of modernity and a love of landscapes, and respond, knowingly and unknowingly, to questions of environmental change, calls for sustainable living, and debates over land use. The bothy ethos comes with its own troubles. Yet in that debate, in the spaces between understandings and misunderstandings, there is a hopeful future. Popularity and awareness of places do not have to result in commercialisation and destruction, and if we want to build futures where more people care about preserving places, we need people to have an engaged, critical, nurturing relationship with those environments. As somewhere set aside from the conventional rhythm of the contemporary world, perhaps the bothy allows a space for exploring this.

As for my part in this, I am the new generation of bothier. I even have a copy of the *Bothy Bible*. I haven't been doing it for years as some people have, I am a good hiker but not an outdoor expert, nor a Munroist (A Munro, in case you don't know, and I didn't at first, is a mountain in Scotland over 914.4 m.) I am never entirely sure if I have all the right gear (although, who is ever sure?). And though I love bothies, I wouldn't call myself a hardcore bothier deep in the inner fold. I haven't done enough, although I don't really know what number counts as enough, and, much to my shame, have done very few in tough, winter conditions and suffered for the privilege of sitting in front of a fire. Covid lockdowns made escapes over difficult winters impossible, and even when we could travel again, my work schedule as an academic - working up until almost Christmas, marking over the break, researching furiously and returning early in January - has never allowed a decent winter trip. As any teacher knows, you also succumb to every illness possible as soon as the adrenaline-fuelled rush of the term disappears.

Bothies arrived in my life when I needed a sense of connection to people and place in a way which I was desperately missing. It would be the simplest thing in the world to say that this is a book about I how got up and walked away from my worries into the wild, into recovery. That I struggled through the pain of difficult journeys of mud and rain and mountain, and in the suffering steps found peace. That I came to rest in the rough refuge of the stone walls of a bothy. It would be simple, but it would also be misleading. Bothies offered me access to inspiring places, time to think, human warmth and encounters with non-human worlds. There was a way in which my focus and priorities shifted through these experiences, but it was not a Damascene revelation, rather a slow, gentle reorientation that is in keeping with bothies. When I look back, it makes sense, of course, that I found bothies, as stories always do when we tell them in reverse. It's never that simple, and accounts of suffering and shelter not so tidy. And anyway, I don't want this be a tale of sadness because it's not, it's one of hope.

Life is not one thing or the other, not purely up or entirely down. I found bothies as I was learning that the hard way, and as I processed the experience, I turned often to one of my favourite poems, Louis MacNeice's 'Entirely'. It ends:

> And if the world were black or white entirely
>   And all the charts were plain
> Instead of a mad weir of tigerish waters,
>   A prism of delight and pain,
> We might be surer where we wished to go
>   Or again we might be merely
> Bored but in brute reality there is no
>   Road that is right entirely.

The words make me consider a way of navigating the 'tigerish waters' of my own life, as well as our response in the current moment of change and environmental crisis. Both have to be able to contain hope and anxiety, loss and gain, fear and love. And I may not solve all the world's problems in the simple shelter of a hut, but it's one place to start.

ONE | CADDERLIE

Stories, Songs

It was the bothy books that got me really hooked. That and the idyllic location next to a beautiful loch. The joyous company. But it was a lot to do with the books. Perhaps it wasn't surprising: as a historian, I love a document. Battered and worn, some with pages ripped out, the books signed by bothy visitors and left in the buildings are a particular kind of archive. Standing in fresh morning air in Cadderlie bothy, I flicked through the stories on the pages. Little drawings. Poems. Short, factual records of the number of Munros 'bagged'. And bagging them, or getting to the top, is a big deal. Narratives of people at a particular time in a particular place. The bothy is a space that lets people tell tales out of the ordinary, of wild adventures, but also of simple pleasures and fellowship. I didn't know yet I wanted to write this book, so now I am kicking myself for not taking better notes on the Cadderlie entries or for snapping pics. It's the historian's impulse, I guess, to archive the archive. Yet I also quite like the fact I can only rely on fuzzy memories, probably idealised, but all the more enticing for the gaps they leave.

Cadderlie was the beginning of my bothy adventure, but it's been multiple things to different people, from a lovers' hideout to a working farm. Many histories and many meetings are braided around this one place. As I walked away from the bothy, I formulated a plan for more trips, more walks, a project on bothies and their archives. I mulled over the bothy books, and I imagined what stories we could tell of the people on those pages, of the landscape and the building, the loch and the burn, or even of the socks drying over the fire. What pungent tales might they reveal.

I rushed to find out all I could about these places with rich histories and wild environments. Here was the beginning of a story. My story. One among many.

Cadderlie's bothy book photographed on a return trip in 2023.

* * *

The journey started with a daring suggestion on a bright afternoon in Oxford, pretty far away from the Scottish Highlands. During a meet-up with friends on the scrubby grass of Port Meadow, Rich was regaling us with tales of a bothy trip he had made the previous year with a friend.

'Fancy coming next time?' he said.

'Of course!' I replied.

And so it began. A whirlwind initiation, and not long after, three of us were on our way to Cadderlie – Rich, me and Charlie. The excitement of adventure as I discovered bothies was all bound up with a time of happiness, promise and anxiety that I remember well as I finally began to free myself from the destructive relationship that had trapped me for so long. There's a strange paradox when it comes to experiences like this, living a life that you know is hurting you and is damaging. You think it would be easy to walk away when you realise that, but you get addicted to the cycle of the pain and the glory, especially with a narcissist. Yet at the beginning of this year something had shifted. I started exploring things for myself, I embarked on new relationships, and then Covid forced me to be removed from London and his presence, finally leaving me space to rebuild myself. Decamping to Bath from London with my friend Zofia, I prised myself away from weary rhythms of sadness, wrote poems about flowers and insects that were just for me, walked through the Somerset fields at dawn and dusk, and embarked on adventurous trips to mountains. As we rushed up to Scotland, I felt like a new page was being turned in my life.

Every bothy has its own story - the most remote, the secret one, the bothy with the best view, the oldest bothy, the tiniest bothy. This title goes to Grwyne Fawr, in the Black Mountains, situated by the reservoir of the same name. Also, incidentally, called 'the horrible bothy' by some because of its cramped conditions and rather grim walls.[1] Luibeilt bothy near Fort William, now a ruin, is supposed to be home to haunted horrors and uncanny happenings, so terrifying that two young men who visited in 1973 could not bear to stay until the morning.[2] We love a good tale. It's often said that we humans are storytelling creatures who seek to make meaning out of the tales we tell, not only in fictions or dramas, but in the stories we narrate to and about ourselves, whether in dreams or glossy commercials. As literary scholar Jonathan Gottschall writes, 'We may leave the nursery, with its toy trucks and dress-up clothes, but we never stop pretending.'[3] What's known as 'the narrative turn' has highlighted the power of stories in all forms of social research, campaigning, advocacy, business, politics and policy, and as a historian, I am familiar with the power of narrative that can include or obfuscate, that can make sense where there seems to be little.[4]

There's an essay I return to often that I remember encountering as an undergraduate, Hayden White's 'The Value of Narrativity in the Representation of Reality' in his book *The Content of the Form*. A historian and literary critic, White questions whether reality is truly represented in seemingly objective historical accounts. Discourses make sense not because they are an unmediated representation of reality but because they conform to moral and aesthetic frameworks that give them coherence. Events never just speak for themselves. What struck me most as an 18-year-old student was the list of dates that White presents from a medieval chronicle called the *Annals of Saint Gall*.[5] There seems to be no arc, no story in the bare list of dates, but even here there is a type of narrative: in the decision to count according to the Divine time of *Anni domini*, to record years even when the entry is empty, to rank violence and battles alongside floods and natural disasters as things that seem to happen to people rather than focusing on human agency. In the blankness and the flatness there is a narrative of prophetic unfolding.

Stories have power, but whose stories we tell, and how, matters, especially now in a time of environmental crisis and social conflict. What do we do with stories that are not human? How do we narrate deep-time narratives and global tales of climatic breakdown or ecological damage? How shall we tell narratives that are fragmentary, disparate or hidden? What do we do with narratives about our own lives when they seem to lack meaning or logic, and when we can't make sense of what's happened to us? I often struggle with this as I try to fit together the ways my own life has unfolded. But maybe that's why White's essay still speaks to me. I think what I liked most about it was the way it conjured the power of imagination to understand gaps and absence. We impose meaning, even in the face of apparent chaos. This can of course be dangerous, and we should be wary of the fictive creations or stories that just reinforce the hierarchies or harm of our world.

But I am convinced too that the way we tell stories about our pasts, presents and futures and about living worlds is central to how we meet the complex crises of our time, which often seem to defy understanding. Reality is real but we cannot comprehend it fully, know it fully. The more we try to approach it, the more it recedes from view. Climate change is what philosopher Timothy Morton calls a 'hyperobject', something distributed in vast ways across time and space, and which we can't quite grasp in its totality.[6] We only see its footprints. We may know ecological catastrophe is at hand, but we struggle to believe it will truly occur. Philosopher Slavoj Žižek talks about this paradoxical gap between knowledge and belief, and this applies to individuals as well as cultures.[7] On a personal level I may *know* that I have not failed or messed up, but I don't always *feel* that way. It's the stories we are telling that create these truths. So, imagination and empathy must shape our responses as we face crises – personal and societal – if we are to truly believe and feel what we think we know about the world, about others or about ourselves.

After driving across to Glencoe from Edinburgh, we spend the morning racing up one of the most iconic Munros in Scotland, rising through the rain and mist that shrouds Buachaille Etive Mòr. Lunch is a hasty affair beneath the wet, pale sun breaking through clouds that illuminate the flat emptiness of Rannoch Moor. The peak is its shepherd. Huddling in a bowl of stone at the top of the mountain, I soon forget the wind and cold as I munch on oatcakes and a cereal bar. We carry on to the shores of Loch Etive, park up the car and eagerly set off. I am a novice, and it is only Rich and Charlie's second bothy trip, but we feel fully prepared for the bothy with stove, kit, pans, lighters, wood and rations. As we start our walk along the edge of the loch, are bodies are beginning to feel our earlier exertions, but excitement at seeing my first bothy overrides any aches or pains.

Cadderlie's stories are many and varied. It lies on the shores of Loch Etive, a sea loch that stretches almost 32 km from its head at Gualachulain to the sea at Connel. Here, the Falls of Lora rise every year, white crests of water swirling in a race that forms when the spring tides rush through the mouth of the loch. Scholar and folklorist John Francis Campbell said you could hear them roar even 19 km away on the Isle of Lismore.[8] The bothy building goes back only 100 years, but a rich history of settlement and community stretches much further. Cadderlie has been the setting for tales of monks and clan leaders, farmers and hikers.

You could tell how it offered sanctuary for Deirdre, the tragic protagonist drawn from the canon of Irish legends known as the Ulster Cycle. She fled Ireland with the three sons of Uisneach, one her beloved, running from a king who wished them dead and from a fate that followed her.[9]

You perhaps would have encountered Robert the Bruce who, so rumour told, laid his head here after the Battle of the Pass of Brander in 1308.[10]

You could imagine the pilgrims who rested here, long before wet, weary hikers sought out the bothy. A further 12 km up the coast of the loch lie the ruins of Ardchattan

Priory. Almost 800 years ago, monks of the now obsolete Valliscaulian order retreated into the quiet of the sanctuary built by Duncan MacDougall.[11] From 1230 until 1602, when the Protestant Reformation brought an end to their community, the monks lived a life of strict simplicity, housed in small cells, without possessions, keeping no sheep, farming no crops, devoted only to God.[12]

You might tell of the farmers who once lived in the hamlet or *clachan* of Cadderlie from the sixteenth century onwards after it was sold to the Campbells, tenant farmers such as the MacIntyres, MacLeans and MacColls. The area was profitable agricultural territory for Clan Campbell for 500 years. On the land, cattle grazed, always a tempting target for rustlers. On the water, the Loch Etive Trading Co., essentially a Campbell smuggling operation, moved tobacco and other luxury goods along the west coast.[13]

Perhaps in the nineteenth century, you could have stopped off on a tour of the Highlands, alongside travellers like William and Dorothy Wordsworth, Romantics who produced effusive accounts of the wild beauty of a land whose 'poorest huts are halls'.[14] Their words have shaped popular imaginations of the Highlands ever since. Not far from the small hamlet was the busy ferry crossing at Bonawe. You might have stood on the shore with Dorothy as she boarded a vessel following the ferryboat to the head of the River Awe. It was conveying a collection of men and women whom she described unsympathetically as 'obstinate beggars'. A romantic sight, she commented, although their 'smutty faces and tinker equipage serve chiefly for a passport to a free and careless life'.[15]

By 1930, you would tell the story of a community that was dying, fading. The buildings started to crumble as people left in search of new lives, with only one structure still roofed and habitable. Finally, in 1948 Cadderlie was abandoned as a permanent home, though the present bothy provided shelter for journeying shepherds and artists.[16]

And in 1994, when it was taken over by the Mountain Bothies Association, you might have written your own story in a bothy book.

But not all Cadderlie's stories are human ones.

It sits beside waters that are home to otters and seals, as well as elasmobranchs (a subclass consisting of cartilaginous fish) such as spurdog sharks. These aquatic predators have the typical submarine snout and wide, dead-eyed stare of all sharks. Slow to reproduce and long-lived, spurdog are vulnerable to overfishing and are listed as Vulnerable on the International Union for Conservation of Nature (IUCN) Red List.[17] They swim alongside salmon, trout and a wide variety of shellfish that attract migrating birds. Below the loch's mirror-like surface, benthic worlds support diverse organisms which can withstand the pressure of the water stacked above them.[18] Cadderlie's four walls are nestled into a band of ancient sessile oaks and birch, and the woods around the loch are full of ash and rowan, with an understorey of hazel. The branches and rocks drip with bryophytes (specifically mosses, liverworts and hornworts that absorb water and nutrients from the air) and other epiphytes (plants or organisms such as lichen that grow on the surface of other plants or objects). They thrive in a bioclimatic zone favourable to the temperate rainforests that once existed in large swathes across the UK.[19]

Cadderlie is on the shores of a loch channelled out by glaciers as they retreated from Scotland, a geological footprint left in the Earth's crust. Pumice that spewed from volcanoes forms the walls of the loch at its western limit, giving way to steely granite ramparts to the east. Cadderlie itself is on a minor fault line, molten rock bubbling below. The creep of the Earth's crust pushed out fingers of rock to form the mountains of Ben Starav and Ben Cruachan at the head of Loch Etive. Cooling magma became trapped on its slow rise to the surface, working according to timescales that are slower, deeper and stranger than those of human existence.[20] It's an entangled, living world of rock, water and green, but everywhere with the telltale imprint of human activity. As we set out on the path to the bothy, it is an unpromising start for a journey into wilderness. Slag heaps belonging to the Bonawe Quarry tower in charcoal and ashen grey mounds.[21] The mined innards of the mountains are being mixed into concrete and asphalt to pave the city streets.

A low-slung, dark building rises out of the grey-green fog of the lochside as the roar of the Cadderlie burn rings in our ears. A column of smoke meanders from the chimney as we approach, packs on our backs, legs heavy from a day of hiking, our feet sticking in the cloying mud. The signs of habitation mean we are not the first to enter the bothy that evening. Some apprehension and excitement accompany our steps to the door. We won't be alone, and we are about to enter the community of fellow travellers who call the little cottage home for the night. Pushing the door as Rich yells hello, we cross the threshold, past the leering stag skull placed there like a ghoulish bouncer.

The windows glow with the steam of warmth against cold panes. The sounds are those of the crackling flames, roaring winds and water, and the musty smell of damp wood and drying clothes fills our nostrils. There are already six people in the traditional but and ben bothy (the name for a two-chamber dwelling with an inner and outer room). A welcoming group who offer firewood and greetings, they are also kind and considerate and leave our group to the privacy of the but.

The men and women do not all know each other but are strangers thrown together in sojourn who now gather in happy communion around a fire with music, dogs and song. Half-glimpsed faces emerge from the flames and twilight, like the indistinct visage of Christ in Rembrandt's first depiction of His appearance to two disciples on the road to Emmaus. In the half-light of the flickering candles, the men do not recognise their resurrected Saviour until He breaks the bread over the table.[22] I'm not religious, but this biblical tale has always appealed to me. There's something comforting about the way in which journeys are often filled with chance encounters of recognition and fellowship, of welcome in places you don't expect if you look past the shadows.

A temporary interloper into the Highlands, I am now a very small part of Cadderlie's story and it's part of mine. As soon as I returned from my expedition, I was eager to recall every moment of the journey to friends and family. Dramatic details were expanded in the slippery process of recollection as I elaborated or romanticised. Recounting tales of the bothy experience is part of the deal. Bothies are deeply embedded in a narrative culture of stories told and retold, round fires, in pubs and on blogs. And these stories mean something. Stories are what make us care, impel us to act, cause us to speak up. They create connections between people and places, and across time. We pass meaning across generations through retelling collective remembrances of pasts we could never know ourselves. Stories that we are yet to finish allow us to envision the futures we want to create.

That first night in Cadderlie, our neighbouring occupants have brought instruments, accompanying the dying light of the fire in the bothy with song. They are no Gaelic bards, but the jaunts are merry. Songs are one of the oldest forms of communal storytelling, a way of recording histories, recounting memories and myths, and brightening dark nights with the sounds of fellowship. Many of the great heroic legends, from the *Song of Roland,* an eleventh-century Frankish epic poem, to the German saga the *Nibelungenlied*, would have been told in verses and melodies, passed down by word of mouth. Virgil's *Aeneid* opens with the famous line 'I sing of arms and the man'.

In Gaelic history, perhaps the most famous bard is Ossian. He is also an imaginative fiction who sprung from the head of James Macpherson in the eighteenth century. Macpherson probably preserved real fragments of Gaelic oral culture, but then attributed them to the mythical blind bard, to give his stories credit and to imitate the epic tradition of Homer. Made-up though he may be, Ossian's popularity was widespread, the poems and verses published by Macpherson in the 1760s sparking a Romantic revival.[23]

There's a link with Cadderlie too. One poem in *Fingal,* a cycle published in 1761 telling of the eponymous noble warrior, describes a conflict on the shores of Loch Etive. *The Battle of Lora* narrates how the Scandinavian King Erragon was slain by the Gaul Morni at the Battle of Lora.[24] Macpherson was probably imagining a scene beside the tidal waters of Etive. In 1801 François Gérard's oil painting of the bard conjuring spirits captured Ossian in a moment of intense passion. His eyes are downturned, fingers straining at the strings of his harp, while a host of ethereal beings bathed in a green glow like quicklime gather on the banks.[25] Churning waters below could very well be the Falls of Lora. The places of the Fingal legends were associated with Loch Etive, and Ossian is now part of the cultural geography of the place. Take a walk across the Moss of Achnacree and you will see a collection of burial cairns, one named Ossian's Cairn, which was excavated by R. Angus Smith in 1871.[26] There's also Ossian's Cave in Glencoe, and if you had visited Loch Etive in the nineteenth century, you could have enjoyed the view from the comfort of a luxury saloon steamer named *Ossian*. With the pride typical of the Victorians when it came to feats of engineering, the *Scotsman* reported that she was 'built of iron, is 121 feet in length, 16 feet in breadth, and 9 feet depth of hold, and is to be fitted with engines of 150 horse-power'.[27]

Through reconstructed fragments, Macpherson conjured a lone male genius in place of stories that were told by ordinary people, men and women whose voices were recorded by other collectors such as John Francis Campbell but who are often hidden in grand epics. Tales told in the songs of working labourers are intertwined with the history of bothies. When young men working on landed estates lived in the bothy buildings attached to farms, the nineteenth-century bothy ballad emerged as a distinct style, although it has become most closely associated with Aberdeenshire rather than the Northwest Highlands. Satirical lines reflect upon the labours and loves of farm-workers. They would not have been written down, as is so often the way with popular refrains, but sung to known tunes on pipe and fiddle. Bothies were spaces that brought men together where they could narrate their worlds.[28] Altogether humbler than the epics of the Romantics, the ballads tell of a different type of relationship with the land, a different type of belonging. The Ossian poems were central to the eighteenth-century idealisation of place; the bothy ballads were part of a popular culture of work and masculinity on the farmed land.

Laughter resounds and friendships are forged in Cadderlie the night we are there. Song is a way of drawing people closer because it's easy to do together. You can sing something you know or set new words to a familiar melody, an easy rhythm that allows others to join in. In 2000 a few members of the Dundee University Rucksack Club (DURC) collected songs they had sung together on trips of adventure into an informal 'bothy songbook'. A long-standing student group, the DURC was formed in 1923 to 'further the interests of the members in all matters appertaining to mountaineering, hill climbing, camping, tramping and similar open-air past times'.[29] Tunes old and new are in the DURC songbook, now housed in the archive at the University of Dundee.[30] It recollects nights 'singing and rejoicing', encouraging readers to hope that 'your beards never grow short and your wits never run dry (or your hip flasks too)', and it's a book made through collaboration and sharing. Mixed in are folk classics, typical end-of-the-night songs, Monty Python verses, Gaelic melodies and tunes that evoke the love of the wild and wandering in other places. Only the lyrics appear on the page, but that's generally all that's needed as I try to make out the soundscape of a DURC bothy night, though a few tunes are less familiar. The absence of notes is a reminder that these are songs that live in memory and people. I can imagine the DURC members sitting together and raising a song, sharing tales, swapping quotes.

As we fall asleep in Cadderlie after our sodden journey, we can hear the sounds of merriment from the ben. It is a comforting murmur against the backdrop of the wind and rain that has slowly grown in intensity.

The next morning, pushing open the door to let in the morning drizzle, we are greeted by scrabbling footsteps as an excited pug careens into the room. The owner soon follows, Bothy Jim, who is keen to know why we have come and to share his story as an experienced bothier. If you go to a bothy and meet fellow travellers, you will almost inevitably be asked a little bit about who you are and how you got there.

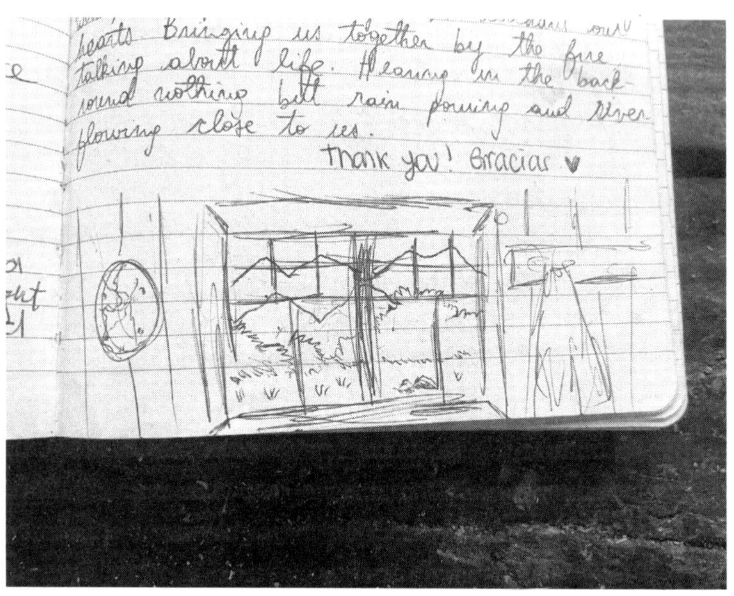

Extract from the 2023 Cadderlie bothy book.

Modern bothy visitors to Cadderlie might not have tales to tell of kings, war and exiled love, but they share accounts of daring feats or of the simple pleasures of walking. On the blank pages of bothy books, ordinary men and women dramatise their adventures. Sometimes it's done with humour, such as someone's sketch of imagined renovations for Corrour bothy as a gigantic castle. (This famous bothy, situated along the Lairig Ghru pass in the Cairngorms, has been in use for decades and the archived books which date back to the 1920s are particularly rich.) Sometimes there's pretension. One man who visited Corrour in 1948,

Leslie B. Bartlett, provided smatterings of Gerard Manley Hopkins and the *Rubáiyát of Omar Khayyám* in his entries.[31] People write themselves into specific locations, and as they take pen to paper, they become connected to a wider world of travellers and wilderness huts.

People compose these stories for themselves, but also for others. The entries in a bothy book are meant to be read, although you don't know by whom. In the summer of 1928, a poem, 'In Memoriam', was scribbled into the Corrour book. We don't know the author: the sign-off at the bottom is merely 'By Gone Before'. Our author addresses anyone who happens to come upon this 'Home of Peace and Light' and tells the fable-like tale of three travellers – a sentimental clerk, a doleful chemist, and a student – who find shelter in the bothy. Three faint little pencil figures march across the opposite page, tracing ghostly tracks. The author (the student) nodded to future visitors, wishing them well.

> Now therefore think, when passing by,
> Of we three who, until we die;
> Will think with tenderest thoughts and pure,
> Of our sojourn in fair Corrour.[32]

Like the anonymous poet of these lines, when you write on those damp pages, you lose ownership of the words. It's a given that they will become entertainment for countless future readers on cold bothy nights, so make them good. James Cunningham from Birmingham, after a lengthy entry in the Corrour book in 1939, signed off with 'Cheerio my public'.[33]

Whether turning the page in a dark bothy after a wet walk or carefully leafing through volumes left in bothies a hundred years ago and now in archives, I love the books. I think it's the way that they try to capture fleeting memories and ephemeral encounters. You come to a bothy for a moment but you don't stay, and yet there's a desire to immortalise that time on the page. Just as you get only little snapshots of people in bothies, you only get little snippets in these notes. Like any archive record, it is only a fragment of these lives or the bothy experience, recorded in decayed books that are damp and fragile. I am particularly fond of tiny, marginal drawings that people do, sketched with a few hasty strokes. In 1929, four visitors to Corrour from Inverey have drawn themselves as tiny stick figures dancing across the page in joy.[34] And these are stories often hidden in other archives of working-class lives, those who were part of the 'proletarian revolution' of hillwalking.[35] They recorded their hopes, fears and loves, for themselves but also for others.

Storytelling is not a private act. Even though we might think of reading as a reverie of quiet isolation, that's a modern understanding. We have always shared stories, whether on the page or through conversations and songs, and that sharing is a moment of participation in a community. From bothy books I have picked up countless poems and quotes from Robert Burns to T. S. Eliot, from American poet Gary Snyder to Scottish naturalist Seton Gordon, as well as rude limericks and funny/unfunny jokes. The bothies inhabit a world of storytelling, interlaced with literature and knowledge, not claimed for anyone, but shared. In the process of retelling tales, overlaying old stories with new, borrowing magpie-like, we produce and recreate the meanings landscapes hold for us in our own memories and in our communities. We tell stories of places entangled with pasts and people.

It was easy for me to sketch out my experience of Cadderlie in a way that resonated with romantic, mythic pasts. I hold close the moments of tender interaction in the shadows of Cadderlie bothy and the flicker of firelight. Preparing a simple meal, warming by the hearth, lovers, friends or family sleeping close and nestling closer as the flames die and the wet and the cold creep in. But Cadderlie's story of paramours, of exiled lovers Deirdre and Naoise, stretches back to a time long before the bothy, before severe Presbyterian churches and shelters for hikers scattered the landscape of the Highlands.

Deirdre of the Sorrows is an archetypal tragic heroine whose beauty was her undoing. She was the daughter of Felimid the Harper, a man of the Red Branch who dared to ask the druid Cathbad about his child's future. Like Helen of Troy, the fair face of the infant was destined to cause war and division, and she was hidden away in a high tower, fated to marry Conchobar, King of Ulster. But she fell in love with Naoise, one of three sons of Uisneach, and the couple fled east to Scotland, along with his brothers Ardan and Ainle. The lakes and mountains of Scotland provided them with shelter and joy. Deirdre of the Sorrows' story would not be a happily ever after, however. Conchobar tracks down the lovers. Naoise is killed, Deirdre forced to marry Conchobar, then given to Naoise's killer. In the end, she throws herself from a chariot onto sharp rocks below.

We feel that Deirdre's story has been told a thousand times, in a thousand other ways, and yet is painfully unique, as is the way of any good legend. The Ulster Cycle was a tale told over many centuries, and the Deirdre myth has had many incarnations, as romantic novels, a play by W. B. Yeats, and in modern songs.[36] The mournful narrative seems to fit perfectly with the wind and rain that whips around the bothy, and it's only added to the imagination of Cadderlie as a wild refuge for those who visit, though it's associated with the happier times of the lovers' legend. Cadderlie's name probably comes from the Gaelic for 'the Burn at Deirdre's Garden'.[37] Cadderlie's legend of Erin's fair daughter is itself a type of loss, not just her loss and sorrow, but an echo of the language and legends of an older world.

I would like to say I meditate on Deirdre as I wander for a morning stroll by the burn, a patchwork of churning eddies flowing between moss-tufted rocks and mirror-glass pools. But I don't know it yet, so instead I brush my teeth, bathe with paraben-free lavender soap, and play on the rope swing, thinking of little more than the berries that livened up the morning porridge. Only later, as I archived the memory and I researched, did my own past become intertwined with these older tales. In later life, Yeats derided his younger self, who had made his 'song a coat/Covered with embroideries/Out of old mythologies.'[38] But that's what we all do. Perhaps the power of your own story in a landscape is the way in which you interlace it with others, with past and present meanings.

As we leave our parking spot near Bonawe Quarry, we follow the coastal path, winding past bottle-green leaves and slate sea on gleaming roads, and Charlie whacks on our road-trip playlist. We have been listening to a fair bit of folk music, old and new, and anything reminiscent of Scotland, from Bruch to Bert Jansch. He scrolls through and puts on Dougie MacLean. The Scottish singer-songwriter immortalised Cadderlie in his deep, rasping tones. MacLean came from the area and his haunting ballad *Eternity* evokes love and loss in the landscape at the edge of the sea loch, the burn rushing by. We certainly weren't the only ones to relive Cadderlie through MacLean's song or riff on his words to recall our experience.[39] It seems fitting that the DURC songbook includes MacLean's most famous song, *Caledonia*. The refrain echoes a familiar sentiment about telling tales of home and homesickness.

Sediments of time and meaning are stacked on top of one another as people constantly narrate and re-narrate the places that they dwell in. Past meanings fade but don't disappear entirely. The process of perpetual transformation and meaning being made is what anthropologist Tim Ingold calls the 'temporality of the landscape'. We shape places, yet they also shape us, because landscapes are never just empty backdrops.[40] They have power to draw people together in imagined communities. When you see a bothy it's hard not to conjure up a story of dramatic wilderness drawn from any number of past tales and possibly personal experiences, but also inspired by the high peaks, the clear lochs and the empty moors.

* * *

There's also a problem, however, one that kept needling at me as I travelled, researched and wrote. I loved the landscapes I saw but it wasn't my home, it wasn't my past or heritage. The way I saw them was influenced by all sorts of stereotypes. As I approached Cadderlie, my view of it came with the baggage of every film I had seen or book I had read about Scotland. These cultural spectres colour our perceptions, even when we don't always know it consciously. Whether it's the romantic literature that constructed legends about the Highlands, paintings like Edwin Landseer's *The Monarch of the Glen*, or even the romps of *Outlander*, there are all sorts of ways in which the Scottish landscape features in popular imaginations. The wistful longing for wild places and fabled pasts is harmless for the most part. But that desire for tradition can also distort and do damage. The much-loved moors of purple heather and green glens, empty of people, are the result of changing land use and the Clearances, the period of forced movement of rural populations of the Highlands and Islands from 1750 to the mid-nineteenth century. In the name of agricultural improvement, people were driven out to make way for large-scale pastoral farms. By the nineteenth century this involved 'assisted passages, as landlords paid for tenants to emigrate across the Atlantic'.[41]

Contemporary romanticisation of Scotland often characterises the post-Clearances landscapes as empty wildernesses. It doesn't recognise the lived past of these spaces, whose depopulation was the result of violence, nor help us imagine what the landscape would have been like before sheep farming or driven grouse shooting predominated. Without always knowing it, the way we see places can bring about narrative erasures of both human and non-human worlds. As a woman travelling up from the south of England, I was aware that there's also a long tradition of the problematic idealisation of the Highlands by those who never lived there as wild, traditional, idyllic and, in the case of past British rulers, also undeveloped and in need of improvement. The outsider's gaze, mine as much as anyone's, can be troublesome, sometimes destructive. After all, the stories we tell are never neutral.

The yearning for an idyllic, pastoral memory of the land can be conservative, exclusionary, even racially and nationally charged. But there are ways of looking back that can tell different stories, whether that's recovering the living histories of bothies that dropped out of use, the landscapes, the working-class lives of bothiers, or the layers of meaning written into Gaelic names for the landscape, names such as Creag a' Mhadaidh or Wolfcrag.[42] There are, of course, no wolves there anymore. The famous anthropologist Keith H. Basso, who spent time with the Western Apache in the United States, noted down the words of Charles, an Apache leader who said of the place-worlds of their ancestors, 'The names do not lie . . . they show what is different and what is still the same.'[43]

In the fight for action over ecological and environmental crisis, the stories that people craft about pasts have an important role to play. Folk singer and environmentalist Sam Lee uses the tales and cadences of folk music to think about what we have lost and what we might rediscover through collecting songs. His work is a call to action, asking us to reimagine our relationship with the land as a living place.[44] Over a sweltering June weekend, I went on his Sussex 'pilgrimage' that returns to the land an iconic folk melody about the turtle dove, first recorded in Rusper in 1907 on wax cylinders. We learned the song, finishing our journey by singing it on the rewilded Knepp Estate in dawn light. From the mists, the turtle doves echoed our singing, but it may not be long before the call goes unanswered. This is the fastest-declining bird in the UK.[45] Walking and singing narrates loss, but also hope and good intention in an age of environmental destruction.

Disappearances and absences surround us everywhere, living things vanishing not only from the landscape but from our books and conversations. The successful collaboration between Jackie Morris and Robert Macfarlane, *The Lost Words*, has become a poignant icon of the magic slipping out of the world and the names that are disappearing from our vocabularies.[46] Reading Yōko Ogawa's disturbing, dystopian dream-like novel *The Memory Police*, where people's memories of things suddenly vanish, it seemed, to me, a chilling warning of the consequences of these types of erasures. The old man in the story laments that even the most wondrous memory 'vanishes if you leave it alone, if no one pays attention to it. They leave no trace, no evidence that they ever existed.' Remnants of recollections are like a flash in the dark: 'that doesn't mean the things themselves come back'.[47] In a world where climate change and species decline are accelerating, stories of fading words and lost things become part of an urgent mission of salvation. Shifting-baseline syndrome means that we assume the depleted natural world we live in is the norm because we only know the 'new normal'.[48] Telling stories is a way of trying to keep knowledge alive.

I wondered how long the bothy landscapes I visited would stay as I remembered them, as glaciers melt, rivers dry up and species disappear. When we alter environments, we change the stories we can tell and the worlds we can envisage. Temporal ruptures occur as things disappear from our world. If climate change chokes Loch Etive or ash dieback withers the forests of the Highlands, different narratives will have to be told. Sometimes stories, such as the prehistoric painted aurochs, wild and massive ancient cattle now extinct, on the walls of the Lascaux cave network in southwest France or the wolves that live on in place names in the UK, are the only reminder of what used to be. I hope that bothies and the landscapes they sit in don't become a flash in the dark, a receding memory of a time when there were more wild places in the world.

After I returned, I wanted to record as much of my time in Cadderlie and to hold the dimming memories of things as long as possible for years to come. We all relay memories as a way of covering over absences and losses because stories are tales of our past, but they are also how we create visions for the future. Perhaps that's why people are so keen to write in the bothy book, to create a record for those who come after, and even for their future selves, if they return. In May 1940, as he went off to war, R. Reid wished Corrour bothy farewell and wrote, 'here's to the next time'.[49] Scientists, activists, writers and creators are also looking to the future to try and drive action on climate change and environment, attempting to write stories that end up somewhere different from catastrophe. As literary scholar Ursula K. Heise writes, 'biodiversity, endangered species and extinction are primarily cultural issues, questions of what we value and what stories we tell'.[50] It matters that we listen to many and diverse stories, to those that come from the dispossessed, the disempowered and the non-human world, and we need to know that the tales we weave matter, as we consider loss and recovery and the future.

The more I thought about bothies, the more I realised that my time in them was bound up with the desire to be part of a community telling bigger stories about the environment and our relationship to it. When I think back, I've always been inspired by tales told about the living world, and I've often wondered why I didn't go down the path of conservation or ecology. As a little girl, I remember being moved by my choir's decision to sing *Ocean World,* an environmental musical by Peter Rose and Anne Conlon. So much so that I put on my own production in my home, got friends and family to pay, and donated the funds to the World Wildlife Fund. Somewhere along the way I lost that connection to places, possibly because I moved so much, possibly because I had little time around busy work or emotional lows.

This time I am not putting on a musical, but bothies and their stories move me. Like White's medieval chronicle, there's no narrative arc in the bothy books, only fragments of lives and dates. But there's also a collective power in the small tales of love and enjoyment that people find in these places, whether they come to conquer

Munros, or just to get away and sit and be in the bothy space, whether they come with kids, or alone, whether they bemoan midges and mice, or eulogise about birds and deer. There are many ways of being in the mountains, but the words and music of these men and women provide a place for connections, for imagination and for possibility.

Philosopher Michel Serres suggests our struggle against environmental disaster has to do away with the idea that there is an irrational past and a rational present, that modernity represents linear progression. It's no good, he remarks, to say that in the past people dreamed and sang, but now we think and experiment. There's no 'us' and 'them'. Now too is a time for dreaming, stories and telling tales.[51] And stories don't have to be grand tales of romance and death. It can be the little details of our remembered lives or simple entertainments, stories of fleas, fungi or walks on the beach. In fact, sometimes it's the small stories that move us, allowing us to develop a particular connection to a place and conceptualise the hyperobject of climate change. I think back to the wet of the dewy morning, the juicy squish of the berries and the gentle call of the birds in the birch trees. Perhaps the small space of the bothy can be a place for just these stories.

What is Cadderlie's story? A refuge for mythical lovers or pilgrims. A working farm. A cosy nook for community and fellowship in song.

It might be all these things, or none, depending on who you talk to. Cadderlie, for me, will always be the first bothy. It was a place where I tentatively explored unfurling feelings for a different future and where I toyed with the idea of writing a book about bothies.

My story or the story of other bothy dwellers is not always the one that others want to tell, either the people who live in the Highlands or those who own the land. The story is different for each person; narratives compete and clash. A critique of bothy culture could argue that the bothy story is simply a vision of wilderness and romanticism imposed on the landscape by outsiders who hike and camp. Yet perhaps the desire for retreat and for a connection with a place and its history can keep alive an imagination of the land that links community, fellowship, ecological thought and heritage. Bothies provide a chance for making stories about places that people value that are both specific and connected. It could be tales of being in nature and climbing Munros. Or it might be more intimate stories, like mine, of relationships and friendships, love lost and found, and the joy of finding new places.

Stories can be both sad and happy, and we don't always know the way they end. I thought this was the start of everything fresh and good in my life. It didn't turn out quite that simply. It took me much longer to prise myself away from the path I was on and to feel content once more. But that time in Cadderlie was the cradle for so many changes in my world, shifting my work and my life into directions that felt positive once more, and it was the moment at which I think I started to retell my own story after feeling lost. Narcissists are called that because they are obsessed with themselves like the beautiful young man in Ovid's *Metamorphoses*. But the other protagonist in the myth is Echo, the nymph who can only repeat the words said to her and who, although spurned, still adores her cruel beloved. She is doomed to wander the woods, and 'only her voice and her bones survive. Her voice lingers; her bones, so people say, were transformed into the shape of stones . . . A sound lives in her.'[52] I often felt like the shade of an echoing voice, fading into nothing. But I found my voice again and I found joyful dreams once more.

We can dream too for the world around us, even when we are uncertain of the ending. As my dad always tells me when I get low, travel hopefully. When it comes to hopeful tales about the climate and environment, bothies might be part of a way of storying the landscape that attends to the past and to loss but also aspirations for a different future. As with other communities that share time in nature, from hikers to surfers, swimmers to climbers, bothies make bonds between people who care about the landscape in particular ways and who have a creative, vibrant connection to it.

The first page of the simply bound songbook of the DURC has a fitting dedication:

To champions of causes, righters of wrongs
Climbers and walkers and singers of songs.
Makers of music and tellers of tales
Teachers and learners and healers of ills.[53]

If we don't have stories of care, about whatever places are meaningful to us, it will be a cold, empty world. We don't all have to visit a bothy. We won't all want to. But we also might take something from the stories that bothies allow us to tell.

TWO | CORROUR

Companions in Refuge

It is 21 August 1940. Charles Drinkwater arrives at Corrour bothy to rest. He has come along the Lairig Ghru, the old path through the Cairngorms that has been trodden by countless feet before him. Taking a traveller from Speyside to Deeside, the route is the most famous mountain pass in Scotland, used by those who lived and laboured in the peaks, by smugglers and thieves, armies and brigands, and now hikers and tourists. Drinkwater arrives from the Shelter Stone, a natural place of protection or a howff formed by gaps between boulders. He has taken the route coming via Ben Macdui and the Tailor Burn. A bit of rain falls, clouds descend to around 900 m to shroud the mountains on the way down, but overall he counts the weather as fair.

Other visitors that summer seemed to disagree, bemoaning the mists, rain and wind that mired and troubled their ascents. Amidst fierce gusts that flung the sand on the top of the mountains 'in all directions', the bothy was a welcome shelter. David Mathieson, who with his companion Biss was forced to give up ascending twice, wrote:

Here we are — brokenhearted
We brought our kit —
But didn't get started.

Perhaps Drinkwater found a window of finer weather, but his contentment might have also been the satisfaction of making good on a promise he had laid out for himself in June the previous year.[1]

He had spent midsummer in 1939 in the Cairngorms, as perhaps he had done in the summers before that one. A walk in patchy sun, hail and snow ended at Corrour at 5.45 pm on 24 June, where he found company and dry shelter. Like others who were repeat visitors to this most famous of bothies, he expected to be able to return year after year, an optimist, hoping for the future. Despite sleep being interrupted by the boisterous antics of the Cairngorm Club, who clattered in at 4.20 am - they had celebrated the summer solstice on the peaks and were now drenched to the bone - his enthusiasm was not dampened. After a hearty meal and a night's sleep, Drinkwater and a man described as a weary, bleeding Lone Sassenach (R. Bridges of Frimley Green, Surrey) teamed up to reach Blair Atholl. The weather had taken a turn for the better. He signed off, 'Here's hoping it will continue.'[2]

Men and women like Charles kept returning to enjoy the mountains, until maybe one year they didn't.

Drinkwater could little have imagined how life would change in the months which followed this expedition. When he returns in 1940, war has been in full swing for eleven months. After a quiet initial lull, fighting has erupted on the Western Front. It is a world transformed, from which Charles seeks refuge, just for a moment. Gone are the carefree days of sipping tea in front of the fire with the Lone Sassenach, and the three young women who later joined them – Margaret Miller, Jean Cruickshank and Christina Murray. Nations are at war, he is enlisted, and he has to make do with his leave from the army, making the trip with his father and sister. His desire for the freedom to wander the mountains is tangible. Towards the end of his entry, he writes, 'Anyway, I'm still hoping to be back here for several days when the war is over.' Still an optimist, but we don't know if he ever did seek shelter again in Corrour. I can find no other entry from Charles.

Sketch from Corrour bothy book, dated June 1939.

* * *

When I set off along the Lairig Ghru for Corrour, it is also approaching midsummer. It is perhaps the most famous of all bothies, with the oldest books, along the most iconic pass in Scotland and host to many visitors, famous and unknown. We are excited to join their ranks, and hot weather in the cities makes the cooler peaks of the mountains seem appealing. My friend Alison and I are escaping for a night from no such horrors as war, just the heat and the intimate stresses of life and relationships.

We all need refuge from something at one time or another, from work, the world or even ourselves. Not everyone seeks it in a small four-walled building or a tent in the mountains, but beyond being a shelter from the elements or the dark, bothies can be a kind of refuge too from fears that plague us or dangers that chase us. In academia, I worked a lot with early modern histories of refuge and refugees, a term that originated in the 1680s from the word *réfugié*, used when French Protestants fled persecution.[3] I would never have wanted to liken my experiences to the exile that these religious communities faced or the horrors that confront the rising numbers of displaced people in the world today. And yet at some level I have come to understand intellectually the desire for flight and the need for shelter from whatever it is that makes you feel unsafe.

It is not hard to see why Corrour bothy appeals if you want to run away for a while. It sits almost bang in the middle of the Lairig Ghru, at the foot of Cairn Toul and the Devil's Point. This high valley that winds between the looming granite once served as a stopping-off point for those moving cattle. Now it's a favourite port in a storm for anyone seeking snow-covered mountains. Not that any snow is to be seen on our trip. It is warm, too warm. Parched grass in Edinburgh parks, tinder-dry forests in Galloway over the last weeks and wildfires in the Highlands make me anxious about the effects of climate change, while certain news outlets merrily report on the sunshine. In winter this pass is covered in deep drifts, a remote place where winds can be fierce, but in the warm and light summer nights, it feels inviting.

We start Deeside, at Braemar. The village at the end of the famous Snow Roads is a pretty little place, iconic in the world of Cairngorms walkers. I had heard it mentioned so many times in bothy books and it must have become fairly used to dirty, dishevelled or injured travellers over the years. Certainly, the small Co-op, well stacked with snacks and Voltarol gel in equal measures, suggests they know what they are in for.

I am glad to be doing this with Alison. We met on a trip to the Peruvian Amazon a few years previously. I'd gone alone on a conservation holiday, a gift to myself after my divorce finally came through, using up the small amount of money left in my bank account after months of acrimonious back and forths. What should have been a simple settlement had ended up in court. Alison, too, was on the other side of a long relationship that had broken down. For distraction and relief, we chose an adventure that involved red howler monkeys at dawn, macaws on clay licks and bullet ants in the shower. I remember tentatively identifying the gaggle of people who were on the trip as we all holed up in the hotel in Puerto Maldonado. We had been due to set off for the conservation lodge up the river by bus and boat, but a sudden cold misty front of weather had blown in. El Friaje shrouded the town in grey and we mooched around. A few conversations over drinks revealed that Alison and I both enjoyed birdwatching and running away from London at times of personal difficulty. We have been firm friends ever since and regretted together our shared penchant for unwise choices in men.

After slathering on sunscreen and midge spray, Alison and I set off late in the afternoon from the shady cover of the trees in the Linn of Dee car park, under the care of the Mar Lodge Estate. I can't get the ticket machine to work, and I pray no estate warden slams me with a fine for parking without permission. The Cairngorms might be a national park, but most of the land is privately owned by trusts or individuals. Mar Lodge, a relic of the ancient earldom of Mar, is now under the stewardship of the National Trust for Scotland.[4]

The sun is slowly descending but still full of heat, and we stop for a quick drink and a picture on the bridge crossing the Dee. I thought of the pairs and trios of companions who had come before us, young men but also women. It's easy to assume the world of climbing and hiking was traditionally a male domain, but there were plenty of female hikers even in the early days of Corrour. In the University of Dundee archives, I deciphered the scrawled names in the old bothy books and saw what they had written, intrigued how the women's experiences differed from those of the men or how they resonated with mine. Women like Isabel S. McKay and E. Marguerite South, who were two 'lone solitary females' who arrived at the 'Corrour Hotel' at 6 pm on 28 August 1931. There was a bit of jostling of gendered hierarchies, as the two men from Dublin already there tried to intimidate them with tales of fleas and brown rats, and they suspected ulterior motives. They weren't deterred and took up their resting spots in the armchair and on the table.[5] I imagined them marching on next morning to Aviemore in fashionable knickerbockers and jackets, unlike Alison and I but not so different either. We tread too in the footsteps not only of hikers but of the fast-flowing ice rivers that sliced through granite, chiselling out the path between the peaks millions of years ago.

No one quite knows where the name Lairig Ghru comes from. The Lairig bit is easy - mountain pass - but the Ghru is a little trickier. It probably derives from Gaelic words related to flow and oozing, *drù* and *drùthaidh*.[6] Nineteenth-century map makers without 'the slightest authority', according to Seton Gordon, the famous twentieth-century naturalist, photographer and folklorist, labelled the route Ghruamach, meaning 'forbidding or gloomy'.[7] It may be an appropriation but it's an apt one for the deep trench surrounded by peaks with names like Creag an Leth-choin (Lurcher's Crag) and Braeriach (Brindled Upland).

Corrour is named after the corrie that sits behind it, Coire Odhar or 'the dun-coloured corrie'.[8] Corries are amphitheatres of rock carved out by glaciers, great stony hollows that often hold snow in their recesses, even in summer. Other corries share the same name as this, including one that has given its title to the highest train station in the UK on the West Highland Line. Corrour was built as a watcher's lodge in the late nineteenth century, a temporary summer home for a man who would count the deer and look out for poachers.[9] It's hard to know just how many deer roamed these slopes, but presumably plenty to support regular stalking parties. By 1912 an astonishing 1,450,784 hectares of land were used as deer forest in Scotland.[10]

When the heyday of the sporting estates was done, the permanent watcher was no longer needed, and as hikers began to fill the mountains in the 1920s, it became a 'haven of rest' for climbers.[11] Corrour is deep in the Cairngorms, almost at the halfway point of the Lairig Ghru, 13 km from Linn of Dee and 18 km from Coluymbridge. While we have easy going of it, it's still steep, and in snow, ice and bad weather it can be an unforgiving place where help is far off. You climb to around 600 m and the winds that whip through the pass can tear at clothes and flesh. In September 1948, J. R. Abbott described it as 'diabolically tortuous country, which seems to be continually trying to force you off some vague boulder strewn track'.[12] Entries in bothy books throughout the years rejoice at the welcome sight of the little building in rain, mist and snow. As E. Rothney wrote in rhyming verse in October 1931:

> Never did Corrour look half so sweet,
> As when viewed from Macdui with freezing feet,
>   Darkness descending
>   Mist impending
> Hasten we down with foot so fleet,
> Into the bothy's safe retreat.
> And so down they rushed.[13]

But it was also more than a shelter from the weather. A few pages into the very first bothy book left in Corrour, in August 1928, D. E. Strand from London scribbled a few lines of poetry, a slight misquote of poet John Davidson's 'The Last Journey'. Deep in the Cairngorms, having escaped London for a while, he reflected on walking and wilderness, and he wrote:

> alone I climb
> The rugged paths that lead me out of time[14]

There's often a strange sense of suspended temporality in a place like this. Because it's a transitory station of respite, time seems to stand still. And that feeling of limbo provides its own type of shelter, beyond the physical enclosure of the walls that protect from rain or wind or snow. A little like hitting a pause button on the strains of life.

People have searched for their idea of shelter in the bothy in different ways. In the heyday of the explosion of hiking among the interwar youth, or what *The Sphere* newspaper in 1930 rather affectionately called 'knapsackery', young men and noticeably also women, many working class, escaped into the mountains.[15] I too enjoy a bit of knapsackery, and we've got pretty used to the idea of getting away from the strains of the city or work for a few days. But this was a novelty for many that came with the freedom of time and a bit of money. As historian Simon Thompson observes, at its heart the hiking craze in the 1920s and 1930s was not so much about neo-romanticism or activism for access, but rather freedom, camaraderie and venturing into the outdoors.[16] Beyond the stuffy spaces of urban parks, the dance halls closed on Sundays or cramped domestic spaces, young men and women found a place to be active, flirt, laugh and bicker, shielded from judging eyes. It is hard to imagine that Isabel and Marguerite could have joked with two lads from Dublin in other contexts.

There's something special about that moment between the wars that was a kind of respite, a sliver of time sandwiched between unbearable suffering and death, when life seemed more carefree. I found it hard to explain, but I was particularly drawn to the books and photographs from the 1920s and 1930s, perhaps because there was a sense of innocence and freedom interlaced with fragile loss. There were, of course, some older visitors to Corrour, part of that tortured Lost Generation of F. Scott Fitzgerald and T. S. Eliot, who entered early adulthood in World War I. But often I meet young men and women on the page who were just too young to serve and who would not have known the horrors of the trenches. Though they may have lost parents or relatives and heard reports of fighting as children, and though the war shaped their generation too, they had not witnessed first-hand the mud and blood.

Men like Archie Hunter. Archie hailed from 27 Angarsk Road, Drumoyne, Glasgow. He first came to Corrour, as far as I can tell, on his 21st birthday, in June 1930.[17] I am not entirely sure I would have got on with Archie. He's pretty dismissive of female travellers – he groans about those not ladylike enough – and gets embroiled in written spats with his fellow bothiers on the pages of the books. And he tends to write long, wistful and, dare I say it, occasionally pretentious essays on the mountains. Writer and experienced hillwalker Ralph Storer calls him the poet laureate of the bothy. I am not so sure. His essays on stroking the granite and God-like peaks err on the side of cheesy.[18]

Yet I also sympathised with Archie when I could get over the fulsome verses. I sympathised with his dream to find respite in nature but also simply to enjoy himself. His home in Drumoyne is the heart of the former shipbuilding industry, so he most likely came from a working-class neighbourhood that must have seemed a world away from the high peaks. One of his fellow visitors in July 1931 joked/not joked about having to go back to the 'soot, grime and smoke' of Glasgow.[19] Perhaps to escape this, Archie came back year after year. Once with a girlfriend in 1935, though she didn't join him on subsequent trips, so I'm guessing it didn't work out. He and his friend Jo Oram jokingly complained about having to bring tea to the 'ladies who lie waiting', Edith Smith and Mary Hawthorn. On his trip the next year, he has made sure to revisit his entry and add a note that they even carried 'the ladies (?)' - Archie's punctuation and choice of word - across the Dee.[20] Unlike Charles Drinkwater, I can pick up Archie's trail after the war.[21]

As the 1930s progressed and war loomed, it started to intrude on people's thoughts, and a sense of anxiety about the future to come infiltrates the Corrour books. On 2 October 1938, men and women from Aberdeen visited the bothy, a few days after Neville Chamberlain waved a famous piece of white paper as he declared concord with Hitler's Germany. The brief note in the bothy book referred to the Munich Agreement by stating simply 'Celebrating PEACE by a visit to the Cairngorms'.[22]

These young people who loved to visit Corrour must, I imagine, have become aware of the possible futures that awaited them. World War I probably still felt like a wound tender to the touch. Or perhaps, like so many of us in moments of impending crisis, they thought the worst couldn't happen, and the as-yet unscarred confidence of youth won through. In June 1939, the same month that Charles Drinkwater visited Corrour, one visitor immortalised the moment of carefree fellowship in the bothy in a pencil drawing. Pipes, sleeping bags, hanging socks, packs, food on the boil, the scratched outlines of the mountains in the distance.[23] It's a moment of peacetime leisure before the war would break out.

As the months dragged on, denial, wishful thinking and warnings abound. On 26 August Klammers Lickle wrote there was no crisis here, 'Peace, perfect peace', while the girls of North London Collegiate on 1 September welcomed the lack of 'disquieting' political news. Other entries from late summer in 1939 make specific declarations about the state of affairs. On 23 August a party of students from Cambridge – I imagine them as young, earnest, serious, filled with ideals of communist equality – brought a copy of *The Daily Worker* as reading material for the bothy 'in the interests of all those wishing to preserve and understand what democracy we have won'. Others do not mention the war explicitly but seem wistful. On 31 August a visitor notes the scents of smoke and heather, reminders of his time there, and he talks of the 'lovely things of the earth around and peace'. Perhaps the most poignant is the entry of 26 August. Edwin Law and Doug McGregor sat reading by the light of a candle. 'There is no sound except the wind sighing through the crags. A mouse has just started squeaking. We have just thrown out a toad which jumped onto Doug's book. Today it is peace. Tomorrow may bring war.' A little sketch of Hitler follows, complete with the trademark toothbrush moustache and a saluting hand. Then the warning 'Time marches on'.[24]

Our need for refuge is, sometimes, from darker realities than work and city air. In times of trauma, personal and societal, the idea of shelter takes on a new, sharper meaning. Collectively we felt that keenly in Covid when we were funnelled into one kind of imposed retreat from the world, yet unable to escape to other places. Home became an enclosed, repeated boredom and while nature has always been a source of respite, getting outdoors for the daily walk permitted by the British government was relief from being shut away. The logic of shelter was in some senses reversed as we sought a sense of safety and security outdoors and not in. It was a place we could forget the pandemic for a moment. A visitor popping by Greensykes bothy in spring 2020 called it a 'wee escape from Covid-19 stress to perch and enjoy our lunch in the sun'.[25]

Other shattering, life-changing events are evident in notes left by visitors to Corrour, though it's often only side glances at the course of global affairs. Peripheral, marginal mentions of war or politics are there, but most people do not want to focus on them as the main subjects of their entries, since these brief moments in the bothy are a time of respite. There's a tension here between escape and reality. Although a bothy may be a shelter from the stream of news or collective anxiety, it would provide no real shelter in a time of nuclear explosion, nor can it halt the return to active service in a war. Three visitors to Corrour in July 1943 write only 'Three Dead Men', followed by their names.

Alison and I walk and talk, we chat about all things relationships and life, passing Derry Lodge, once a shooting lodge, then used by the army, now boarded up. The weather is clear and perfect, the fords we have to cross are lightly trickling bands of crystalline water and the trees glow emerald-gold. After crossing the Luibeg Burn, which is gentle and not in spate, not a rushing 'snaw bree', the path begins to wind higher into the mountains.[26] Tree cover disappears and all that remains is sun, granite and river. Meadow pipits quarrel, an impossibly large moth settles near us, horseflies stick to our legs like needy children. We see a few people on our way, groups camping, enjoying some time away. Just like Archie, escaping for a moment, knapsacks and all. Because of course, time doesn't stand still and the retreat Corrour provides is only temporary.

The bothy is just round the corner. We are hot and a little thirsty but not too tired as the craggy granite of the Devil's Point looms ahead of us, a sharp, shorn, jagged tooth. By contrast, everywhere you look, the heads of cotton grass form fluffy, golden-white pom-poms. The glen's curves and crags are shelters not just for climbers but have long provided respite for animals too. In every pool and channel of water we come across we find common frogs, small and large, glossy-backed and beady-eyed. They proliferate in protected habitats in the Cairngorms, often on their own trek through the mountains looking for sustenance, shelter and somewhere to breed. In search of food, they may make journeys of up to 10 km.[27] In Coire Odhar above the bothy, rich earth, green pasture and water made it, so hiker Alexander Copeland wrote in 1901, 'paradise for frogs'.[28] Good grass in sheltered hollows was a place where cattle grazed in summer. The name of a nearby mountain hollow means 'corrie of the maidens', a reminder, as poet Alec Finlay writes, of the young women who worked in the mountains long before the climbers claimed it.[29] Hidden and forgotten, stones in the ground nearby mark the remnants of summer shielings.[30]

Drawing of Corrour pinned to the wall of the bothy.

Alison and I turn into the cooler air of the valley, and while it's still impossibly light, the line of shadow is creeping down the edge of the mountains. Finally, we rock up at Corrour at about 8 pm. Alison has never slept in a bothy, so we wanted to give it a go, but we have brought the tent just in case the bothy is full. We realise, however, that a bothy night is undoubtedly a lost cause long before we get close to Corrour. There are tents all around, a sure sign of a full house. Restoration work was undertaken in 2006, but it's still a small bothy which can sleep only a few. The extension of the toilet block was a sure sign of its popularity.

I am a little disappointed. Perhaps it is a mark of the increasing pressure on outdoor spaces, but, in truth, Corrour has been busy and popular for decades. On New Year's Day 1937, after a cold and arduous walk across the Lairig through a bitter snowstorm, the Creagh Dhu Mountaineering Club arrived to find the bothy full and were forced to sleep out. They had been racing to be 'first footers', the first people to stay in a new year. Much to their disappointment, they had no chance of winning the race as A. Lavery and D. McGovern (Corrour stalwarts who turn up in the books almost as often as Archie) had arrived only fifteen minutes into the New Year. There was plenty of merrymaking later, as the two groups joined forces, another sketch poking fun at the 'also-rans' who couldn't get close to the fire.[31] We didn't have to battle with any snow, but like others who have found the bothy full over the years, we pitched our tent instead. Then, as now, all just looking for a place to lay our heads.

Though we can't fit in for the night, Alison and I wander up to the bothy to say hello, though, unusually for bothiers, people aren't that friendly. Maybe there are too many groups for a sense of fellowship. Maybe it is late in the day, and people are tired. In the bothy itself, we chat to a couple of other travellers, and I note that tucked into the sleeping platform is one hiker who has already bedded down for the night and is snoring soundly. I wonder if he has reveries of the high peaks or if he is in the dead dreamless sleep of exhaustion. We return to our tent, lay out our beds and after toasting the day away with red wine, we try to shut our eyes to the light of a Scottish summer night. Alison has remembered her sleep mask; I have not. Lying awake, I regret my poor packing choices.

A shelter may be a place to hide away, a retreat from the stresses of modern life, a retreat into time and space, an escape from personal trauma or war or Covid, but at its most basic it's just somewhere to rest for the night. It struck me how a bothy is deeply intertwined with the need to sleep and to find a place to lay your head, with some protection from the dark, the weather and the wind.

The bothy offers more room and comfort than the nearby Shelter Stone, though ever since the late nineteenth century, rock hideouts have been a favourite among climbers. Many are dotted around the mountains, but the Shelter Stone is the most famous, and played host to the founding of the Cairngorm Club in 1887. It is a giant granite rock that tumbled from the cliffs of Carn Etchachan millennia ago, snapped off by ice, to come to its resting place on the rocky shores of Loch Avon. Clach Dhion, as it is called in Gaelic, balances seemingly precariously on smaller stones, and the dark space beneath offers protection from snow and storms in the heart of the Cairngorms. With an earth floor, limited ceiling height and only 12 sq m of usable floor space, it is a harsh sort of shelter, but much loved by Cairngorm climbers. It too has a series of 'howff books' which are full of joking complaints about damp and cold but also an affectionate familiarity.[32]

Compared with the tough respite of the Shelter Stone, Corrour bothy was, as one visitor commented in July 1937, luxury. Another recounts his bothy experience with succinct clarity: 'I slept inside the bothy instead of in my tent.'[33] We came, we slept, we went. It's what bothies offer, alongside youth hostels, tents and even shelters of rocks and boulders. If the 1930s were the time of hiking, they were also the time of sleeping out. For most people that feeling of safeness and security in rest comes from having some barrier between the dark world outside and its weather, even if that is only the cold stone wall of a howff or bothy.

There's also companionship in the need to sleep. We all need to do it – as do most living organisms – though in truth I have always been terrible at it. Thinking of the frogs we saw earlier, I'm reminded of how their American relations, the bullfrog, along with animals like dolphins, are thought to have unihemispheric sleep, one half of the brain always awake, one at rest.[34] And that's the problem on a long walk or a hike. You need water, of course, food too. But with all the provisions in the world, you can't keep going for days unless you lay your head down. There will always be a moment of vulnerability when you close your eyes and drop your guard. There may be no one keeping watch as the flames die and you nod off, and for the most part, there's an odd trust in the space of the bothy that you can sleep alongside strangers. Perhaps there is a shared sense of community in the simplicity of sleep, a chance every day to retreat into dreams, to reset and go again.

The following morning, I wake up before Alison. It's light, but the sun has not yet reached the valley. A sandpiper bobs in the cool water of the Dee, and I feel that lovely synchronicity you get of waking up with the world around you. Sleeping out is supposed to be good for you, a reset of your circadian rhythms. No glaring artificial lights here keep me awake, no artificial darkness keeps my eyes closed. The birds, too, are not confused by the false dawn of bright lamps. It's a still moment, a sense of companionship in sleeping and waking with the day, and a respite from the disrupted, constant orange twilight of the city.

Across the bridge at the bothy, tent flaps are twitching, gas stoves clicking, and bodies moving.

Sleeping out comes with its dangers, of course, and not just exposure, but if you believe the stories, the ghouls and ghosts that supposedly lurk in the dark and the shadows of the Cairngorms. There are plenty of bothy horror tales of strange spectral beings and fearsome apparitions in the mountains from whom you might need to hide. After all, we are camping below the Devil's Point, its angelic counterpart a few hundred metres away. Both are nineteenth-century monikers. The Gaelic name of the peak is Bod an Deamhain, which actually translates as 'the Devil's penis', but when Queen Victoria asked her ghillie for a translation, he protected the queenly sensibilities with this tamer euphemism.[35]

Camping under a demonic rock penis certainly seemed a likely place for chthonic apparitions or evil spirits. Apparently if you are in Corrour, the one to watch out for is the Grey Man of Ben Macdui, or Am Fear Liath Mòr. The eerie phenomenon, reported for decades by walkers, tells of some monstrous, supernatural presence that haunts the peaks. High up on the snowy plateau, where light, sound and weather converge in otherworldly conjurations, it can most likely be explained as a strange optical phenomenon, but those who have seen it swear that Am Fear Liath Mòr is real. Professor Collie's account in 1925 first brought the Grey Man to fame as he told of the heavy footsteps of an unseen companion that crunched behind him. Since this, numerous others have reported they sensed something hovering at the margins of perception, and these horrifying moments are often associated with the edge of sleep, a dream world of waking and moonlight. Syd Scroggie, a famous hiker who later lost his sight, claimed he saw the Grey Man one night beside Loch Avon pacing 'slowly out of the blackness at one side of the water into the blackness at the other'.[36]

Entries in bothy books are a little more sceptical. The group who had failed to be first footers in 1937 joked that Am Fear Liath Mòr should be Corrour's keeper, while in 1958 Sandy and George drew some rather cute little doodles of a little yeti and a friendly Grey Man who came to tea.[37]

Fortunately, Alison and I survive the night and live to tell the tale.

In the morning we tidy up and pack away. Our home for a night is quickly removed, tent city cleared. The community camped around Corrour disperses, although the bothy still squats in its hollow, waiting for the next visitors. We chat with a couple of people as we overtake them or are overtaken in turn, back and forth on the walk away from the bothy along the Lairig Ghru.

The sanctuary the bothy provides is supposed to be temporary, not a permanent state of being. A poem from the very earliest bothy book, in August 1928, declares that it's not exactly a 'home from home' but a place of shelter for those who roam.[38] I think it's part of the attraction. Bothy life is, as geographer Rachel Hunt writes, a form of outdwelling beyond conventional patterns of settlement.[39] A requirement is that you do not stay too long in a bothy. There are no clear guidelines, but it's agreed wisdom that it's a few nights at most, so much consternation was caused by James McRory Smith or Sandy, who occupied Strathchailleach to the south of Cape Wrath for thirty-two years, against the code of bothies.[40]

A bothy is more than a tent or a bivouac bag, less than a hotel. It's a semi-safe shelter for transitory visitors, situated at the threshold between two states of being, outside and inside, settled and moving. In such places and times of in-betweenness the rules are often different, and this fleeting edge state has often been associated with demons and danger. In early modern Europe, people believed that unbaptised and unnamed children, not yet enclosed within the fold of the Christian community occupied a liminal position between both life and death, and between naming and anonymity. In this precarious state, they were prey to all manner of malign spirits. Doorways and thresholds were spaces that had to be protected from the Devil.[41] When people come through the door into Corrour there's a sense of crossing over for a moment into a space of safety, but perhaps also still a peripheral place that is not quite secure. Mountaineer and author Affleck Gray, initially sceptical of the Grey Man legends, recalled his visit to Corrour in 1932. The inner door was closed, the outer open, but as he dozed, he heard it slam shut and the bar swing into place to lock him in. Gray jumped out of the window to inspect the scene, but nothing stirred. When he re-entered, he dared not do so through the door but clambered back through the window.[42]

There may be uncertainty and danger at these times. Yet play is perhaps also more possible when you feel in between things and when the expectations of home, adulthood or city life seem only partially to bind you. Life does not seem to be one thing or the other in the bothy, as you are gathered with people you will not see again and trying on behaviours that are perhaps new. Playful stories of ghosts, of relationships, of recipes and of revelry in Corrour are bound up with the liminality that is often associated with carnivalesque festival, a time when hierarchies and structures are for a moment overturned. Bothy book accounts sometimes read a little like accounts of carnival with people, so one visitor recalled, arriving at 1.30 am, with four bottles of White Horse whisky, to find sixteen people enjoying the bothy.[43] Everyone returns eventually to the world they came from when they leave Corrour, but in the transient moments, there's play and release, and a time of escape, keeping the monsters from the door.

This transitory state is quite literal for some people. On a visit to a bothy on Rùm, Guirdil, I read one entry in the bothy book from a man who described this and other bothies as a temporary home, as he had recently been made homeless.[44] The bothy provides a physical shelter but perhaps also a place to process transition. I thought again of Sandy in Strathchailleach, whose wife had died in a terrible car accident. Robert Macfarlane calls him the 'irascible, contorted opposite' of contemplative monks.[45] Perhaps, but I felt for this man as someone stuck in the grieving process who, it seemed to me, neither physically nor emotionally transitioned from this place of refuge.

For my own reasons, I have also often been drawn to places like this in pain and grief, and I feared at times that I would become stuck in the in-between. I've thought a lot about shelter during the darker moments in my life. As I ached from the broken future of divorce and then quick on the heels of the separation, the destructive rollercoaster of a relationship that came next, I wanted to hide away. I kept returning to a poem by Edna St. Vincent Millay, where she describes a torturous relationship as akin to the sharp fierceness of diamonds and icebergs, the constant pierce of 'lightning or a sword'. She writes:

Such things have beauty, doubtless; but to me
Mist, shadow, silence – these are lovely, too.
There is no shelter in you anywhere;
Rhythmic intolerable, your burning rays
Trample upon me, withering my breath;
I will be gone, and rid of you, I swear:[46]

I have felt something similar. When trying to explain the sensation of being with an emotionally volatile partner, I thought about a twisted version of the fairy tale *The Happy Prince.* I was casting away parts of my body and soul until I felt blind, naked and with nothing more to proffer, except that my sacrifices were not for any greater good. At those moments not even sleep provided relief. I remember dreams that occasionally still plague me. I am in the house I owned with my ex-husband, sometimes sharing the space with him, sometimes the man who came after. I want to leave, just walk out of the house. But there are no doors where I remember them, and any pleas are met not with anger or denial but just blank incomprehension.

Often I sought escape; I tried to run away for a moment, and looked for refuge in strange places. In the year before Covid, I visited thirty cities in eleven countries. Keep moving and you might find the way out, I told myself, while all the time not leaving behind the place or the person that was at the heart of it all. I found comfort in temporary spaces, public places, even, where people looked oddly at the tears I shed or the despair that I wore visibly, but who would never see me again. A tissue, a cookie, a kind word from strangers, but no pressure to explain oneself. An escape to a hotel or temporary space for a while could feel like living a parallel life where I was free.

I felt the same way about the transitory space of a bothy that is a unique kind of shelter. In these situations, the stakes are low, the meetings casual and so without pressure, and yet also strangely intimate. You are holed up together for a short period and you all take respite together.

It surprises me, sometimes, that what we need to feel safe or that the shelter we crave is not always what we expect. The walls of home can feel like a concrete enclosure when home is unhappy or violent, or when it is a place full of grief, as it must have been for Sandy. It had become, perhaps, a home like that in Larkin's moving poem 'Home is So Sad', 'Having no heart to put aside the theft'.[47] We all need shelter from the elements and to feel safe we need to be able to take care of our basic needs, and so many do not even have that in a world with increasing numbers of refugees and hostile regimes.[48] But we need something more than these fundamental needs to be satisfied, to flourish and to feel secure. The philosopher Martha Nussbaum talks about these as capabilities – the chance to play, to affiliate, to feel emotions, to live with the non-human world, to sense, imagine and think.[49] I did not expect bothies to be a soothing respite, but as places where I was able to outdwell, to stay beyond, I have flourished there.

Despite the transient nature of bothy interactions, there's a strong sense of community among bothiers born out of the shared connection of coming to a place, full of laughing and arguments, tensions and friendships. You never quite know who you will meet and how you will react, which can be exciting, nerve-racking and freeing all at the same time, and characters pop in and out of people's lives. On our walk to Aviemore, Alison and I keep meeting two young women who have bivvied out on Devil's Point. (Bivvying is one rung down from camping in simplicity terms, sleeping under the stars in a sleeping bag with a waterproof cover.) We share pleasantries and a joke. We say 'Hi' each time we pass. But we never find out their names.

It might seem an unstable sort of fellowship, but there is something comforting in that transience. I thought of a line from Jessica Bruder's astounding book *Nomadland*, documenting people in the US left behind by industrial decline who are now constantly on the move. Of course, for these communities, transience is a permanent or semi-permanent condition, but even that transience has hope. They have, she writes, a 'bone deep conviction that something better will come. It's just ahead in the next town, the next gig, the next chance encounter with a stranger.'[50]

I still feel that pull now to a place of temporary retreat at the first sign of personal conflict in my life. I never get enough detail to know, but I wondered if any of the women, in particular, I read about in the old bothy books shared this need; if they had difficult homes, or were simply glad to be in the hills. I was drawn to the sense of freedom they felt. Kitty Kinnaird and Mary Stephens who visited Corrour in 1936 delighted in their visit to this 'home from the home', signing off as 'Two of the Musketeers'.[51]

* * *

Alison and I continue on the pass, over scree and boulder fields, until finally we reach the Pools of Dee and plunge into the water, whose freezing clarity burns our fingers. We are gleeful. The hard work is done. Our skin tingles with energy from the cold water and the sun. But then Alison slips on the scree and sprains her ankle just beneath the shadow of Lurcher's Crag. There are still 10 km to go, and though Aviemore is visible on the horizon, it seems an awfully long way off. Suddenly it becomes a place of danger and distance again, far from help. I am worried the ankle is broken, but after a rest and some pills, we conclude it is just a really nasty sprain. We strap it up and she is able to walk with the help of walking poles, a dose of Kendal Mint Cake and some tactical underestimating on my part of the distance left to go.

This is still a dangerous, remote place, and there are plenty of tales of sprained ankles and worse in the books. Tragic tales are entwined with the bothy's history and that of other high shelters. In November 1971, five Edinburgh schoolchildren on a navigational trip died high on the Cairngorm plateau after getting caught in bad weather. Their school leader attempted to lead the six students on the trip to the Curran shelter on the plateau in the driving snow. They never made it. Bivvying in a blizzard, only one of the 15-year-olds and the leader survived. In the aftermath, the shelter was dismantled. It had acted, so some argued, not as a place of respite but a dangerous lure to those who were inexperienced.[52] The Cairngorm plateau can quickly become a bleak, lethal expanse of white, and animals and birds too succumb to its ravages. Seton Gordon described finding a frozen robin near the Pools of Dee, caught up in a blizzard on migration, that had fallen 'exhausted amid the unheeding snows'.[53] We are lucky. Weather is great. We get down. No need for Corrour to save our life.

As soon as we are over the ridge of the main point of the pass, the phone signal picks up again and I am pretty relieved, in case we do need to call for help. Even in places of retreat, the reality of the world quickly intrudes. During World War II, Andrew Innes came up to the bothy on 21 September 1940 from Braemar. It was a time of respite from the conflict, but on the way out to Cairn Toul and Braeriach, the drone of a German plane filled the air.[54] In our case, reality comes in the form of social media and WhatsApp. The pinging sounds bring us back to a world of boyfriends and emails and work. The transience ends, the spell broken. We start to think about what snacks we will eat when we finally reach the M&S in Aviemore. I fantasise over what was my meal of choice after a Brazilian jiu-jitsu competition – BLT, Diet Coke and salt-and-vinegar crisps.

Perhaps we are always doing this dance between reality and escape, indulging in just enough escape to keep reality at bay. In this way, the in-between space of the bothy becomes a place for physical shelter but also a space for dreaming, even disassociating.

I think of Archie's last entry in 1952. He talks of the 'pale beauty' of the moon 'drowning everything in its magical cloak'. And he wishes that he could die here knowing 'that we have worked and our wages are taken and to sink into peaceful slumber in a place like this and know that we are not dead'.[55]

In the playful threshold spaces of these edge places maybe we find, as anthropologist Victor Turner argues, the room for 'revolutionary manifestos',[56] a way of dreaming of different realities, new futures, and other possibilities, for us and for the worlds around us.

THREE | GREENSYKES

Living the Good Life

I look around at the cosy home we have made for the night. The fire is glowing with amber warmth. The cooking pans are empty after we have scraped them of lentils and couscous. Above our heads, clothes and socks hang, watched over by a small, fluffy ladybird called Spotty. Our sleeping bags are arranged snugly on the sleeping platforms, music plays, the night deepens and our conversation trails away into the dark corners of the room. It is, I conclude, an evening well spent within the wood-panelled walls of Greensykes bothy on a gloomy Saturday in autumn. The weekend away with my friend Debbie to this bothy in Dumfries and Galloway was not a perfect idyll, it didn't suddenly remove all the stress and anxiety that was going on in our lives, but in that moment, I don't even think about whether I am happy. There is simply a deep content. Other visitors seem to agree. One person before us has written:

'What a Place, Words cannot describe the peacefullness [*sic*] of this place one bit. Thanks much like.'[1]

Conscious or not, the journey to a bothy is about what happiness, fulfilment and living the good life might mean away from the constraints of the contemporary world, its technology and hectic rhythms, and its urban hardness. The idea of the 'good life' is old – it goes right back to Aristotle. And it's pretty simple in theory: to live a good life and to flourish is part of the goal of human existence, and for Aristotle that also meant being virtuous. A good life is not just about untamed hedonism, it's the sense of constructing a life that you value, that feels a life well lived and 'the good life' presents an ethical position about our place in the world. Indeed, hedonistic pleasure and eudaimonic pleasure (living well) might be at odds with one another, the latter suggesting a slower, more sustained, more attentive way of living.[2] Maybe Debbie and I found that in Greensykes, or perhaps we were just playing at it for a moment, giving up some of the complexity of our lives for a night of open fires and camp food.

If you ask many people what it means to live a good life, they might agree on a few things like love, purpose, dignity, a sense of control. And many of us may well include getting out into nature and a connection with the living world. But although it might seem a simple idea, working out what the good life means is complicated. We disagree about what we need or want, we have different notions of values and virtues, and there are nagging, worrying concerns about how or even if we can live well in the contemporary world. The lifestyles of the Global North have led to the accumulation of stuff, but no discernible increase in happiness. And as academics and authors Karen Lykke Syse and Martin Lee Mueller ask: 'What does it mean to live a good life in a time when the planet is overheating, the human population continues to steadily reach new peaks, oceans are turning more acidic, and fertile soils the world over are eroding at unprecedented rates?'[3] The question of what it means to live a life well lived is an old one, though it seems we are no closer to a definitive answer.

Bothies present a vision of living well that is very different from how we might imagine it in the consumerist twenty-first century. They seem a world away from the comfort of a modern dwelling – no running water, no electricity or heating, the nearby watercourse for a sink, and for the most part a shovel and the wide outdoors for the lavatory, although Greensykes is one of the luxury bothies with an outdoor composting toilet just across the bridge. It's all part of the experience of making do, getting back to simple things, and venturing out into places that seem remote from the modern world. You can only take certain things into a bothy and there will only be limited creature comforts, but I wonder what we might gain by thinking about what we choose to leave behind, even for just a night. A momentary slice of the good life, or at least the bothy version of it.

The Greensykes bothy book holder, just inside the door.

An easy starter, that's the impression you get of Greensykes in the various bothy guides in books and on blogs. A pretty new MBA bothy, it is nestled in the gentle hills that border the valley of the River Esk in southern Scotland and has been kitted out with love and care, wood cladding and a composting toilet. The walk from Glendinning Farm is not too long, it's close to a road, and the whole shelter is very well maintained. This was the first bothy I did with Debbie, her initial venture into the world of bothying. She is about my age, a little older but not by much, and we have shared a great deal together. We had met a few months ago on the 'pilgrimage' organised by folk singer Sam Lee and immediately clicked as we talked about the shared experience of our marriages breaking down. She said she had been wanting to go to a bothy for a while but was nervous about doing it alone. Despite the fact I am also a newcomer, I feel like the experienced old hand compared to her, knowing what to bring, how to behave, what to expect.

Not that Debbie needs looking after. She's an adventurous, exciting person who climbs, bivvies and dances her way through life, and is always up for a new challenge. I ask her after our trip whether she would have come by herself to a bothy.

'I don't know,' she answers. Hiking or walking alone feels different from solo urban expeditions or work, a little bit scarier. But something changed after she went through the divorce and the psychological shift of making her life for herself as a single person.

'Don't wait for someone else to want to do the things,' she says. 'If there's something you want to do, go and do it.'

I admire her for that, and I love that her way of living life after her divorce has been to make the room for adventure, affection and thrills in whatever space she finds it. We are very different, an introvert and an extrovert who find a meeting point in the acts of care we give each other, but I think we share a love of finding joy when we can, in simple things as well as grand expeditions.

We set off on a grey October morning. I feel guilty for driving, especially as we do so during a national fuel crisis, unsure if pumps will be empty or full. There's a wonderful short story by Italo Calvino written in 1974, at the height of an oil crisis caused by an embargo targeted at countries who supported Israel in the Yom Kippur War. His character worries about running out of petrol. He worries too that we will all run out of resources and time. He and others like him have been irresponsible, thought too little and acted too late.[4]

The tale hardly assuages my guilt for driving to the bothy, that often-present anxious struggle between the need - or is it just a desire? - to get out to see the living world or to get away, and the impact of my decisions to do so. What price the good life? After all, there's really no other way to bothies or adventurous places for many people than to get in the car, at least for some of the journey.

We know this won't be a particularly long or gruelling trip. Constraints of time, the working week for both of us, and childcare for Debbie as a single parent means we have only a couple of nights away. I am conscious how different is our rushed outing from the idyll of wandering wild for weeks on end, like travel writer Patrick Leigh Fermor or lone adventurer Chris McCandless. The trip is squeezed between tense arguments at work and family strains. The start of a busy academic year in the midst of a pandemic means endless queries from distressed students trying to juggle illness, grief, insecurity and anxiety with academic study. Running departments in the new strange online world of Covid is no easy feat. I worry about my little sister too and her new son; Debbie has the demands of her children. We are grateful the trip is an easy one.

The journey up is broken with an overnight stay in Old St Leonard's Church in Langho in the Ribble Valley. I should say, we didn't break in or seek sanctuary. You can hire some old churches for the night via the Churches Conservation Trust initiative called Champing. After an evening spent amidst the smell of slightly damp hassocks and half-melted candles, we continue up, the driving rain thankfully having given way to weak sunlight. A highlight of the trip is a rather fine breakfast at Tebay services, a favourite pitstop of mine on trips up and down to Scotland, since you are almost over the border, and it has a good farm shop. Debbie normally stops off at the Lakes just before this part of the M6, so this was a new adventure too. Bacon sandwiches overlooking the lakes of Tebay. Dreamy.

After some debate about whether we are in the right parking spot, we set off. Our walk from the Thomas Telford Birthplace Cairn near Glendinning Farm was a mere 50-minute stroll up a gentle hill along a path that followed the top of a small valley. The Megget Water twists below, sun peeking out to illuminate it in butterfly-wing blue, and we ford the trickle of water that is Green Sike, the stream that gives the building its name. After pushing through a forest gate, we arrive at a spick-and-span building sitting next to the point where the Megget Water meets Loath Sike. We are not the only ones there to enjoy it. A bounding little terrier, whose name we later learn is Jeff, greets us merrily, and then his owner and friends heave into view. They are already gathering and chopping wood for the stove in the main room.

Greensykes is quite a new acquisition by the MBA, going back only to 2011. In the nineteenth century the building was once home to the Anderson family, two adults and six children living in a two-room cottage in 1841 and working as shepherds.[5] Different families came in and out over the next 100 years, all tending to livestock, until forestry replaced farming. The dark, dense pines that dominate the land around are a reminder that it is forestry territory. There have been people using it as a shelter and later a picnic spot for around seventy years, ever since the last permanent resident moved out when John Beattie left Greensykes in 1961 for a new life down under. Forestry workers took advantage of the building to rest, and even when the roof fell in, local resident Kenneth Irving came with his family for outings. In this century, the MBA restored it as 'a grand little cottage (bothy) to give shelter to many a weary traveller'.[6]

Greensykes has three sleeping and living areas, but the main one with the stove and cooking apparel left over from previous trips is occupied, so we fling our bags into the smaller room on the other side of the bothy. We marvel at the wood-panelled walls, clean fire, sturdy sleeping platforms and the bathroom facilities. As you do, we chat with our bothy companions, Gaz, Chopper and Dave, who hail from the North of England, just over the border. They often visit bothies as a group, they tell us, trips that allow them a weekend away from the humdrum and stresses of modern life by coming to somewhere a little simpler and slower for a few days.

After settling in we poke around and gather wood. In a bothy you will find yourself being busy with not too much. It doesn't take long for you to settle in, making it a temporary home if you stay overnight or even if you just pop in for a visit. It no longer becomes a remote shelter, but a strange, transient parallel home filled with domestic tasks. There are the Boy Scout rituals of making do with what you find, washing up the pans with tufts of grass for scourers and searching for the stuff to make a fire. As is often the case, even on Forestry and Land Scotland territory, we spend a good amount of the afternoon collecting dead wood.

We try to light the fire with homemade fire bow and flints, completely unnecessary since we have perfectly good lighters, but I have been watching the TV show *Survivorman*, so the prospect of a more adventurous way of igniting the fire appeals, while Debbie wants to test out skills taught on a recent campfire night.

A lot of people seem to like the little tasks of bothying. I know I do. I have always found respite in doing things. Soothing the soul by being busy, I am by nature restless and active. I always joke that I inherited my mum's night-owl tendencies and my dad's early-bird rising, leaving only a few dark hours in between to squeeze in sleep and rest. A million projects are always buzzing through my head, ideas half finished, still forming, discarded or waiting. It's not always a good thing. It leaves me tired and annoyed, if also productive. So the activity needed in a bothy appeals; it keeps you busy but there has to be a slow method to it. The more you do it, the better you get at it. Going to a bothy has this aura of being something traditional and straightforward, stripped back. Yet there's also considerable expertise behind the apparent simplicity, as geographer Rachel Hunt has explored. She calls this 'the simple as skilful'.[7] And that too provides a feeling of living well, engaging in the act of crafting and the agency that comes with it to make your own comfort.

There's a sense of adventure and of exploring for us, but it's a different satisfaction from the lone adventure into the wild or the thrill of danger. Debbie and I talk about what constitutes an adventure, how lockdown taught us to find the adventures on our doorstep, not just thousands of miles away. She adds, 'Parenting is a bit like that, suddenly there's this constraint . . . so how do you make adventures work within those constraints?'

This matters for our fellow bothiers too. The trip is only possible because it is close. Their male bonding over years of friendship, away from the demands of home, is no great test of the wild but a happy communing of friends in a simple spot, surrounded by nature. Getting outdoors is, too, part of the good life.

Our tasks done, we sit drinking beer given to us by our fellow bothiers, munching on cakes bought from the Eskdalemuir community centre earlier in the day, and avail ourselves of the luxury that is the Greensykes toilet, crossing the blue ribbon of the stream. Luxury is such a relative concept. The concessions to comfort such as a composting toilet or a nice stove are about as far as the MBA is going to go when it comes to adding equipment, and although in any other context these might be seen as basic, simple, even sustainable solutions, here they represent an added frill brought in from the outside world. By making places a little more accessible or welcoming, it makes it possible for people to enter the bothy world who might otherwise not have been able to do so – families, newcomers and those who are a little nervous. Even with this concession to modernity, accessibility and creature comforts, a bothy is still not going to be for everyone, no matter how cosy it seems in its present form. I wondered what would happen if you tried to sell this idea of modern luxury to someone who likes spa weekends. Not that there's anything wrong with a spa weekend, but there's no way my older sister would go for it if I proposed a bothy. Candles for light, water taken from the stream and wood gathered from the ground might not be an aspirational lifestyle for most, but Debbie and I enjoy the make-do life, at least for a night or two.

The bothy ethos is about keeping out or leaving behind bits of the modern world because, for bothiers, that's a large part of what makes the experience worthwhile and fulfilling. The bothy space seems suspended in a strange limbo between past and present, where there's a different idea about what a happy or fulfilled way of existing might mean without loads of stuff around. Rough as they may be, though, they are not places of hardship, but of joy and happiness. Jasmine Mawson, visiting a few months before us, wrote in the bothy book that 'we made the place home for the night, got cozy, fire on'. Her boyfriend and his mate were happy, and she enjoyed it too, especially the nice breakfast in the morning.[8] Bothy books are filled with accounts of treats and food carried in for sumptuous dinners. In the back of one of the Corrour books from before World War II there's a list of rations for five people for two days, including cocoa, sugar, jam and four loaves of bread.[9]

At the heart of these conversations are debates about how much or how little you need to feel happy. The bothy's stripped-back aesthetic is not necessarily concerned with macho displays of survival, though there's always a bit of that in any area of the outdoors world.

There's also the desire to live simply, to enjoy the strange fullness of a day of making do, to enjoy these landscapes without too much distraction, to have little impact, to leave no trace. Because of this balancing act between simplicity and comfort, enclosed within walls but in the outdoors, bothying is special and different, different even from getting outdoors in some other contexts. I love camping with my sister-in-law and brother in Canada where they live, for example, but when you pitch up at the spots on campsites deep in the British Columbian forests, it's not exactly like being in a bothy. We come in the pick-up truck and bring the gas barbecue. I'm yet to see a large gas cooking station at a bothy.

Aside from the obvious fact that it's too much effort to be lugging a load of stuff to make it a glamping experience à la Tom Haverford in *Parks and Recreation*, it also isn't in the spirit of a bothy. Despite that, I love the little accommodations people make to inject homely comforts, and the reminders of the outside world that haunt a bothy. This could be a string of twinkling fairy lights in Penrhos Isaf, a musical instrument like a pink guitar at Uags, a copy of a favourite book – I've seen many left behind, ranging from *The Lord of the Rings* to Mark Powers' photobook *The Shipping Forecast* – or (more controversial) a speaker. There may be things that we want with us. We don't need them for survival, and yet we still need them. *Bothy Bible* author Geoff Allan prides himself on being a packhorse who is able to carry in all the food he desires, though he baulks at the idea of an iPad in a bothy. My treat often is a little glass jar of fancy spices and coarse sea salt that enlivens the one-pot meals, and if I am by myself, a book or two. In the bothy you crave a distinction from the comforts of home to be assured you are in the wild, in nature, and yet you also surround yourself with the security of stone walls and a fire. As Debbie said, it's about the subjectivity of reduction.

As a result, the things you find on the mantelpieces and shelves of a bothy are a strange mix. Some seem to be straight out of another older world, others are plucked from the domestic comfort of our twenty-first-century lives. Debbie and I sit amidst that usual jumble of old and new. In a very different context from the world of bothies, the hodgepodge of the modern and the traditional reminded me a little of another community I have spent years studying. The strict religious communities of Mennonites and Amish in North and South America often spurned the norms of the world around them but made strange compromises about what they chose to welcome, what to reject. 'Black Bumper Mennonites' are so called because they decided to use cars but paint over the shiny chrome that's too bright and too modern.[10]

But don't we all do this in some way? Make our pact with what we want to take and what we leave behind? The modern world is constructed from ways of looking back as well as forward. Modernity isn't just a dismissal of all things past, as if we progress from one way of living to another and dispense with older habits and practices. Time flows in funny ways, and we all make adjustments to the time we are in, with a sense of what's to come but also what's been.

A bothy is no different. Its idealised space gazes back

to an idea of simplicity but it is also inhabited by people from the world of outdoor adventure, a world that loves modern gadgets and gear. Whether walkers, climbers or bothiers, I have rarely met someone who goes outside a lot who doesn't take an interest in stuff. The way we engage with nature now is through the medium of a certain set of technologies that all change the way we experience the world. Whether it's the ease of navigating on a GPS that removes the thrill of finding a hideout, or an expert scoping lens that brings the birds and animals closer than ever before, our perceptions are shaped by stuff. Whether that's a lighter sleeping bag or fancier bivvy bag, this is gear which generally gets you closer to the outside world rather than removing you from it or hiding you behind an electronic screen, but it's still high-tech equipment. If you are talking to fellow travellers, you swap notes about bags, pots, devices and shoes. It can also be exclusionary, says Debbie, if you don't have the right boots or bags. There are no hard and fast rules about what is too much gear and what is too little. But amidst all the stuff in a bothy, there's a tussle over simplicity, comfort and technology, a certain uncertainty perhaps about modernity and what it offers, and desire for something straightforward, satisfying and getting back to nature.

It's why, in the twenty-first century, two women enjoying a modern craft lager in front of a wood fire in a restored shepherd's cottage, watched by a toy ladybird, Debbie's keychain Spotty, can make a kind of sense. Spotty actually belongs to her youngest daughter and is a way of feeling less alone on a trip, like the girls are there with her. She doesn't need it to survive, but it's a treasured, important object for her travels.

In its simplicity, bothying is also pretty environmentally low impact, though that's probably not a way most bothiers would talk about their experiences. Even with a car journey to a parking spot thrown in, the carbon footprint comes in at a fraction of most other expeditions, and is radically less damaging than say flying from London to Scotland. In a recent photo essay, Murdo MacLeod argued that bothying is the perfect model for sustainable tourism. The MBA huts, he points out, have some of the lowest environmental impact of any shelter and accommodation system in the world, although this would not even have been on the radar of those who went out into the shelters in the 1930s, or even the 1960s.[11]

Living a good life is also about ethical responsibility, and eudaimonism has come to sit at the core of much environmental thinking, especially among activists and writers who argue that virtue should shape human responsibility towards the non-human world. What kind of person would kill the last whale in the ocean, cut down the last tree in the world, or squash the last mosquito? These are the types of question posed by environmental virtue ethics, and are the opening parry of Thomas E. Hill's important essay on the subject.[12] Most people have a sense that there is something wrong with such acts of extermination but cannot quite pin down why. Virtue ethics, with its attentiveness to character, attitudes, our way of existing in the world and our complex responses, attempts to answer this. And because virtue ethics asks not what is the right thing to do, but what does it mean to live well, it seems particularly pertinent in our current moment of environmental crisis. So many of us are thinking about sustainability and impact, and there's no end of discussion about what we need, what we can do without, and what we might be able to engineer in order to reduce our footprint. In short, how can we live well and flourish, but ensure the non-human world flourishes also. Bothies are a microcosm of these wranglings between sustainability, modernity and comfort. I don't think most people go into the bothy world thinking: 'This is a statement on sustainable tourism,' but the bothy does represent something different, a way of thinking about the world in an unusual way.

We all make concessions and compromises about what we keep and what we relinquish when faced with responsible consumer choices. The problem with living sustainably is that it sometimes seems to conflict with ideas of the good life. Being sustainable seems to demand that we strip away the comforts of modernity to which we have become so accustomed. Sustainability has become a fractured idea in environmental thought. The idea of living within one's means or reducing use of limited resources has been reframed in the language of 'sustainable development', a new terminology of growth couched in the framework of green thinking.[13] In contrast, there are those who argue we can only really hold onto an idea of sustainability if we actually consume and use less. Less is more is the motto of the degrowth movement, which has become a powerful force in Green politics. It lays the blame for the central crises of our world, both climate change and inequalities, at the door of capitalism and its mirage of continual progress.

There's also plenty of research to suggest that we might be happier if we lived more simply. Beyond a certain level, rising wealth and rising wellbeing don't go hand in hand. There's no romantic vision of the upward curves of GDP, income, equality, happiness, kindness and love all stretching into a rosy horizon.[14] Writing this at a time when the FTSE was peaking at over 8000, as oil and gas companies announced record profits, while inflation and the cost of living were leaving so many in poverty, it's hard to disagree. Instead of the continued pursuit of growth, a sustainable good life might lie in getting off the hedonic treadmill. Instead of living well by various means of engineered survival – think something like the thoroughly eco-modernist urban building project called The Line in Saudi Arabia – degrowth advocates that we should dispense with the 'false god' of wealth and reorientate our ideas towards a simpler life, one more connected to the living world.[15] Perhaps we should listen to poet Mary Oliver, who suggests we fall down not in prayer, but on the grass, knowing how to pay attention, 'how to be idle and blessed, how to stroll through the fields'.[16]

It's easy to poke holes in the idea of degrowth, as many people do on social media, by saying it's all about going back to huts and darkness and is preached from a place of privilege. I get that. Sometimes there's also a sense that people are simply trying on simplicity for the optics, virtue signalling their commitment to ecological aims. Moreover, sustainable solutions are rarely straightforward. Borrowing or appropriating something because it looks simple or close to nature doesn't necessarily provide answers when it's thrust into urban lives. Consider the recent debate about wood burners in affluent middle-class homes compared to ones in a truly off-grid location. I think people like them because they feel traditional or authentic, whatever that might mean, but in urban areas they have become toxic polluters of city air. However, it's also easy for people to condemn wood burners when they don't live in rural areas without other heating options.[17] The cult of simplicity can also be as expensive and problematic as the cult of stuff. A stripped-back lifestyle which may be low emission or low impact may often be more costly, simply unaffordable for many people. The relative cost of trains and flights remains a case in point and a perennial source of annoyance. In theory we might want to get away to the wild by sustainable means, but as Debbie says, getting a train is often not feasible. She would prefer to do that rather than drive. Often, though, it's just too expensive, not to mention unreliable when you have to be back for childcare.

It's easy to say from the position of affluence that life should not be concerned with material wealth, and it's enjoyable to experience the simple life in the temporary retreat of a bothy before going back to the comforts of the 'real' world. But degrowth is more than that. It's about a vision of the good life based not on growth or just acquiring more stuff but recognising that human and indeed non-human wellbeing might lie at the end of a different path. In her collection of essays *Dancing at the Edge of the World*, Ursula Le Guin once said that in questioning the rational, linear road to a utopian future, she was not 'proposing a return to the Stone Age'. She argued that utopian thinking is doomed, like markets, industrial output and people 'in a one-way future consisting only of growth. All I'm trying to do is figure out how to put a pig on the tracks.'[18] When the Western lifestyles we have created don't seem to make us happy, perhaps we do need a kink in the track that supposedly leads us to modernity.

That's the thing that underpins all these trends for simple or off-grid living, the feeling that the lives we are leading in affluent countries, for all their material advantages, don't quite cut it when it comes to happiness, and are also destroying the world that makes those lives possible.[19] Anthropologist Thomas Hylland Eriksen quotes the Norwegian folk singer Ole Paus who wrote, 'We have everything, but that's all we have.'[20]

In the evening, Debbie and I sit in front of the fire as music plays from a small speaker. I am pretty sure that we are in contravention of some people's bothy codes, and I wouldn't have used it if we had been sharing the space with others, but Gaz, Chopper and Dave are in the far room separated by a hallway. Music is important to us both and we wanted the space filled with notes, but as Debbie says, not everyone can bring a guitar up the hill. Nick Drake's lilting strings and gentle baritone tremble in the air, and there is contented quiet. Like the song lyrics suggest, a salve for our troubled thoughts.

Debbie stares at the fire, seeming to enjoy her first slice of bothy life and she later comments on how conversation flowed in different ways, interspersed with companiable silence. She expressed some anxiety that if she had been alone, she wouldn't have known quite how to fill her time. Listlessness, rather than being alone in the wild, worried her more.

In the thick of the bothy experience, when life is reduced to the tiny flame of the camping stove or the ordered laying out of mats and sleeping bags, it's hard for me not to feel that I am living the good life. I don't want to get all romantic about it, but I defy anyone to declare that camp-stove lentils flavoured with fajita mix after a day in the wet is not one of the world's greatest delicacies. The good life is not always simple, and living simply is also not straightforward. We might want to choose the simple, sustainable solutions, but they aren't always possible. Refraining from buying and consuming more, making do, embracing the natural world, choosing fellowship – these are all noble ideals. They seem obvious in front of the fire but are less straightforward when we return to our busy lives. And yet, in the moment in Greensykes, it is also simple. One reason Debbie said she liked the bothy was the simplicity, that she likes finding the essence of things. She has reproduction Picasso sketches hung on her walls that are a few lines only; she enjoys poetry that is concise. The stripped-back essentials of a night on a sleeping platform in front of a fire appeal. A house, as she says, reduced to its most essential elements.

The flames have died back to embers. We are about to settle down for the night when our neighbours call out to us. The clouds have cleared, and the canopy of stars is revealed above us. A moment later they are gone, shrouded once more in the rolling pillows of cumulus. Dark night skies are becoming rarer in the modern world as light pollution drowns celestial brightness. Old light twinkles down at us for a few brief moments, the smeared cluster of the Milky Way's stars stamped across the night.

I think how many people using bothies as a shelter in wild places have done this before, stared out at the light of deep, dark time and enjoyed it just for a moment in their transient time of dwelling. And I am glad, as I so often have been on trips like this, that while we have warm modern sleeping bags, lighters and a good gas stove, we have left enough of the contemporary world behind us that the darkness is still lit up by stars, not streetlights or lamps.

We sleep well and deeply on benches used by others before us. If to live well is to feel part of a community, then it's something you may also find in a bothy. There are always things that seem to draw people together, simple mundane acts and things common to most bothy experiences. You are enclosed away from the elements and the wild but also with the living world ever present. There is usually, for example, a bothy mouse from whom you must protect your food. In another context you might try to rid the house of these little visitors, but it's pointless here. There are socks hanging over the fire, soaked in peaty water. The smell of wood smoke. The sound of wind and rain. The light and the dark.

In a bothy there's a bodily connection even when there's no touch, no intimacy of a physical nature, no closeness that we might think of as corporeal closeness.

I think back to a trip at Staoineag with my friend Rich, both of us a little troubled by things in our lives, both in need of companionship. We drank port and whisky, searched for firewood, ate cheese, bathed, laughed, and talked and talked and talked. After all, there is little else to do in a bothy. There was a quick arm around a shoulder when I was feeling tearful one day, but aside from that, no other physical contact. And yet there was a connection between me and him, between us and people who had come before as we shared space and matter. Smoke from countless fires is on the chimney. You sit in a chair used by many people, sleep on a platform that has been a bed for many others. The stuff that lives in a bothy has a material quality imbued with emotions and memories, materiality that has the power to move us.

There's something about these places that produces a kind of legacy and connection. They are small spaces of intimacy and I love that. Debbie and I talk about touch too and its comfort, and how necessary it is to have a physical and bodily connection to feel sustained and nourished. Bothies helped me to replace relatedness I was missing: to places, to people, to bodies and to community. To leave a marital home was hard, an unrooting, the ripping-up of a stability that I thought I had wanted, yet didn't. But it was the relationship after that left me untethered. Twice, three times perhaps, I moved to escape, and when I finally did break free, it was at the expense of friends and things that I had come to love, in order to cut ties. I stopped doing the martial art I enjoyed so much, that I had excelled at, and with it, something disappeared. When you do a sport like that, there's a trusting physical intimacy between training partners and friends, even fellow competitors. You trust your body too, and the work it can do. Silly as it seemed – after all, it was a just a hobby – I missed it dreadfully. I did not immediately find a community that welcomed me and changed everything. Bothies did not always feel like my world, even though I am an MBA member now. But now I have come to recognise the sense of community and closeness that it has helped provide.

Many bothies are undoubtedly in incredible locations, but I think what makes them special is not necessarily the grandeur of the landscape but the little connections to place and people. Bothy users have a sense of creating a space for people they will never know, and for futures that are not theirs. Most people would agree that to live well means meaningful connections and an ethical version of the good life is one that cares for others. Environmental humanities scholar Kate Rigby argues that we live in a time when ordinary notions of dwelling have dissolved with dislocation and environmental destruction. In unsettling times, we have had to reimagine new connections to landscapes and environment 'because any unselfconscious connection that we might once have had with a particular dwelling place has been lost'.[21] Perhaps bothiers have found a way of claiming a different type of dwelling, just beyond, at the edges of things. The bothy life does not just entail excursions to remote, beautiful landscapes, but is built on a humbler sense of people sharing community in places that are a little damp, sometimes muddy, often smoky and dark.

As I leaf through the bothy book in Greensykes, touching

stories come to me of others who have experienced the bothy this way, and for the first time, like Debbie. As might be expected, Greensykes, as a relatively new bothy that's easy to get to, has a few first-timers in its pages, all finding their own way, all shaping their own experiences. Some visitors are surprised about how pleasant and easy it is to be there, and they make jokes about their fumbling attempts to cope without running water and electricity. One Londoner comments on the happy difference from his urban life. Children and parents come, such as Sharon, her friend Kay and their little dog Jack (complete with drawing), or Fraser, who popped in over the summer of 2020 for the first time with his wife and little five-year-old. One visitor even remarked upon the new composting toilet.

There are also the returners, and you get the sense of these new people entering a community that shares the love of making do and warming by a fire. Perhaps the most touching entry was a note from Roger, signed off with a kiss. He had come alone, back to a place that he held dear, as he had visited bothies with his wife. They hadn't known it, but their trip in 2019 to Greensykes was to be their last. She died the following autumn of cancer. Even in the deep sadness there is a sense of something shared, a fragment of a life well lived.

Michelle, a visitor a few months before us, has an entry in the bothy book that makes me rejoice. She's drawn a large simple heart, scrawled 'freedom' diagonally across the page. Her first bothy; she was shocked by how nice it was, and she cleaned up because she wanted to keep it nice for those to come. For her, it was a reminder of her childhood spent outdoors.[22] Personally, it doesn't bother me too much if someone brings a few creature comforts into a bothy, because there's something still so heart-warming about the idea of all these visitors finding ways through the world without mod cons, existing for a while in a simpler way. As Debbie says, 'How minimal you can get and still feel comfortable, still feel human.'

Sometimes the idea of the good life is a return to pasts and to feeling unconstrained by the things that bind us. Sometimes it's being outdoors. Sometimes it's small daily acts of care and love that bind us to others.

As we explore the lush valley of the Esk the next day, we wind our way along the side of the B709 to another place of shelter and retreat. Kagyu Samye Ling Monastery, with one of the first Tibetan temples to be built in the West, is a surprising collection of coloured, golden Buddhist temple buildings and prayer flags in southern Scotland.[23] Normally welcoming to visitors, it is shut for Covid to protect its vulnerable older members. It wouldn't be my choice to live my life like this, but the community too are finding their own way to navigate the strains of our world, to do good, to feel connection, and to flourish in simplicity.

In my work as a historian, I have always been intrigued by religious communities who grappled with questions about what of the world to take and what to leave behind as they sought salvation. The answers are always different, but it seems an inherently human thing to understand what it means to live a life well, and for everyone it is about more than just mere survival. Medieval monks in Benedictine orders may have been committed to silence and quietness in daily interaction, but they raised their voices in song, and Gregorian chants echoed around stone halls in worship. I love Gregorian chants, their soaring tones and fluid rhythms have provided soothing sleep music on many nights of anxiety, so much so that the monks of the Abbey of Notre Dame, Fontgombault topped my Spotify 'most played' one year.[24] Our bothy music vibe in Greensykes is different but equally important to us, though not as some salvific dedication. Debbie said that music is pretty low on her list of things she would be willing to give up.

We've all got different ideas of the good life, from monastic retreat to bucolic idyll, from fine things to family. Maybe you'll find it in a bothy, or it may be some other place. But the fact that some people do chance upon happiness in places like bothies in the modern world, pulls at the unravelling threads of that troubling narrative of linear progress that is arguably at the root of so many problems. Maybe it's not so much a question of what shouldn't be allowed in a bothy because it's too modern, but rather what bothying tells people about what they can live without, live with, and how they can make do. What surprising accommodations can we come to if we strip back a little and rethink our relationship with modernity.

I guess it's why I don't mind the odd fairy light or speaker. When all's said and done, it's still a joyful, simple way of experiencing the world. Simplicity is not supposed to equate to poverty or hardship. It's about freedom, not oppression, a voluntary giving-up. It's easy to say that, of course, when life is not a struggle, but recognising our positions of privilege, especially in the Global North, is going to be crucial to any sustainable solutions in the modern world. A sustainable good life should also be about pleasure, not just inputting lives into the 'utilitarian calculus', weighing up one thing against another, or buying off a hedonistic deed with some offset. But bothies show us that pleasure might be found away from the world of urban consumption. After all, bothying is about fun, friendship, fellowship, and there can be such joy in the immediacy of the tasks it demands.

We get back to the car and enjoy the touch of warm, dry clothes and the taste of a sweet snack. As often as it is repeated as a mantra, I sometimes struggle to live in the now, to appreciate the things in front of me, and to believe I am living a good life when I become consumed by thoughts about what I have lost or the errors I have made. Recently, at one low point, where I worried about being single in my late thirties, Debbie suggested that I listen to Anna B Savage's song 'Orange'. She intones the simple sentiment that it will be alright, that she needs nothing more than she has. The song in turn draws on a Wendy Cope poem that we both love by almost the same name, a poem that is an exquisite, restrained exercise in the celebration of simple things. After describing the contentment of sharing an orange, Cope concludes with a paean to the simple things in life, such as love and a full day of little tasks.[25]

We can't always live in the now and we don't always succeed in celebrating the little pleasures before us, but I keep on trying as I think of what it means to lead a life well lived.

FOUR | SECRET HOWFF

Hiding in the Hills

Bothy Jim eagerly shows me the shaky screenshots of his GPS OutDoors app that marks every bothy, known and secret, that he has been to.

'These aren't the ones you find in *The Scottish Bothy Bible*', he grins happily, pointing to some little purple flags on the map. 'You should try them.' (It was only my first trip and yet I was quickly getting initiated into the ways of the bothy.)

Every bothier who has been doing it a little while has a list of bothies not on maps or in guidebooks. I'm not going to give out mine; suffice to say I got them by word of mouth and a bit of research. I have to admit I liked being in the know too, part of the community, party to the secret. Who wouldn't? Most of us want to be in the inner circle, the VIP club.

Bothying always used to be something that was done by word of mouth, whispered secrets of huts and howffs between those who had the hidden knowledge, but that's not been the case for years. In 1998 the MBA put all locations online and most bothies are plotted on Google Maps. Bothying has become cool, and the increasing presence of bothy adventures in print and on social media has created a new buzz around the experience.[1] I have seen Geoff Allan's *Bothy Bible* everywhere. At a service station and chocolate shop near Applecross. Hata Café in Edinburgh, where I buy tiny but delicious and very expensive flat whites. In the hands of people on trains. Some bothies even have signs pointing you in the right direction. Grwyne Fawr is helpfully listed on the maps in the Blaen-y-Cwm/Mynydd Du car park for the reservoir and named as a place to stay if you are out too long.

But there are a few spots which remain hidden or secret, or at least don't turn up on Google Maps if you put them in. Not all of them are well-kept secrets, but they are secrets nonetheless. As soon as I heard about them, I too wanted to find a secret bothy, not just a normal one. On a mission, I tried to decipher the locations on the screenshots of screenshots given to me by Bothy Jim.

In the end, I realised many of them really aren't so secret after all. Most on his list are not MBA bothies and that makes them a little harder to track down, but if you were walking in the region, you would probably come across many of them. But that's part of the nature of a secret. Once told, it seems obvious. Previously unknown, completely opaque and obscure, but now revealed, the signs seem clear. All that I know is that I know something, to misquote Socrates.

Part of the fellowship of bothying, or indeed any community, is being in on the rules of the game, and once you are in, you get to know the club secrets. It's for that reason I haven't said exactly where I went on secret trips. Get into a conversation with me and I might tell you, but not on the page. I will keep the code.

Some traditional bothiers feel their world, the sacrosanct inner circle, is under threat in an age of Instagram posts and online blogs.[2] They have a point, and perhaps the hidden nature of some parts of the world would have kept them protected if they had stayed hidden. On the other hand, though, maybe keeping the secret is just gate-keeping, a bit of elitism. Secrets also have that power to push up against the hierarchies and structures of the world that we know and to challenge ways of knowing. A secret is all about knowledge. Secrets are both knowledge and ignorance all at the same time, and as philosopher and psychoanalyst Anne Dufourmantelle writes, 'the secret always makes three: the guardian, the witness, and the excluded'.[3] Knowledge held by only a few.

Initials carved into the bench at the Secret Howff.

* * *

In the darkening days and cold of late winter 1952, a group of men made a clandestine journey. Past the Gothic spires of Invercauld House, they lugged concrete and timber on their backs and made their way up the valley that leads up to Beinn a' Bhùird. They were waging a silent battle with the landowners, the mighty Invercauld Estate, with a 500-year-old lineage. In 1539, Finlay Mor Farquharson was listed as the sole tenant of Invercauld, and the Farquharsons have had the title ever since, although the estate is now run as a business and operated by a partnership of owning trusts.[4] The men were building a shelter from which to explore the mountains but without the permission of those who owned the land. The Shelter Stone and Smith-Winram Howff in Coire nan Clach, alongside various other howffs, provided access to explore much of the Cairngorms without having to bother with the cost of a tent, but to access the corries of Beinn a' Bhùird a new hideout was needed. The group consisted of mostly working-class men from Aberdeen. There was Ashie Brebner, a car mechanic, the shipwright Charlie Smith, stonemason James Robertson, a dental mechanic, Jack Innes, a steel erector called Jack Doverty and council worker Doug Mollison. Choosing a spot that could incorporate the rising cliffs of the land into the building, over the coming months they transported the materials needed, often in the dark, and by the spring of 1953 there was a cosy little howff. At a height of 630 m it was snug enough to protect from the wind and snow, that is until the gales blew off the roof in 1956 and it had to be replaced.[5]

'Howff' is an old word for an enclosed space, but it's taken on its own particular meaning in the world of climbing and mountaineering to mean a rock shelter squeezed in between boulders, a favourite haunt. At one time it was used as a label for a burial space, an association I feel a little uneasy about when sheltering under heavy rocks, but in more recent usage it referred to meeting places of disrepute. There's an old verb too, to howff. I too wanted a weekend away to 'howff'.[6]

When the Secret Howff was built, it was the tail end of the golden age of the search for howffs and shelters that stretched from the 1920s to the post-World War II era. At the same time that Corrour bothy was becoming a popular haunt, climbers were also seeking out places such as the caves in Glen Loin. This network of natural howffs in the Arrochar Alps, north of Glasgow, became the stuff of legend, whispered about, found only by the wisps of smoke seen from fires or half-heard instructions.[7] The secret shelters were not just places of play and fun. Rather, the coded hierarchies and counter-society that the caves created were a way of challenging the oppressive realities of working lives. In the same way, the Secret Howff challenged the dynamics of landed power and wealth by defying the unwillingness of those in charge to allow access. Secret knowledge subverted the hold that rich elites had on access to places and landscapes.

The Secret Howff, something between a built bothy and a rock shelter, is all that remains of the age of hidden constructed howffs in that part of the Cairngorms, for there were a series of them in this area. It's well known among climbers and has been well looked after. The roof had to be replaced again in 2017, a task undertaken by a team known as the Olifab Boys.[8] Remarkably, the exact location has never been mapped and though it's well known among the world of bothiers, so far everyone's kept the pact of silence. Despite the amount written about it, it remains unmarked on any chart.

In part a secret hideaway for men playing in the hills, in part a testament to the inequity of access to property and land, it's become part of bothy legend. I was eager to share it too with my trusted circle, to bring them closer by letting them in and to find fellowship. I planned a trip with three friends, but they too remain anonymous. After all, you might end up quizzing them for the secret.

A hangout that is a secret is a slight oxymoron, but the notion of a hidden favourite haunt sums up the howff/bothy perfectly. Keep out. No non-howffers allowed.

It's not giving too much away to say the Secret Howff is in the hidden folds of Gleann an t-Slugain. That much is common knowledge and there are plenty of hints online on numerous websites, but it won't come up on Google Maps. I pored over all the online blogs and reports, got out the Ordnance Survey (OS) map to trace the route, guessed where I thought might be the likely spot and then told my friends we were going on a trip to the Cairngorms, but I couldn't tell them exactly where. Pitch up and search were the instructions for the day.

It was a fun trip, I remember. A warm summer's day, the complete opposite to the weather that Smith and his friends must have experienced, when we park in the Invercauld Estate car park. There's no need to hide any more from the landowners, and the estate now maintains the place for cars and provides maps of the area. Access to the mountains is no longer a covert operation under the shroud of darkness.

Off we go in the pursuit of hidden knowledge. The walk winds past the estate buildings, following a well-marked track through the lower reaches of the wooded valley with tumbling burns before the land opens up to barer slopes. As we climb higher, the path forks, the upper route stretching to the peak of Carn na Craoibhe Seileich, the lower tracing its way into a lush green valley known as the Fairy Glen. It's well named. Shielded from the harsher weather and nibbling deer, it's a refuge for the trees and plants, an explosion of vegetation and waterfalls pouring from the rocks. Steep banks protect small grass plains with spreading rowan and birch. Trickling streams invite us to drink in the afternoon sun. We stop for a quick break sprawled out on the grass but then initiate Mission Find Secret Howff.

We search in vain for an hour or two, winding up the path in the glen. We reach the ruins of Slugain Lodge at the top of the valley, the old hunting lodge for the Invercauld Estate, now fallen into disrepair. In the great age of shooting for sport in the nineteenth and early twentieth centuries, it was a famous place for hunting both grouse and deer. One guide for travellers written in 1873 described the area around Braemar as 'one vast deer forest'.[9]

'This can't be it?' I ask.

That would be too easy. No, this is just the reminder

that the people who owned this place used to use the land for sporting entertainment. They still do, of course. Driven grouse shooting and red deer stag hunting are still popular pursuits for paying visitors.[10] Slugain Lodge has been abandoned since the 1930s, and although the MBA talked about taking it over as a bothy, nothing has come of it.[11] I stand atop the walls of the ruin and imitate the pose of a scout looking out for the enemy on the horizon.

We continue the hunt, first lazily, then with more purpose as it seems fruitless. Surely it is supposed to be more obvious than this? All the blogs said so. But the outcrops of stacked rock, naturally formed, look like the edges of buildings, and we investigate each one in vain. It is hot. Three of us give up temporarily and recline on our packs while we eat apples and drink water, the final valiant member of the group doggedly continuing the search. Birdsong and the still heat of the afternoon surround us. Then a *woohoo* echoes in the glen. Or at least we think it is a woohoo. We listen. There it is again, for certain this time. It is the missing member of our party, signalling that he has found something. Woohooing back to one another, we scramble up and follow the sound, and after climbing through heather and ferns, find a path. And there it is, perched on an outcrop, almost seeming to grow out of the rock, imitating the stacks of quartzite that jut from the sides of the glen. The door is tiny, hobbit-sized, and a confident, insistent frog guards the threshold. We have disturbed his place of repose. We are pretty sure he is the last inhabitant, cursed for being about to reveal the location, transformed by the magic of the mountains and spirits of bothiers pasts into a ranine guardian.

Despite walls of thick stone, it's a surprisingly light space with its skylight roof of corrugated plastic, and a rough floor with about enough room for three to comfortably sleep. Its walls and the wooden bench at the back are covered with etchings and engravings, but there is also a bothy book kept in a rusty old ammunition box. It seems appropriate. I don't quite know why. It's quiet, still, enclosed, and I could see how on a cold, stormy night it would fold you in the darkness of the mountain. Snuggled in a bothy or in a howff, without your phone and technology, there's a sense of what Dufourmantelle calls 'the intimacy with the self'.[12] There's perhaps time to contemplate or imagine, to play in a way which becomes difficult amidst the engagement and display that the modern world demands of us.

The usual collection of odd objects is arranged on the shelves. Batteries, cards, tins, fairy lights, an old 99 Flake poster and a battered, slightly tatty archive of the restoration project, tucked into a plastic document wallet. Just my kind of archive, displaying the signs of wear, discoverable only at the coalface of research. Plenty of visitors had only found the howff on the second go, I discover, reading the book. We'd done well, and we reward ourselves with a celebratory pork pie.

I sense the familiar thrill of discovering the undiscovered. Archives always hold that possibility of the uncut page, the letter unopened, the object hidden away for centuries. We are drawn to the new and the novel, each revelation holding the possibility of something more. I feel that here as I leaf through the pages which only those who got to the bothy would ever see. An archive is never just a passive collection of documents, but a place where ideas about power and knowledge play out. How and why information is archived shapes not only what we know but also how we think about the world, since an archive gives voice to some things and silences others. French philosopher Jacques Derrida wrote that 'what is no longer archived in the same way is no longer lived in the same way.'[13] I recognise how it only increases the sense of thrill to access arcane knowledge in this way, to consult an archive in a secret place, hidden in a rusty box, and to uncover what secrets the secret place might hold. As Luke D. B. wrote in the bothy book: 'If you are reading this, you are part of the club.'[14]

But I also think about what it means to discover secrets in this way, to reveal not just the place but people's stories written in bothy books. We face these dilemmas as historians and researchers much of the time about the ethics of what we uncover in archives, but also the value of reading into the silences, considering what might be hidden by the sources we use.[15] The tales of working-class leisure I have found in bothy books are not always told in other accounts of great estates and the Highlands. Archives so often silence voices of the marginal, the Other, or those who do not hold positions of power, and lives and stories sometimes hidden are revealed in bothy books. But people also do not write in the bothy and howff books with an expectation that their words will be archived and studied, though they are aware that others may read what they have scribbled. Secrets are always about power and knowledge. The space of the bothy is almost like a confessional, a place for intimate sharing, and to reveal all the details of conversations I have heard and things I have learned would be unfair to those that imparted them.

Who didn't have a secret hideaway as a kid? Maybe it was a treehouse, a cubbyhole, a bed wreathed in curtains, a den in the garden, or even the stories in a favourite book. Mine was the imaginatively named 'prickly bush', a monster evergreen shrub in the back garden of my family home which enclosed me in its dark innards, where I could search for bugs and bones and pellets from owls. A child's clandestine retreat is a place to play, where the adult world of hierarchy and order is othered and suspended.[16] The caves and howffs would have perhaps been a chance to escape not only the streets of Aberdeen, but to claim a younger part of the self that gets rubbed out and blunted as the cares of the world weigh us down.

As I leaf through the entries in the book in the Secret Howff, I recognise that impulse for infantile fun and for escaping for a moment from the world. A group from Stornoway can't believe their luck in finding the place of legend. Gemma and Alasdair walked in on New Year's Day in snow, the full moon lighting their way on a 'wonderful adventure'. A stag appeared, silhouetted against the night sky, the glare of the moon illuminated the snow in a magical blue shimmer. Children who visited with their father in 2017 admired it with childish wonder.

Isla, aged eight, loved the door. A small door, she writes, and very friendly. 'What about the hobet?' she adds. The door to the howff is small, a portal to secret space of another world.[17]

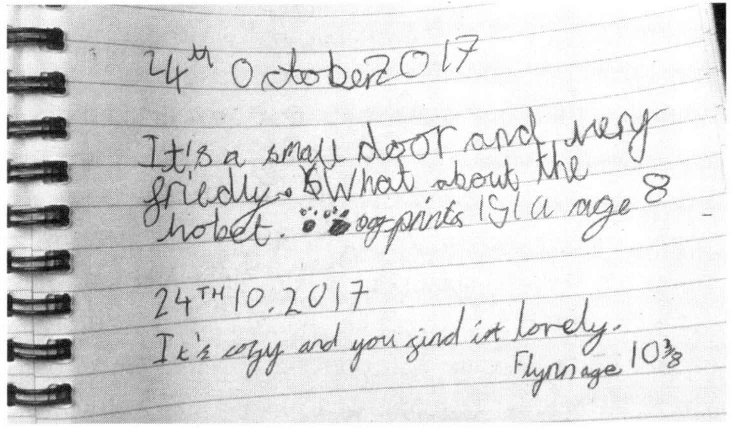

An extract from the Secret Howff book.

I think I longed for a time when secrets held this childish joy because for me the world had been filled with unpleasant confidences and painful reveals. The damaging relationship remained a half-secret in the shadows for a long time in a strange, unsettling dynamic of thrill, control and antagonism, and I could not always talk about it. With no one I felt I could turn to, I could not make known the full reality of what I was going through. Even as I moved on, I often kept things quiet from others, things in my past, things I became ashamed of and that I wished I had not been through. I wanted secrets to be magical again and a place to hide away.

The frog still sits stubbornly at the threshold, gazing

with bulbous stare. We always knew it was going to be a squeeze to fit us all in the bothy, and especially with a couple of other visitors whose bikes are parked at the bottom of the hill, we decide against a night in the hideout. A little disappointing, but I vow to return. We leave our croaking froggy friend to his lair and we spend the rest of the day enjoying the green calm of the Fairy Glen. Gleann t'an Slugain translates as the 'glen of the gullet', a place swallowed up by the folds of the mountains. My friend affectionately calls it 'sluggy glen' (and there are plenty of slimy slugpals). It feels like a hidden place itself, a flash of verdant green in granite and heather, that's tucked into the rock. Here the Slugain burn hides underground for a stretch, watering the land around it. It's what's known as a 'defile', a term for a narrow gorge where troops would have needed to march single file. Though it's not a local term, the name Fairy Glen seems appropriate for the place and its magical emerald softness. Some call it eerie. but it seems entrancing to me.

You only get a vague sense of the contrast between the plateaus, the peaks and the valley from the symbols of the OS map, unless you are really skilled at translating shapes into landscapes in your head. On the paper, a thin stretch of green follows the edge of the burn, a brief respite from the arcing orange of the contour lines. It is a surprise when you come upon it, bursting into life and growth. The whole glen certainly feels like a secret place. I understood why people lusted after it, but I also wondered what it is about novelty and the undiscovered that thrills us so. We revel in the excitement and yet also we are often unable to keep a secret completely. I wasn't going to reveal the route publicly to the Secret Howff, yet I too thrived on that strange tension between the known and the unknown. Even though the howff remains unmapped, I recognise that dynamic balance in the way other people write about these places in the bothy and hill-walking world. Just enough information to reveal that you know the secret, that you have conquered the place, climbed the crest.

The desire to find the hidden and the unknown, yet at the same time to proclaim that act to the world is an impulse that has shaped deeds of exploration and discovery. German cartographer Martin Waldseemüller's famous printed map of the world as it was known to European explorers in 1507 was the first to use the word 'America'. The only surviving copy in the Library of Congress, Washington D. C., has only the suggestion of what America is, the north of the continent a thin jagged wedge of coast with land marked only with the Latin phrase '*terra ulteri' incognita*' (land beyond unknown).[18] Mapping and the act of exploration sit at this intersection of the unknown and knowing, and it has always come with a desire to know the world, to measure it, possibly even control it. Hollowing out the secrets of a place was intimately connected to the act of exploration and conquest. I thought of legends of El Dorado or the search for the supposedly Lost City of Z, all fuelled by a desire to uncover something secret and hidden. Knowing the secrets means mastering the mystery. The projection of palaces of gold onto places unknown to the Western world, seen for example in Willem Janszoon Blaeu's mapping of El Dorado in his seventeenth-century atlas, made a claim for the discovery of secret, magical and enchanted places.[19]

Visitors to the Secret Howff are hardly conquistadors on the search for gold. But for those in the know with the mental map, the hidden howffs and places of shelter become a way of unlocking the landscape and its secrets. In some senses, they too are mastering its mystery, enchanting and disenchanting the land at the same time with symbols and markers that make sense only to those who are privy to the secret. My own OS app now has a series of purple flags and red routes, not for public consumption. As I tick off the Secret Howff on my iPhone screen, I worry I am turning into Bothy Jim, thrilled only by the conquest of cool, hidden places.

Yet the fact that the howff remains unmapped, even if not unknown, in some small way seems to be an act of resistance to this impulse to vanquish the secret places in the world. The eighteenth century, with its insistence on ordered landscapes, straight roads and enclosed, regular fields, not only changed the way in which people accessed the land but also made it known and knowable, dismantling the secrecy of irregularity, hidden caves and winding paths.[20] Preserving a howff shelter, not marked on a mapped path, keeps a little corner of mystery in the world.

The next morning, we wake, and embers are still warm from the night before. We carry on along the path to summit the peak of Leabaidh an Daimh Bhuidhe, the highest point of Ben Avon. Technically, though, we don't bag that Munro. We stop at the ridge of granite tors known as the Sneck, the bealach (a narrow mountain pass) between Ben Avon and Beinn a' Bhùird. We look out at the glacial depth of the valley below, wind gusting away breath and voice. I think of those who have camped out in the Secret Howff to attempt these ascents in previous years and how important it was then to hide from the estate. Secret meant secret for these men, but now the idea of secrecy has become a byword for popular honeypots.

Everything seems to be a secret or undiscovered place in the language of contemporary tourism. The websites Undiscovered Scotland or Secret Escapes are hardly a list of unknown places and yet the undiscovered place has become the holy grail of much exotic tourism. Going to 'undiscovered lands' now feels like a little bit like internet dating. The illusion of mystery, yet all the surface details known beforehand and an expectation of how to behave. So often our knee-jerk reaction is to put everything on social media, advertising the victory of discovery. There's definitely more than a little bit of the legacy of colonial conquest, now translated into contemporary tourism. And I do chuckle when I see people talking about finding amazing hidden gems if they are photographing the Buachaille Etive Mòr from the road or the Old Man of Storr on Skye.

Once-secret bothies are subject to the same trends. Put in a search for bothy (or some variant such as wilderness hut, shepherd lodgings, cabin) and you will come up with no end of results. Do it now and see. Wikipedia, of course.

The MBA website, and then a strange mishmash of articles recommending holidays in various spots in Scotland. From tiny pods to luxurious cottages with hot tubs and beautiful kitchens, the tourism bothy is a 'thing', a trend. Lists appear of the Top 10, Top 20, most remote, top-secret bothies in Scotland.

Perhaps my favourite is a Condé Nast rundown of the best bothies, an odd mix that starts with high-end, simple-but-expensive places: Inverlonan Bothies, on the edge of Loch Neil, which have buildings bought from Bothy Stores, versions of simple huts sold by the commercial arm of Bothy Project, and Loch Venachar Cabins, low-impact hideaways in the Trossachs. Then also on the list are places with a pretty different vibe, 'trad bothies' we might call them – Kearvaig, Cadderlie, Glenpean, and, of course, the Lookout on Skye, whose panoramic views rival any luxury holiday retreat. Kearvaig might have a 'secluded bay' and a 'beach on your doorstep', but getting there isn't really comparable to rocking up to a luxury holiday home. There's no need to create a hierarchy of ways of 'doing Scotland'. Go to a traditional bothy or don't, or stay in a fancy hotel. But something seems more than a little odd when Kearvaig is summed up as the best spot for 'a secluded summer staycation'.[21] Speaking as someone who loves the place, I am not sure how long you could – or want to – staycate at Kearvaig which is located in an active military training area. Presumably only until the Ministry of Defence (MoD) started firing exercises again. Besides it's against the bothy code.[22]

It's understandable why there is some anxiety from

some bothiers about how many people use bothies, but there are also some pretty uncharitable, aggressive reactions such as the Kearvaig Pipe Club who have a picture on their website of a burning of the *Bothy Bible*.[23] I was glad they were not present when I visited Kearvaig. Geoff Allan, as author of the *Bothy Bible*, has borne the brunt of the blame, rather unfairly, for people piling into bothies to party. If people do see these places as a holiday destination, tourism websites and newspapers talking about 'secret Scotland' have helped create this situation just as much as Allan's book or blogs by thrill-seekers. The language of secrecy has become big business in tourism.

There's always a contradiction here in the desire to get away to remote places, which puts pressure on them and their status as places of natural wilderness. Anywhere that attracts more visitors potentially increases the damaging impacts from repeated feet or flattened ground, waste, or things thrown away. While on Orkney to visit a bothy museum, I encountered stark reminders of this. The famous Ring of Brodgar on the Mainland was fenced off, as the ground was wearing away from too many steps taken. I wondered if my Instagram photos of the trip were only perpetuating the problem. The more these places get photographed, idealised, pictured, written about, the more people want to visit them. It's for this reason the one bothy on Lewis, privately owned, requires that you don't post about it on social media. No such luck for other bothies that have become iconic, recognisable, and featured in image after image.

With all these narratives of momentary discovery,

there's a doubt about how much you can know a place when you don't live or stay there, when you visit just for a moment to tick it off the list. People love the thrill of discovering something but perhaps that's not really knowing the place at all, but rather the illusion of secrecy, which feels like revelation and unlocking patterns of meaning. As Le Guin writes, 'to reconstruct the world, to rebuild or rationalize it, is to run the risk of losing or destroying what in fact is'.[24] Perhaps all that thrills us is that the place was hidden, unknown, and the layers of meaning of others, human and non-human, who have known this place before us are erased. Environmental humanities scholar Kate Rigby writes that there must be something in the land that remains 'latent or undisclosed' if it truly is to have its own agency and value, not only given over to our wants and needs.[25] If we discover the secret place anew for the first time, what room is there for layered memories of settlement and living?

We leave the Fairy Glen, and back home I certainly understand why people wanted to keep the secret, partly out of the thrill of community but also to protect the howff. I wasn't going to post anything on socials this time, conscious that the 'secret' label, while intended to keep the knowledge closed to only a few, may actually be advertising the howff further. And there are genuinely good reasons for keeping things secret.

Other places are unmapped in the world, some because they are top-secret military sites but others because they are important conservation areas that need protecting from human interference and impact. The location of the ancient Bristlecone Pine, Methuselah, high in the mountains in Inyo Park, California, is kept secret, known only to a few because the tree is so precious at almost 5,000 years old. His brother, Prometheus, was felled by accident in 1964 when Donald Rusk Currey got his tree corer jammed inside it.[26]

Some places, like the deep ocean floor, remain too alien, too strange, too deep to be fully knowable. The language of secrecy, however, is also intimately related to ecological endeavours and the study of the natural world. We often talk about uncovering hidden worlds of trees or insects. Like the bothy, we want to know and not know all at the same time, to be aware of hidden worlds, yet also we try to preserve these worlds from too much damaging attention. Uncovering the arcane knowledge of the natural world was once all about mastering that universe. *Libri secretorum* were medieval and early modern books that had formulas and experiments for revealing wonders. The occult properties of all manner of substances that were connected in a cosmological hierarchy could be understood and tamed if one realised how outward appearances and attributes pointed to 'hidden similitudes'. Once known, the secrets of nature could be used to heal ills and bring about marvellous effects. Wolf skin, for example, was thought to heal bites from mad dogs because of the antipathy between the two animals.[27] But now, connected as it is to the world of conservation and preservation, I wondered if the language of secrecy speaks not so much to uncovering hidden mysteries but tells of our sense of things that seem to be vanishing from our world.

We talk about secret pockets of green and gardens in urban spaces as if they have a life of their own. Coming upon them in a concrete jungle is a form of playful fun, a way of enjoying secrets that seem unlikely or unusual. The little-known Chicago nature writer Leonard Dubkin spent a lifetime searching for the secret places of wildlife and nature in his city. He rejected the idea that you had to travel a long way to find these hidden treasures or to find wonder, truth or joy. They could be discovered in humble urban spaces as much as in jungles or forests:

> for they exist in the common, simple, everyday things all about us, as well as in the rare and exotic.[28]

His descriptions of these daily urban places delight me but also make me sad. Alongside finding a sense of wonder in the everyday, here the language of secrecy also grasps at the retreating places of nature and greenery in city spaces. They are not so much secret as rare, unusual, and this is true too of places that are kept under a veil for conservation reasons. The secluded spots where some species retreat to, such as steep valleys and rocky slopes for aspen and birch in Scotland, where it's harder for deer to tread, are known as 'refugia' in the world of conservation. Secret places where things cling on even under threat.[29]

When I returned home, I didn't post about the howff, not because I needed to hide from the estate but because it seemed the right thing to do. The location of the Secret

Howff may not be entirely hidden any more, but it still is a secret.

I and others still keep that hidden knowledge. Maybe it's comforting to have some things that remain hidden in the world, not fully exposed to the glare of the day. Or perhaps it is more than that. A secret is not just an inert thing but a dynamic, ever-changing act caught between ignorance and knowledge which creates and shapes our ideas about the world. Secrets are something disorderly, not mappable, not knowable, and so they can be radical and disruptive. A space for play and imagination, for protecting precious things.

FIVE | SWEENEY'S

Creative Communities

Sweeney is a man made of feather, untethered and light as a bird. He is the tortured Irish king of the Dál nAraidi, cursed and damned, who roams land and sky in a frenzy. On the run, in the wild, eating acorns and berries, he writes and sings, a poet forged in the harsh crucible of nature, and at the eastern-most point of his travels from Ireland, he settles, just for a moment, on the Scottish Isle of Eigg.

> I'd build my cabin
> among the bluebells
> if only you'd all vanish in the mist.
>
> But I swear, I'll never
> come off the mountain
> to live again in the township of men.[1]

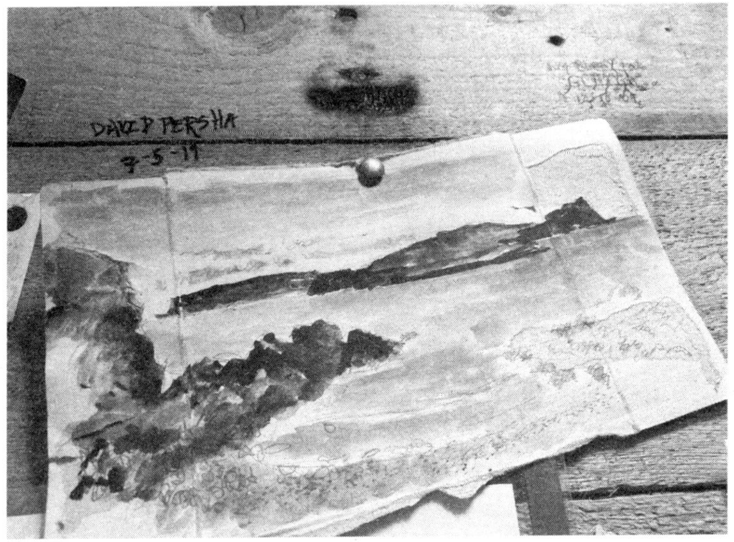

A painting left in Guirdil bothy by a visitor.

It's October when I visit Sweeney's Bothy on Eigg, a snappy holiday in the mid-term break. Nights are drawing in, days of clear sun becoming rarer in between grey clouds and rain. The sea and sky are no less beautiful in those slate hues, though, when the sun wreathed in cloud glows in a haze.

If Rùm is the rugged volcanic big brother, Eigg is more like its wee sister. Born out of the lava flows that spewed from the calderas of other islands, it is smaller and dumpier, although dominated by the impressive outcrop of the distinctive peak of An Sgùrr. The mountain's crested ridge is a volcanic wave frozen in time, in mid-air, the ignimbrite rock the result of pyroclastic flows that rushed from eruptions on Skye 58 million years ago.[2]

I only have a few days on the island, the end and the beginning of the week squeezed out by work. I hope it might get the creative juices flowing, staying in Sweeney's Bothy.

The bothy doesn't quite trace back to mad Sweeney, also known as Suibhne, the legendary - and possibly mythical - seventh-century king drawn from Irish medieval literature. Sweeney's Bothy is a modern off-grid residency built in 2014 as a poetic evocation of Suibhne's story, conceived by an organisation called Bothy Project and designed in conjunction with artist and writer Alec Finlay.

You can book it as a holiday hideout which you pay for, very different from an MBA establishment. Wake up to sea and sky in a private, beautifully kitted-out bothy all to yourself. Woodburning stove. Outdoor shower beneath the stars. Views of the islands. It sounds like the same advert you would get for any Airbnb or rental on a Scottish island, but Sweeney's Bothy is rather different. You can only reserve it for a week or two for six months of the year, as for the other half, it's an artists' and creative practitioners' residence. Simply furnished and off-grid, with only a living/kitchen room and a sleeping loft, yet it's not a bothy in the sense that most hikers and outdoors people would understand. Rather, it's a space that plays with the wider cultural idea of a bothy as a place of retreat and in some ways is part of the zeitgeist for cabins and shelters in nature.

Since 2011 Bothy Project has worked to provide residencies that allow artists to work and think while living simply and exploring the landscape. Sweeney's is the focal point of their work, though until recently residencies also took place at Inshriach Bothy in the Cairngorms National

Park, and Pig Rock Bothy, erected temporarily on the grounds of the Scottish National Gallery of Modern Art as an exhibition space. Bothy Project was the brainchild of architect Iain MacLeod and artist Bobby Niven. Niven's own time spent in bothies inspired him to explore the creation of small-scale off-grid living. It also owed much to Lloyd Khan, who pioneered green building and green architecture. At the core of the organisation's activities is the desire to work with the environment, with sustainability and the local community, and inspire creative practice that does the same.[3]

In many ways, Bothy Project stands in an established creative tradition. Bothies, shelters and shielings have long been a source of creative inspiration and creative connection. We might think of the idyll of a place of shelter in weathered landscapes, like poet Edward Thomas's poetic conjuring of a shieling, or Romantic landscape painting with a building nestled neatly in the fold of the mountains. American writers Gary Snyder, Philip Whalen and Jack Kerouac retreated not to bothies but to remote fire watchtowers in the North Cascades.[4] Now, in the bothy books, people turn their hand to artistic renderings of the mountains or their adventures, while contemporary Instagram drooling, too, is born out of a particular bothy aesthetic.

The notion of retreat to a shelter in the wild appeals to many and to our aesthetic sensibilities of the connection between nature and creative practice. Like Sweeney wandering in the wilderness, the romantic notion of the artist, the writer, the poet as tortured and alone in a retreat in nature is hard to shake. Henry David Thoreau has a lot to answer for. The nineteenth-century withdrawal to Walden, stunningly evoked in his writing, was an exercise in solitude and creativity that has shaped much popular imagination about what it means to write about and be in nature (although he outsourced his washing, so he was not that far removed from the modern world). 'I have my horizon bounded by woods all to myself . . . and a little world all to myself.'[5] As Dan Richards writes, Thoreau has 'seduced the modern psyche'.[6]

The bothy building too, nestled in the crook of the mountain or amidst the heather, takes on its own persona in image and word of a lonely stone-dweller. Yet it's a portrayal that can cut the bothy off from the world around it, relishing in a creative impulse that is centred solely on isolation and loneliness. I always baulk at this a little, while also feeling torn because, don't get me wrong, I love the dream of writing for weeks in quiet solitude, and I also long for places where birdsong and waves replace the soundtrack of Teams calls and trains. (I swear if I have to hear amend to: 'See it, Say it, Sorted.' once more, I may start a small rebellion.)

But life rarely affords that possibility for most of us. I am a little grumpy that my trip to Eigg can only be three days long, and feel pressure to be optimally, sublimely inspired now that I have those three days here, alone, dedicated to the purpose.

I arrive on Eigg on the small ferry with a gaggle of others, a couple day-tripping and a few residents returning home. The crossing is uneventful, the usual mix of hearty ferry fare and a few moments standing on the salt-sprayed deck to wildlife-watch. Minke whales, grey and black with small fins and ribbed throat grooves, arc out of the water alongside the hull, dolphins chase the ship like aquatic bodyguards. I watch as the ferry jigs itself delicately and artfully around the turning pillar, covered in barnacles, to dock at the new pier that has only just opened.

Charlie's Taxi service picks me up – a guy named Charlie and his hardy minibus. He offers me a dram of whisky, of course, from a bottle stashed in the side of the vehicle, and takes one himself. Then we make a stop-off to collect the local parcels and post, pause to pet one of the local dogs, and are off across the one road that leads to the end of the island and back again. It winds past the school, the old church, the red post boxes that still have 'GR' marked on them, having been put up for the reign of George V and then never updated. Charlie stops to point this out, and soon after we are travelling under the towering notch of An Sgùrr, then descending into Cleadale bay on the west of the island.

Sweeney's Bothy is up a small track winding behind the croft of its custodians, Lucy and Eddie. A short walk passes through heather and bracken, coming upon the small shelter perfectly placed on the arc of the sloping ridge. It's a simple building made of timber and metal with a large window facing you as you approach that stares out west towards the looming peaks of Rùm: Askival, Hallival, Anshival, Trollaval, ancient volcanoes with spiky yet lilting Norse names that seem to match their titanic form. Inside the bothy, everything is warm wood and simple designs. At the back, through the narrow gash of a window that's at eye level when you crawl up into the sleeping-platform bed, the sheer cliffs of Beinn Bhuidhe rise. You wake to a morning wall of rock and heather on one side, a pane of sea and sky and peaks on the other. Cliffs and waves dominate your senses from the safe interior of the bothy, your gaze always drawn to the tall glass looking west. The poem that Makar (National Poet of Scotland) Kathleen Jamie composed while in the bothy goes:

> for too long I haven't
>
> glanced at the sea.[7]

Sweeney's tale, Buile Shuibhne or Suibhne's Frenzy, was the inspiration for the building, not just in terms of its design and its location, but also its intended purpose. The legend tells how Saint Ronan cursed Sweeney after the Battle of Moira and fated him to wander into the wilderness in madness, where he would recite poetry of suffering. The tale comes down to us in three manuscripts, the oldest of which is the one written in County Sligo between 1671 and 1674. But the linguistic clues take us back possibly as far as 1200, and literary and historical evidence seems to suggest that the stories circulated in the seventh century, the time of the Battle of Moira (CE 637) when Sweeney went mad.[8] In Seamus Heaney's rendering of the legend, *Sweeney Astray*, the frenzied exile makes avian leaps, and at the furthest point of his journey he reaches Eigg. Here he shelters for six weeks in Donnan's cave.[9] Bothy Project residencies are intended to some extent to mirror his fleeting dwelling in a place of shelter where ideas, words and images might be created.

Months later, nestled on the sofa in his Edinburgh flat drinking a warming infusion out of beautiful porcelain, I talk to the artist behind the bothy, Alec Finlay, about his vision for the dwelling. It is, he says, a thorn-made building. When he conceived of it, he envisioned a place that would stand:

> square and plumb
> on a hill facing
> a rugged mountain skyline
>
> the hut-yet-to-be-built
> has found its home
> in the vale of Cleadale
> on the Isle of Eigg
>
> the furthest of the leaps
> the outcast Sweeney made
> in his mad journey.[10]

Alec is a quiet, thoughtful speaker. His measured words display a precision of language that is mirrored in his work, a careful consideration of place awareness and bodies, form and naming.

The design of the bothy is full of intention. A thorn-shaped column at the centre arcs to serve both as a strut to support the bed - a cradle to sleep in - and higher up, a sheltering canopy. I snuggle up there as soon as I arrive, read, eat snacks, play a computer game (only something I can entertain as I have my laptop and electricity, unlike a traditional bothy), and read a bit more. The curving wood echoes the tales of Sweeney's nights spent in a tree.[11]

Alec describes the bothy's placement as a rare spot between the granite rocks and the ever-changing sea. A perfect shieling. We talk too about access and vulnerability. Alec himself has ME or chronic fatigue syndrome and is unable to visit MBA bothies because of the distance and the damp, so this too is interwoven with his design. It is a place that allows for recuperation and engagement in place - without difficult travel and the slightly wet walls. We talk about whether it would be oppressive for some, in this enclosed quiet. He asks if it would be painful for me if I was suffering from a bout of depression or anxiety, a place to go mad or escape madness. Perhaps both, I think.

He likes that Bothy Project, in their renting of the bothy, have stayed true to the ideal that you don't go for long. This is not a place to retreat for months, creating an entire work in isolation. It's trying to curate a moment to pause, reflect, create and recuperate. It's different from an MBA bothy, in some ways more accessible because it's dry and comfortable, in some ways less because you have to book and pay for it. Traditional bothies, Alec says, are not really buildings that encourage viewing, since they are enclosed away from the elements. Yet they also share something with Sweeney's, in that sense of temporary settlement, engagement with place and a caesura that produces creative connections. A particular type of aesthetic inspiration comes from being in the Highlands and conquering the peaks, but Alec's work asks what it might mean to experience place from the point of view of dwelling and encourage different understandings of place-awareness. He devised the term 'hutopianism' for an exhibition called 'Machines à penser', that explored the relationship between exile or retreat and places that favour intellectual creativity, grounded in the work of three philosophers, Theodor W. Adorno, Martin Heidegger and Ludwig Wittgenstein.[12] As a term, it has now become part of a wider movement where artists create huts, shelters and viewing platforms, not simply to gaze upon the wilderness but as a way of offering chances to discuss new ideas about living, new ecological, architectural, social and technological models.

As I settle into Sweeney's for a few days, I do a lot of sitting and looking, as well as walking. There's something about the space that invites you to view and to consider, but also does not dictate the form of that viewing. The bothy is simply set up for whatever you need, but without distraction. Calum Wallis, a Dundee-based artist who spent time at Sweeney's in the winter of 2022, said he liked the way the bothy didn't tell you what you are supposed to do – there are books and a cosy reading nook but no towering, intimidating, commanding library.[13] A desk or dining table, but it can be moved wherever you please. A simple kitchen, the large stove that heats the tiny building with surprising speed, one snug armchair to curl up on. There's also plenty to keep you occupied as you attend to the daily acts of living. In the gazing and the chopping and the caring for the house there is a form of creation, producing its own kinds of work and thought.

Perhaps I imagined I might retreat into the wild and then sit down to write endless pages of beautiful prose. I don't.

It's so hard to shift into the mode of 'now I shall be creative'. I read and make some notes, then stop for tea while I gaze at Rùm, or tend to the stove, but in general I feel at times discouragingly unproductive. Yet maybe there is use even in the seeming inaction. I was comforted reading writer Kaddy Benyon's account of her time on Eigg, worrying about the little she wrote.

> I walked, chopped, daydreamed, combed, wept and baked . . . interspersed with long stretches of just looking, staring through the window at the view of Rùm in quadriptych.[14]

Anyway, though I love the dream, I am not sure that in reality I draw from the wellspring of isolation. Rainer Maria Rilke is one of my favourite poets, but I take issue with him when he says, 'The necessary thing is after all but this: solitude, great inner solitude.'[15]

I have found inspiration in bothies but not in the way I expected, not through solitude but rather creativity born out of connection and collaboration. But perhaps that is entirely the point of Sweeney's. It stands in a long tradition, as Bothy Project director Lesley Young says, of the bothies as not 'purely retreats', but quiet places of caring and doing, even when you are seemingly doing little. Creativity always seems to hover somewhere in that gap between silence and noise, or between loneliness and the peopled life. A life lived in complete isolation, with nothing to occupy our time but our own minds, would provide little to inspire the imagination, and yet we all need that quiet that allows us to hear thoughts or craft dreams. Even then, what good is a dream when you have no one to tell it to when you wake in the morning?

It's for similar reasons, I think, that traditional bothies can also be creative places. Although they don't offer that same space for viewing and contemplating as a retreat, there's still plenty of thinking and making. Lots of people suddenly become impromptu poets or artists when presented with the blank space of the bothy book and time to write, a lack of distraction or possibly a lack of other entertainment. Leafing through the archives, I couldn't help but be drawn to the doodles and the drawings in bothy books. Some are as simple as sketches in the margins, stick men and stick dogs, others are full-scale portraits. There are pencil outlines of landscapes and vistas, such as a quick drawing of Camasunary bay from 2002.[16] Others are whole comic-strip narratives of their time in the bothy, such as Mary and Helinka, who had come to help work on Maol-bhuidhe in 1973, lured, they said, by Roy with the promise of sunshine. Corrour's books are full of cheeky figures inside the building. Bare bottoms bend over in the rapid scramble to pull on clothes before getting too cold, while socks hang on a line. You can almost smell their delightful, musty, sweat-soaked aroma that in a few hours is going to mingle with wood smoke.[17] Bottled scent of bothy, one might call it. There's a similar variety in what people write too, from staccato entries about weather and food, to long day-by-day accounts of what peaks were climbed, to those with more literary aspirations.

As I read and note my thoughts down on Eigg, I wonder if it's not the isolation which allows people to be productive but simply having a space to play and to be busy, but busy in a different way from the day-to-day. Given a chance to write, a lot of people do, and perhaps it was my imagination, but the more I looked at the bothy books, the more I realised that the type of notebook chosen moulded how people expressed themselves. Small narrow-lined books result in truncated reports, whereas the wedding-guest book, actually celebrating a bothy marriage, put in Corrour in 1996, with big blank pages, results in verbose entries and sprawling illustrations.[18] In some places the bothy itself has become a canvas. Entering Claerddu bothy along the Cambrian Way, you are treated to walls that shout and sing the reminders of people's presence, covered in engravings and messages. I guess it's technically graffiti, but there's no bothy book in this building, so the wood cladding has become the pages on which people etch their words. On the walls someone has artfully drawn the tree that grows outside the bothy. Crooked, leaning like the Tower of Pisa, with a thin, long trunk and twisted crown of branches, atop which is perched a corvid of some kind, it's been given a caption too. *Don't cut the tree.* And no one has.

Space and matter in bothies seep into people's thoughts in surprising ways, and even the material to light the fire becomes the artist's tool. People grab whatever is to hand and scribble, write or draw. A lovely entry in Corrour in 1938 has been written with charcoal because there was no pen or pencil.[19] I liked the continuity between the creative acts entertained in MBA bothies and artists' retreats, which defies easy definitions of high and low art. Calum's large canvases of the cliffs near Sweeney's Bothy were also made using inks ground from charcoal and seaweeds.

Creativity, as record producer Rick Rubin writes, is something that is common to all humans, not a special gift given to a few, and creative acts do not have to be bought, sold or seen to be art.[20] I was drawn to the democratisation of form, function and process here. It's the art of the ordinary - made with things around, depicting everyday things. The romantic landscape certainly excites people's imaginations in these places, but bothy art also pushes against that. Alongside misty peaks and snowy skies, people write about dirty socks, tinned food, dogs, mud, buildings and bodies.

It's why, too, I was drawn to Nicholas J. R. White's photographs of bothies. His series *Black Dots*, shot on a Chamonix large-format 5x4 field camera over the course of a couple of years, documents the world of mountain huts. His book includes achingly beautiful images of bothies in winter landscapes amidst tumbling mountain screes, but this is not a simple cliché of towering peaks and romanticised buildings. His photographs pick out the black dots, old shielings and crofts as they historically appeared on OS maps, of the bothy network as a chain of places that connect the landscape. But he also documents the eclectic assemblage of people and things that constitute bothy interiors. Intimate portraits sit alongside still lifes of stacked shelves with books and tins or glowering deer skulls on wax-covered mantlepieces, and even the Penrhos Isaf toilet outhouse makes an appearance.[21]

After coming across his work, recommended to me by a friend when I first started thinking about bothies, a quick email exchange soon saw us arranging a Zoom call. Nicholas opened the call with what I have come to learn is his typical dry humour.

'So, bothies hey?' he presents as his opening gambit, and laughs.

The professional conversation quickly turns into a two-hour-plus natter about bothy culture. Bonding over the buildings, we have become firm friends ever since. On the call, we share a few tales about characters we have met and objects we have seen. His personal favourite is a massage book in Warnscale bothy in the Lake District. He found it an amusing addition to the bookshelf, but it also speaks, he says, to the layers of human history in a bothy.

'They are sensory places', he adds, 'filled with the scent of a thousand fires.'

That feeling of bothies as places you can almost touch or smell is present in his photographs too.

Perhaps my favourite image is a shot of Shenavall, a much-beloved bothy, in what is known to many as the 'Great Wilderness'. Morning sun hits the peaks, still ringed in mist, the bothy below, and it seems as if you could reach out to feel the dew that sits on the grass of the glen of Allt a' Chlaiginn. It seems to encapsulate the empty loneliness of the mountains, until you spot a small figure hovering at the door, interrupting the scene of wilderness, an accidental interloper, Nicholas explains, when speaking at an event I organised a few months later. The bothies in his photographs are not empty places of the sublime imagination, nor are the people in the portraits isolated creative geniuses retreating to cabins like Thoreau or Wittgenstein. Rather, these are ordinary men and women, writing in the bothy books, doodling on their pages, making their mark in a space and part of a particular community of hikers and Munro-baggers. In the bothy, they are turned momentarily into writers, diarists and, sometimes, artists.

Sweeney's Bothy on Eigg.

* * *

Every morning in Sweeney's I wake up to clear light shining through the window, looking west to the ridges of Rùm and the waves. Sometimes it's the bright morning sun, sometimes the dark shadows of looming clouds. In a bothy you become very aware of light and the limits of light, whether it's a traditional MBA bothy or an off-grid retreat. Sweeney's has a couple of lamps and a kitchen light, all run off the solar panels. But even so, as the day fails, the glow of these lamps only just seems to hold the night at bay. We have become so used to the glare of lamps whenever and wherever we need it, but as day fades, so too does the ability to see the page or the canvas.

I think about one winter in the house I lived in with my ex-husband in Oxford. Floods and dodgy repairs had resulted in no heating or light, but the deadline was pressing for my first book, so I found myself huddled over my laptop and notes with fingerless gloves and candles. Academia to the max. I thought of monks in their scriptoriums peering over illuminated manuscripts, hurrying to finish in the daylight hours, flames flickering in the gloaming, compared with being up all night to meet deadlines. How different things might be without the ability to light into the dark hours.

That fading light of Scottish skies and the glowing glimmer of a candle or fire is part of the thrill of a bothy too. As problematic as all the romantic visions of the Highlands and Islands often are, there is something undeniably special about the light at these western edges of Scotland, where horizon and sea merge, and pink, orange and red bleed from the sun into the water at daybreak and sunset. It's a light that's inspired countless people over centuries. Artist Winifred Nicholson came often to the west coast of Scotland, including Eigg, with her friend, the poet Kathleen Raine, first in 1950 and a final trip in 1980 just before Winifred died. Drawn to 'the clear sea-light of May' but also the brooding darker skies of colder months, both women found inspiration here.[22] Raine wrote of love and light on Eigg, penning her lyrical poem entitled 'Love Spell'. 'By the way of the sun/ By the dazzle of light/ By the path across the sea,/ Bring my lover'.[23]

Perhaps this was a paean to her unrequited love for Gavin Maxwell, author of the *Ring of Bright Water* and famed for his fondness for otters. Maxwell became the more famous writer and naturalist. It was Raine, though, who had gifted him the name for the work which was to become famous. In her poem 'The Marriage of Psyche' she writes:

He has married me with a ring, a ring of bright water
Whose ripples travel from the heart of the sea[24]

The relationship was a difficult, fraught one, bitter on both sides. Maxwell was gay, and could not return her affection, and there was conflict over work too. I could not help but feel a pang for Kathleen, who sought meaning in the hopeless love and devotion. She wrote: 'I had clung to that role in part for self-righteousness, in part from fear of losing him; only by being needed, I thought, could I hope to be wanted.'[25] I read just a little of myself in some of these words, as different as my world was from Raine's. As a woman who has often struggled to feel creative, when I am told I am practical, able, intelligent, capable but not artistic, and who has balanced my need to be wanted by the men in my life with what I want for myself, I have made myself smaller, smudgier, painted myself out.

I found inspiration in the way in which these two women knew joy and creativity through each other, in the bond between them. Nicholson also suffered heart-ache as her husband, artist Ben Nicholson, left her for the sculptor Barbara Hepworth. If not, too, for the women who have buoyed me up, I would have given up the ghost of writing: my sisters, my caring and fearsome academic mentor Lyndal - it was to her I turned when I left my husband - and the quartet of four female academics with whom I talked and wrote during my postdoctoral fellowship, aka the 'wilderness years'. Raine and Nicholson forged a connection with the landscape of the west coast, mirroring one another's work, one crafting with words, the other in colour. The little cottage they had, not too far from Sweeney's, was somewhere they wrote about and painted light, a place of colour and sound. On their first trip together to Eigg in July 1950, staying in the manse, Nicholson wrote out in her notebook versions of Raine's poems, including 'Love Spell'.[26]

Neither was Scottish but both talked of the inspiration they found in one another, and also in the community of the islands and their crafts, in Gaelic culture and language. Nicholson spoke fondly of the women on Uist who spun and dyed the wool 'with wonderful dyes from lichen, yellow iris root, waterlily root, coal or peat fire soot'.[27] They went to church and listened to Gaelic services.They walked to Cleadale, witnessed the remains of destruction wrought by the Clearances, the few remaining crofts left behind, and Nicholson painted the Sound of Rùm from the Bay of Laig.[28] It's the view I look at also as I walk down in the evenings from Sweeney's, but Nicholson depicts it in her glorious chromatography of shimmering lights of yellow, blue, white and green.

The light that mesmerises me when I wake in the morning and snuggle into the bed in the evening, is the same light that drew Raine and Nicholson, and Nicholson was disappointed, when she returned in 1980, that the Gamekeeper's Cottage in which they were to stay had been modernised, and she no longer had to use candles. Yet all was not ruined, and one of her last works was the luminous painting *Candle, Eigg*, created on a dark day, in her small bedroom where the window was darkened by larch trees. Her final painting was of the blue gate to the Gatekeeper's Cottage, *The Gate to the Isles,* a reference to the Highland myth of sons of the dead making the journey west to live with gods on the islands of the blessed.[29]

There's something more meaningful in such work than simply the inspiration of the wild. Sweeney's location in the miraculous, weather-hewn place of granite and sea moved my soul, but I was always loath to fetishise such locations, acting as if they are the only place we can create, alone and in the wild. If that's the case, what hope is there for beauty and art for most of us? Must we also imitate the 'strange migrations' of Sweeney and feel the pain of solitude to wander, to write?[30] I hope not.

For all the fact that the bothies are in glorious and wild places, the thing I like about bothy art in the bothy books is the licence to create and be creative in whatever space and with whatever tools you find yourself. Hunched over a fire with socks drying, or nestled in the cosy nook of a cramped sleeping platform in a sleeping bag.

I've often felt guilty for writing at awkward times, on bus journeys, trains, squashed into cafés between meetings. I still maintain that the Oxford Tube bus service and Caffè Nero should be the headliners in acknowledgments for my PhD. As I was writing this book, facing yet another house move and couch-surfing for a while, facing another break-up, coffee shops were my friend. I don't have children, but I know that my friends who do, particularly those bearing the brunt of the caring, talk about the way in which the snatched hours before children wake or the nap time become moments when writing just has to be done. It's impossible to go on retreats for days, and carers (more often women) have always had to do this juggling act. Some artistic residencies now recognise that this is a difficult balance to strike and Moniack Mhor, a creative writing centre in the Highlands just south of Inverness, has developed a programme specifically with childcare attached. If it seems that women like Nicholson and Raine retreated into isolated glory, this was not the case. Nicholson balanced bringing up three children, and after devoting the morning to work, the rest of the day was spent in domestic duties and care.[31] We get so used to the space of an artist being sacrosanct and separate, but this is the preserve of the wealthy, the privileged, those without caring responsibilities. Maybe I would be a better writer with an isolated studio, but maybe not. I have always enjoyed the collaborative side of work too, inspiration that comes from incidental encounters, chance observations, and the fire of conversation.

Sustained projects need time and often quiet, but they also are borne out of daily interactions and can emerge in the strangest places. We can write in a studio or café, draw on a canvas or scribble in the margins of a book, sing at a concert but also in the shower or with the family in the car. Each and every act is a creative one. I know how much I and many others would value more time to work on artistic endeavours (although, then again, it's easy to imagine another day or another week would make a project better). But perhaps we should also not be too hard on ourselves when they get put together piecemeal, fitted around the reality of busy, caring, active lives.

Eigg is unique, and it's no surprise that Bothy Project developed one of its residencies here. It's a special island, which overturns lazy images and expectations of islands as cut off or fading or isolated. The word 'insular' has come to mean an inward-looking backwardness, but it has not always been so. It simply meant 'of the island', from the Latin. He might not have been quite the first, but Dr Samuel Johnson of dictionary fame bandied the word about in his account of trips to the western Scottish Isles. He wasn't particularly complimentary about them and complained of the penchant for rumour in these 'narrow countries' and the 'penury of insular conversation'.[32]

But Eigg challenges all that as a place where community, creativity and energy combine, and it underscores that an island can be seen as a place of change, not a backward-looking remnant. It's been owned by the community since 1997, administered by the Isle of Eigg Heritage Trust, after a three-year bid for a buyout. Despite initial enthusiasm for the plans by Keith Schellenberg, a former Olympic bobsleigher-turned-rich businessman who had bought the island in 1975, patience had worn thin as housing and livelihoods dwindled. Embryonic plans by the Trust for Community Ownership had failed in 1992 due to lack of funds, but patience that 'the land will be returned to the people in time' paid off.[33] This form of community land ownership is rare but could be at the heart of reinvigorating local communities and restoring landscapes, as it ensures locals have a say over land and its uses. Community Land Scotland is an organisation which represents and collects such efforts, listing the benefits as the chance to 'develop economic opportunities, enable the development of vital housing, build on a growing awareness of environment and heritage to enliven the social life of its people'.[34]

As I walk across Eigg, I feel this community energy. On the second day there, I decide to pop across the island to the shop by the pier to pick up supplies, a 16 km round trip, but one which let me see and feel the contours of the place on foot. Descending through the collection of houses at Cleadale, I stop off at the little blackhouse museum, which documents crofting life in the village. The building that stands there now is fairly sturdy, as it was improved in 1893. Originally, however, this was a *tigh dubh*, a traditional blackhouse thatched with rushes and bracken, possibly named after the soot that would accumulate inside them. Inside, the exhibits document the history of the families who lived in Cleadale.[35] Before crofts became the norm, the fields were held in joint tenancy by a handful of farmers. From May to September the young people took the cattle to the north of the island to pasture over the summer. It was a time for courting and love and fertility. When the narrow crofting system was put into place, this practice stopped, and when the potato famine hit, many young people left for Canada, where there was land and work. Ageing populations and the disappearance of young people has plagued the Highlands and Islands for decades.

But Eigg is reversing that trend. Outside the museum is a box with a small collection of objects gathered by the local primary-school children during excavations of croft number 7. The delightful little monument made by the young people who will be the future of this place is a mix of bones, crab claws, bottles and jars, the everyday finds of ordinary lives. Making my way up the hill out of Cleadale, An Sgùrr on my right, I come to the school itself. It's also home to the local archive, run by Camille Dressler, who moved to Eigg over twenty years ago and put down roots there, becoming a champion for the island's past and heritage. Archive and school, past and future, sit side by side. The school is vital to an island like Eigg, and the other Small

Isles. Without a school, it's hard to see a future for places like this as the link to generational inheritance is severed. It is a weekend day, so the playground is quiet, the classroom empty, but it is heartening to see the life of this place in climbing frames in the garden and the finger paintings on the windows.

Ever since the community buyout, Eigg has worked hard to create a sense of community. Creativity and art and culture have been a crucial part of that as much as shifts in land ownership and work patterns, and Eigg has its own record label and craft workshops. And since 2014, through Bothy Project, its own artists' residency. It matters that the bothy is not a second home, rented out at extortionate prices, but a small residency run with and for the community. The artists who come may spend a week alone, but they create work and ideas in dialogue with the place and the people.

The connection between creativity and place is most keenly evident in Bothy Project's Neighbourhood Residencies, specifically designed for people who live close to the bothies in the Small Isles, Assynt and around Inshriach. After the residencies finished, all participated in a series of recorded conversations, and speaking with startling honesty, they talk about the problems and potentials of rural and island life, and I am particularly struck by the conversation in the third episode of the podcast about island life between Norah Barnes from Eigg, Fliss Fraser from Rùm and Isebail MacKinnon from Canna, all of whom stayed in Sweeney's and who make plans for how some of the challenges facing the Small Isles might be solved. Bothies seem to be away from people, but this bothy is entangled with the community around it, and we hear voices from that community. Norah speaks about how it really was a 'neighbourly thing', the residency, and Fliss comments on how ideas fly around and inspiration flows when the Small Isles residents meet. Life, as it emerges in these conversations, is not concerned with the romantic retreat that people sometimes imagine is the norm on a beautiful island. Rather, their conversation flows over housing trusts, boiler maintenance, work and tourism.[36] Yet also something seems to have emerged from the breathing space to think in Sweeney's. Fliss said that 'Going to Eigg gave me space just for me to explore what I wanted .... I spent time doing things that the voice in my head says I'm not good at or I've not got time to do, like writing.'[37] Romanticism and reality don't always have to be opposing forces, perhaps.

The space of Bothy Project offers the time and place for a different kind of creative community, and it underscores the fact that the responses we mount to the crises we face, environmental, social and cultural, have to be aesthetic as well as scientific and practical, and they must be collective and connected to places.

All the participants from the Small Isles are also women. A coincidence, but it made me think again of the importance of generational connection, fertility, inheritance and futures. The name Eigg is a hybrid of Gaelic for island and the Norse word for a notch, but thinking about these women, I like the old Gaelic name, Eilean nam Ban Mora, or 'The Island of the Big Women', after the Pictish female warriors of the Queen of Moidart.[38]

* * *

On the last night on Eigg, cloudy skies clear and I sit out in the chilly October night. A pitch-dark sky and the creamy smear of spangled light tell their stellar stories of bears and hunters and brotherly sacrifice. I always think looking at constellations is a little like doing a *Magic Eye* book – squint, shift the gaze, then they appear. Sometimes you just have to look from a different angle.

Being in bothies has made me alter my perspective on so many things. I didn't spend the time in Eigg retreating into the quiet solitude of writing. In some ways I wish I had, but my brain has never been quite like that, racing through ideas and projects and plans. I have come to realise how much I need others for creative inspiration. Sweeney's Bothy does not offer isolated withdrawal from civilisation but a sense of contemplative retreat and wilding, in conversation with the community and the place.

In the darkest moments of depression, I have worried I would not be able to research and write again. If a tortured soul is supposed to be the sole wellspring of a creative mind, I never found it so. It terrified me that this ability to write and craft with words was gone. But piece by piece it came back. New projects emerged. Strands picked up. Habits remembered. I definitely didn't retreat into the wilderness and the suffering alone to find my inspiration. I am not down with Rilke's emphasis on solitude, but I have always found solace in his idea that the dragons in our lives are really princesses and that love and courage will transform them.[39] This I have found to be true. Not romantic love, not necessarily, but love and support from all who travel with you and who make you see the world with fresh eyes.

When writing this book, I gathered many of the people who had inspired me and nurtured my ideas or discussed the work. I treasure the kind words from my colleague Lesley, an archaeologist whose gentle encouragement always left me feeling assured and calm, and from whom I learned to look at the earth, the land and the assemblages of things. I can taste the quiet tea I had with Alec, and I carry with me now, in the way I view the world, a sense of the awareness of place that he nurtures through understanding names and language. I feed off Nick's humour and energy and endless love of images of places, people and abandoned ruins, and though I cannot replicate his skill, I try to put myself in his shoes as a photographer, working with a camera that requires him to see the world upside down as he frames the image.

Nan Shepherd's famous passage about viewing the world differently by changing your perspective, whether tilting the head or bending to look back through your legs, is much quoted:

> By so simple a matter, too, as altering the position of one's head, a different kind of world may be made to appear . . . How new it has become![40]

Yet shifting our gaze and seeing in other ways, with the eyes of others, matters. Bothies can be places of collective creative inspiration but not because they provide an isolated retreat, not because I found myself in a place of genius solitude, but because there I and others found a community who cared collectively, creating together.

We experience companionship and connection through creative acts, and the words or images of others allow us to visit landscapes we will never see, or places we may long to get to, although life for now is too busy and too full-on. We go as comrades alongside them, sharing in their travels and joys.

I look over Alec's small volume that he produced on Sweeney. In delightful, neat handwriting, it's got a dedication – for Kat. A gift. I skim over it and imagine myself under the shadow of Beinn Bhuidhe once more, the evening sun setting the cliffs aflame. Next to it is Nick's *Black Dots* and I stare at the images, picturing myself in bothies I am yet to visit. It too is a gift. Reciprocity, generosity and care in the act of creation. The dragon is a princess again.

SIX | MAOL-BHUIDHE

Walking the World

What are all the ways you can walk? Think of them now. All the ways you will walk today. With purpose to work. Sluggishly from bed. Dragging around reluctant children. Idling with a lover. Pacing anxiously to nowhere at 2 am. Striding to conquer a fearsome route.

There are as many words for walking as there are ways. Mosey or ramble. Mince or prance. Saunter, stroll, stomp.

And many reasons to walk.

In a warm July, as I work out the final months of my role at the university, my friend Debbie and I walk to Maol-bhuidhe bothy in the Northwest Highlands. We go with striding steps, but we also idle and deviate, stumble, and then amble. There's no one way to walk. Even when you are on a mission to get to a bothy. And I love that. There's something expressive in the many ways we can walk and wander in the world that resist the ordered structure of our contemporary lives and the pace of modernity.

There's also no way into a bothy other than to walk.

Or possibly cycle or kayak some of the way. That's part of the joy. You have to put one foot in front of the other and trust the path, even when it's unclear, undone by weather and rain. Walking to bothies made me think of author Torbjørn Ekelund's idea that you are 'moving in the way we were meant to move'.[1]

But walking, too, can be an act of conquest, a way to map the world. It can be destructive and aggressive. The way we walk in the world, the way we may be allowed to walk, matters.

A drawing from the bothy book for Loch Chiarain bothy.

I think I had built up the route to Maol-bhuidhe in my head to terrifying proportions. The building is nestled amidst the peaks of the western side of Ross and Cromarty. Though it's not an official designation, most people know this area as Wester Ross, a romantic name of Highlands imagination with one of the lowest population densities in Europe.[2] Maol-bhuidhe is one of the most remote buildings in the UK, nestled amidst mountains between Glen Carron and Glen Shiel on the 25,000 hectare Killilan and Inverinate Estate. Situated on the Cape Wrath Trail, a long-distance route that stretches from Fort William to the northwest tip of Scotland, it's a popular spot at which walkers pitch up to break the hike. I say popular – I mean by the standards of the Highlands (and the pretty remote Highlands). Initially when I scouted out the path, I wanted to take a route that starts at Morvich, winding past the Falls of Glomach, where water crashes down from a height of 113 m in a haze of rainbow-infused droplets. I think I had in my head dramatic images of Sherlock Holmes and Moriarty at the Reichenbach Falls. Exciting, definitely, but also possibly lethal, especially as I had planned this first as a solo trip. Every report I looked at warned of the precipitous scramble down the sides of the waterfall, past a sheer drop into the thundering torrents. Without heavy packs and with company, fine, I thought, but maybe not this time. I wanted to get to Maol-bhuidhe, but there was no need to die in the attempt.

Fortunately, I recruited Debbie to the cause. I was glad to book her in around her hectic schedule as a busy working single mum and a wonderful, sociable friend. We chose the Camas Luinie route, more fords and steeper climbs, but a little shorter than the walk in from Killilan. Driving up from Glasgow and past lay-bys of tourists drooling over the peaks of Glencoe from the safety of their camper vans, we park up around 5 pm in the Camas Luinie picnic area. There's still plenty of time in the light evenings of a Scottish summer, and we are lucky that the threatened rain has disappeared to leave only golden-blue skies. We walk for companionship, friendship to beat out the worries of the world through pacing and prattle.

As we set off, Debbie says she is glad that the walk is long and that a winding road lies ahead of us. There's plenty of time to get into the juicy stuff of our lives. After a few kilometres of walking, feet and tongues become looser, and the freedom that comes from speaking to someone as they stride beside you is a funny thing. From Thoreau to Rebecca Solnit, there's no shortage of writers who have explored the mind-body connection of pacing feet and an active mind.[3]

Debbie and I had started our relationship walking. I remember distinctly the moment we clicked, passing under pine trees somewhere in the Sussex countryside. I told her about my divorce, the troubles that came after. It had been similar for her, she said. Both recovering from difficult relationships with difficult partners, both now in a much happier place and relishing the joyful freedom that comes from dumping emotional baggage. Or trying to. We walked side by side that afternoon, and the parallel lives we lived connected us in a way I could not quite understand but that has made me grateful ever since. The freedom found in our pacing companionship has stayed with us. We always walk to meet, meet to walk, or walk to talk.

We pass along the edge of the River Elchaig, following the winding water, first through midgey woods of dappled light, then across the bridge at Coille-righ into the high-sided valley. My memories of this part of the walk are sensations of light and heat and stone amidst laughing conversation. The yawning blue ribbon of the river widens into a loch. We hear the sheep complaining for their dinner. A charm of goldfinches flits frantically in the tops of the bushes. I don't remember every word of what we talked about, but conversation flowed like soft evening light, about boyfriends, love, sex, walking, writing, bodies, poetry, children. A friend once told me that when I needed to have any difficult conversations with my partner, to do so on a walk. There's no face-to-face confrontation, and the painful words spoken seem to settle gently in the landscape around you rather than being thrown as daggers in a duel.

People have always found companionship in going to bothies together, by walking along the path and building something in every step taken and mile covered. Perhaps because of the remoteness, especially when it comes to somewhere like Maol-bhuidhe, it is a place for fellowship forged in the walking. These are stories woven with love and friendship, but also loss, because climbers and Munro-baggers lead dangerous lives. Maol-bhuidhe became an open bothy in 1970 and it was dedicated to people who had walked and worked together. The renovation project was launched as an act of commemoration to Brian Ripley, a climber who made the first attempt to bag all the Munros in a continuous trip. Along with his brother Alan, he made it to number 230 of the 282 peaks before bad weather halted the cause. Not long after, in 1968, he died when hit by rockfall on Malubiting Peak in the Karakoram range in Pakistan.[4] There's joy as well as grief in these tales. Two of the couples who visited in the early days in February 1970 were both married a few months later – one was Bernard and Betty Heath of B&B MBA-founding fame, the other Penny and Mark (hitched via Bernard's 'Marriage Bureau', they joke in the book): 'Join the M.B.A. & find a mate.' But another in that party, Dan Elliot and his dog Whisky, came to a tragic fate. They died on Ben Nevis a couple of years later. 'RIP Whisky II.'[5]

As we pass Loch Elchaig, we are joined by a stranger called Patrick. He's walking the Cape Wrath Trail, he says. He always wanted to do it but never got round to it and he just picked up the book one day and said, 'Today's the day.' His rhythm is a little faster than ours, he's caught us up from somewhere, but he slows to match our step for half an hour or so.

'Lemon sherbet?' I say, putting out my hand, having retrieved the sticky gift from my bag. He accepts, passing over some kind of coffee sweet in return.

The Cape Wrath Trail isn't really a trail at all, not a marked one, anyway, but a rough route traced out by Denis Brook and Phil Hinchliffe in 1983.[6] It's what photographer David Lintern calls a 'desire line' that winds up the northwest side of Scotland from Fort William to the tip of the coast, where nothing stands between you and the Arctic. It has its own special mythology and has become something of a must-do route for Highland hikers, with many ways and paths and layers of legend.[7] Most people we encounter that weekend, either on the path or in the pages of the bothy book, are doing the CWT - and yes, you do have to give the acronym if you are doing it properly - in one way or another.

We all stop for a quick rest where the path splits, one way going up to Maol-bhuidhe, the other following the line of another river, Allt na Doire Gairbhe, and past the peak of Aonach Buidhe. Patrick's going to press on, but we decide to explore a bit. Just a few hundred metres away is a cream-coloured building with a red door. This is the Iron Lodge. I don't know who last lived in the abandoned house, but this whole estate on which it stands is now owned by the ruler of Dubai, Sheikh Mohammed bin Rashid Al Maktoum.[8] It sits at the bottom of a steep slope with some vicious switchbacks, a route that leads to the Falls of Glomach. The name doesn't exactly inspire confidence, conjuring up something out of *Game of Thrones*. A YouTube video I found, while researching the route, of someone doing a found-footage horror-movie impression only adds to the sense of apprehension. The windows are smashed, the red door forbidding. We step inside.

If the place were completely abandoned it would be less weird, less unsettling. But the old estate house doesn't look like it has been empty that long. The unplugged Hoover in the middle of the lounge, the unfolded ironing board on the landing, and the blank TV in the kitchen, whose sideboard is covered in the rubbish left by people who have stayed overnight, give us the feeling that it is a house that hides a terrible secret. In the bedroom, a blackened pool of mould spreads into fibres of the red shagpile carpet. It seeps out from the centre like dried blood or sticky ectoplasm. We run out gratefully into the evening sun, away from the cold shudder of this strange building. Midges gather everywhere, the nemesis of any camper or hiker out in a Scottish summer. The Gaelic name for them is *meanbhchuileag*, meaning 'tiny fly', but as I try to bat them away in vain, I think of a line from Shakespeare's *A Midsummer Night's Dream.* 'Though she be but little, she is fierce'.[9] If you are wondering, it is only the females that bite. Little vampires searching for fresh blood for their eggs. Despite the swarms forcing us to move on fairly swiftly, we stop for a moment as the sun hangs lower in the sky and the shadows lengthen.

The climb up the short, steep track away from the Iron Lodge to the bealach is more arduous than the route so far. The rocky path veers in front of us, but the rivers that need fording are pretty dry. The higher we climb, the more impressive the views, and it feels as if we are stepping upward to catch the last rays of daylight from the peaks. I have that irresistible urge to look back, to see the path climbed, the distance covered. I want to see the veil of shadow slowly edging down the mountainside as the light fails, but I also want to reward myself with a reminder of how far we have come. I wonder if it's a little like tempting fate, congratulating yourself on the distance already covered rather than focusing on the journey ahead, like the Greek myth of Orpheus glancing back to his wife Eurydice in Hades, too eager and too soon. Debbie and I peer up at what feels like a near vertical 30 m stretch to the top of the pass. It isn't anything so dramatic, of course, just a slightly steeper bit of the path when we have tired legs and heavy packs, but nonetheless we curse ourselves for thinking the worst is over.

We reach the top and rest a moment. If we were different types of walkers, we might now peel off to the left to summit Faochaig, a peak of 868 m. But we aren't, so we don't, and besides, it's late. Plenty of people walk because they want to get to the top of every mountain or bag every bothy. Walking in this way can be an act of conquest, a way of claiming the land by stepping onto it. There are goals you have to hit and routes you have to walk to consider yourself a proper climber. In 1891, Sir Hugh Munro published his table of the peaks which now bear his name and, ever since, the craze for completing them has inspired countless hikers.[10] Even if you get pretty high, if you are a Munro-bagger or summit chaser, you will be disappointed if you get almost to the top of a mountain but fail to make the last few metres to the 'real summit'. There is, as Robert Macfarlane has written, a way in which mountains 'exert a considerable and often fatal power of attraction on the human mind'.[11]

Maybe there's nothing too much wrong with that but I have never really wanted to walk that way. I don't have much interest in it as the sole purpose of any hike or trip. It seems a strange way to see the world to focus only on the high goal above you. Nan Shepherd's famous poetic meditation on the moment 'ere consummation, ere the final peak' allows you to view the 'mountain shut within itself, yet a world,/ Immensity'.[12] She summited many heights, but wrote more about the clamber down into the innards, recesses and cracks of the mountain.[13] If there's a peak there, I'll maybe do it, but I also love the view I get from walking below and seeing the jagged etching of the rock against the dusky sky.

It's about 8 pm when we reach the top of the pass. The path becomes fainter as we descend onto the wet, high moor, where green sphagnum moss oozes water and peaty puddles glimmer with an oily sheen. The heads of bog cotton blow like little ghosts in the evening sun, barely tethered to the stalks, and yellow stars of asphodel glitter alongside. The delicate floral carpet, light as air, seems at odds with the looming mass of the mountains and the earthy downwards pull of the peat.

We try to read the tracks and work out if anyone is going to be in the bothy when we get there. On a walk over difficult terrain you tend to spend much of the time looking down. There are footprints, some barely held by the soggy moss, others clearer in the mud. Dog prints point away, footprints towards, but we reckon Patrick will have pushed on to Strathcarron. There's always a bit of divination as you approach a bothy, working out who has trod the path, when and how many. We want the bothy to ourselves, really, to chatter intimately without hindrance, though we aren't too bothered, but I think of all the people who wanted to be first footers at a bothy in the New Year and the friendly race of conquest to arrive. John Hinde, arriving in January 1974, was a little piqued to have been beaten to the title by Hamish and co.[14]

Arriving at Maol-bhuidhe. Photograph by Debbie.

That moment of arriving at a bothy is normally worth waiting for, the end of a pilgrimage of sorts to a place of relative isolation. And, like a pilgrim, you nod to fellow travellers on the way, you acknowledge their journey, their step.

Pilgrimage, secular or spiritual, to mountains or shrines, is rooted in the moment of arrival as much as the travel, for without the arrival the journey cannot function as an act of completion, transformation and fulfilment.[15] We turn the corner and see the bothy: white walls, white roof. It is a welcome sight, and after fording the final river, the last act of endurance (although in truth it is not very challenging), we tumble into the bothy and are pleased to find a well-appointed, beautifully clean building with wood floors and walls. We think it is empty, but we realise soon that the occupant is only sleeping, like the princess in a fairy tale, though we are not there to wake them up. By the morning they are gone, and we learn their name - Jess - but they will never know ours, even though we are bonded by a funny sense of trust. We are quiet so as not to disturb their slumber, but ascend the stairs opposite the front door, which opens out into the cosiest nook of a loft with a Velux window. Sleeping bags at the ready, we throw ourselves down for a long night's rest.

If I do sometimes imagine bothying as a form of pilgrimage, however, for me it is more than about idealising the moment of arrival at some far-flung sanctuary. It is a way of walking where you meditate on ways of moving and being in the world, both human and non-human. I don't think walking necessarily has to be seen as an act of spiritual communion, more that as you feel the weight and rhythm of your own body in the world, you perhaps become a little more aware of that world.

The step of our feet over tumbling scree and into soggy pools is along paths that might also be burns and we watch the passage of day to night and the crescent moon. Our path sometimes follows and sometimes deviates from the winding way of the river that flows fast or swirls in eddies around glittering rocks. We think about our own journeys through life alongside these ways, paths that circle back and return, with dead ends and roads not taken.

It was a long trip in. The next morning, we realise the camel packs and bottles are empty, and we go down to the river to fill up. The track down to the water is clearly visible, where others have walked before, doing the same tasks as us. People have probably been doing this short trip to the banks of Allt a' Creachail Mhoir or Allt na Sean-luibe for hundreds of years, for Maol-bhuidhe has been used as a summer shieling for a very long time. Men and women drove cattle here to graze the summer pastures, and on this site, they would have tended to them and led them to water. Pastoral paths of montane transhumance, the seasonal movement of livestock, have shaped Scotland's uplands, a landscape dotted with the names and remains of shieling sites.[16] In Wales, too, there were *hafodydd* in the high hills. No longer do communities come to these high places for seasonal grazing, but in the Alps, you can still witness the festival that accompanies the return of people and animals from high places, *Le retour des Alpages*. As snow comes back to the mountains, they then retreat downhill, just as alpinists and winter hikers make the reverse journey to seek icy pinnacles for pleasure.

At some point, Maol-bhuidhe became a permanent dwelling, though it is not clear when. As land was reserved for hunting or sheep farming, seasonal grazing had been given over to deer stalking, shepherding and gamekeeping. By 1841 the dwelling appears in the first census and then on OS maps in the 1870s. It was inhabited by the MacRaes, the MacLeans, the MacLennans, Renwicks and finally the Burnetts. Halbert and Mary Renwick brought up ten children here at the end of the nineteenth century, in a small building with three rooms with windows and a rent of £2 a year. In the winter, this would have been a harsh place, cut off for months by snow and storms with no options to walk out. You would need to take in enough food for the winter months, and schooling was undertaken by what was known as a 'side teacher', who came for a week at a time, rotating between here, Pait Lodge and Lunard at the head of Glen Cannich. The distances were substantial. Many of us have never known what it is like to live so far from others, making long journeys for labour or learning, without any routes out in harsher months.[17] Both Debbie and I feel the remoteness, thrilling and terrifying in equal measure, even though we are only there for a couple of nights. She checks her phone hopefully from time to time to see if there are any communicative pings, but we are, of course, a long way from any masts.

Retreading the footsteps of old paths recalls the different rhythms of the past. Perhaps the small act of going for water brings to mind something of the meaning of paths in an older world, a time when 'people and trail grew up together, sharing both hardship and hope'.[18]

The day with Debbie is spent in small tasks. We definitely do not have enough food for a winter but enjoy lunches and dinners of apricots, lentils and chorizo. We take trips to hang the clothes to dry, stretch our legs after writing and reading, pad up the stairs for a long, deep nap in the afternoon. Walking, but for no particular purpose other than to complete the quotidian acts of living.

In the evening we wander away from the bothy to explore the small loch nearby and the mountains. I'd spotted a small beach on the far side and was determined to investigate.

Wheatears and skylarks fill the air as we make our way down to the water's edge. The beach glows and glistens with flecks of mica. Northwest of the Great Glen, the massive rift that scythes a diagonal line across Scotland, the rocks are part of the Moine Supergroup. Once upon time, 500 million years ago, there was a shallow sea here that lapped the edges of the bloated supercontinent Rodinia, into which mud and sand were deposited. Heat and pressure as continents collided transformed the muddy silt into hard schist laced with mica.

Transparent flakes embedded in the sand, they make the ground sparkle like a street covered in confetti in the aftermath of a glorious gala. Under the water of the loch, the light is refracted and reflected in a thousand miniature constellations. I try to capture it on my phone's camera, but it can't possibly contain the ephemeral light show.

We sit for a while, idling by the water, making time to play with the sand as if we are children again. I pick up a handful and let it drain slowly from my fingers as it catches the evening rays. Our hands and arms are covered in dust, and we shine like selkies. Deer tracks lead away from the beach, and this is clearly where they come to water. I trace the outline of their footprints in the sand, and I imagine them walking off into the heather with dazzling hooves, leaving a shimmering trail.

Deer prints in the glittering sand of Loch Cruoshie.

Later we bathe in the river, naked and unashamed, lying in clear pools. I have always admired Debbie's comfort with her own body and we bask as if we are seal women. I remember that Debbie has told me earlier in the day about a statue she likes. It's a monumental 9 ft sculpture in bronze of Kópakonan (the Seal Wife) created by Hans Pauli Olsen and installed on the rocks in Mikladalur harbour on Kalsoy, one of the Faroe Islands. Like all selkie in the legends, she can return to the land temporarily from the ocean and shed her seal skin. But a fisherman steals her pelt, and she must stay upon solid ground until she can once more recover her skin.[19] Most selkie stories follow this bittersweet arc of the woman returning to the depths, leaving behind her husband and children. Debbie likes the sculpture, she says, because she looks like a woman just being human, beautiful and unrobed yet confident, ready to take tasks in hand. She steps out of the water, undamaged and strident even when the roaring waves engulf her. I want to face the tides of the world like her.

After a second night of deep, long sleep, we wake early in the bothy, as you normally do. A combination of wood floors and natural light are not conducive to lie-ins, but it's no bother. Anyway, we are keen to be up and away, as the weather looks set to change.

We walk the same way as the men and women did with their animals as they came off the mountains, returning for the winter. Yet others had made this journey, never to return. In 1916, the last inhabitants of Maol-bhuidhe left the shelter of its walls. Will and John Burnett, only 12 and 14, departed for the last time, following many other Highlanders who emigrated or went to the cities for employment.[20] It has been empty ever since.

It feels if we are just outrunning the rain at every step. We pause on the top of the bealach once more, surrounded by a crowd of meadow pipits chattering busily, and look back to the moor and the valley where the bothy sits, mist and rain shrouding the land.

The act of walking in reverse always feels uncanny to me. It's not just the same thing backwards but, rather, seems like being in a different dimension. Time taken to ascend disappears, and sweaty uphill sections that we toiled over for an hour or two vanish in the quick, stumbling canter of the downward return. As we descend the slope, past the Iron Lodge, the world appears to have changed in the morning light. The golden softness of evening has given way to the primary-colour brightness of midday and it's hard to judge the markers.

The patter of our talk changes too, or it does for me as we return to what waits, to messages and demands. Daydreaming explorations of loves and lives float back down to Earth. Waiting for us both are some difficult conversations with partners. Debbie asks me if I like falling in love. I say, yes, but then there's a pang too. I know my relationship is at an end and the return is to a moment of reckoning.

I ring my mum as soon as we get back to somewhere we have signal. She loves to walk vicariously with me, along routes she can no longer make, but would do if she could. A few weeks before we had been on Arran together, with my dad and brother, and we'd all done a walk up to the high loch on the northwest of the island, Coire Fhionn Lochan. Dad and I swam in the cool water collected in the bowl of the hill. We have always shared the love of plunging into the sea or lakes. He taught us all to swim at a young age, throwing us into pools with water wings or without, but of the four children I am the only one who will brave waters with him that are not artificially heated. In the turquoise light, I am transported back to being a little girl paddling frantically and gigglingly away from my dad, who is pretending to be a killer shark. I relish sharing that quiet, liquid space as an adult. I am glad we all got up this far. The path was fairly steep and long, but both my parents made it. I was conscious they might not be able to do so for much longer.

But even people who cannot get to places might still be able to experience them. For centuries we have made journeys in our minds to lands we cannot visit. In the medieval world, pilgrimages could be undertaken by nuns enclosed within walls they could never leave. The women cloistered in the city of Ulm in the fifteenth century went on spiritual sojourns to Rome, Jerusalem and Compostela as they traced the virtual routes mapped out by the preacher Felix Fabri. In the sixteenth and seventeenth centuries, armchair travellers who owned monumental cartographic compendiums such as Georg Braun and Frans Hogenberg's *Civitates orbis terrarum* or Joan Blaeu's *Atlas Maior* could visit most corners of the known world from their homes.[21] Author Judith Schalansky has mapped remote islands she has not visited and never intends to with artful narratives of their troubled pasts and futures woven from the stories on maps and in travelogues. Google Street View lets us pace streets far from our homes.[22] There is walking without walking that might be possible for anyone.

Not everyone can climb Munros and walk to bothies, whether because of illness, disability or lack of time or resources. Covid-19 suddenly made us aware of what walking meant, and for those who developed the chronic form of Long Covid, journeys on foot that had once been normal became impossible. Poet and artist Alec Finlay's charting of Scotland's landscapes through names new and old is a way of walking with these locations even when it might not be possible to physically get to them. Proxy walks for others can make a gift of energy, experience and imagination. Whether places live in our memory because we once walked to them or because we can simply grasp a sense of their shape through the words and actions of others, an imaginative experience of viewing and walking is possible. As he writes in a small volume created for Macmillan Cancer Support, 'when we can no longer walk place-names offer a path that leads into inaccessible landscapes'.[23] Maybe it's why I document it all for my family. Or for my future self, when I will retread the paths in my head that I can no longer walk.

The day I return, news breaks of the successful campaign to restore the right to camp on Dartmoor and all the debates that entails about access to land, trespass, paths, roads and land in the UK. It hinged on debates about what constituted recreation under English law and whether camping could reasonably be allowed under that definition. As campaigns are waged by organisations like Right to Roam for greater access to land and common spaces, advocates often look to the Scottish example.

The right to access land in a way which is not possible in England has been long in the making in Scotland, and its story often told.[24] In the late nineteenth century, the campaign for access was first taken up in Parliament. On 28 February 1884 James Bryce, Liberal Member for Tower

Hamlets, stood up to introduce a bill in the Commons, arguing for the freedom to roam to be made a legally protected right.[25] Bryce, too, was interested in defining what might be considered permissible recreation, and excluded poachers and egg collectors, but also dog walkers. The bill didn't pass. Year on year, until 1914, his Access to Mountains (Scotland) Bill was read and debated, transforming in the process to include England as well as Scotland. Only once did it get to a second reading, never making it through.[26]

After the interruption of World War I, it popped up again and again on the parliamentary agenda, until finally, in 1939, a bill was passed. By this time, it was so watered down that gone was the grand vision of being able to walk every path and paddle every waterway. Access to land was seen as an attack on land ownership, and with so many vested interests in Parliament, the bill made for unpopular reading. Yet campaigns for permission to roam persisted, and it was not just powerful politicians who spoke up, but walking societies and ordinary people who protested and jumped fences. In 2003, some 120 years after Bryce's first efforts, the right to roam was enshrined in law in Scotland by the Land Reform Act. England has yet to match this. The CRoW Act 2000, while a major victory, is a pale shadow of the more far-reaching access granted in Scotland and elsewhere in Europe. The Right to Roam movement, with peaceful trespasses, is aiming to change that. Like the legendary Kinder Mass Trespass in 1932, the purposeful ramble organised by the Young Communist League to protest against the closing of access to areas in the Peak District, the simple act of putting one foot in front can be radical.[27]

The freedom to walk in Scotland or other European countries such as Norway creates a different relationship with the land, even though that land is not necessarily publicly owned or held in common. Walking becomes an act of freedom, not of trespass. Scottish legislation covering access to the countryside in Scotland is without question more progressive than that in England, and land reform is an urgent concern for some in England. However, the question of access remains a live debate in Scotland too. Old arguments persist, as landowners have tested the limits of what is meant by 'curtilage', the common-law principle of land immediately surrounding a property that can be enclosed. The land around Kinfauns Castle has recently been shut off as a private garden, while the Glen Lyon estate of 2,630 hectares isn't keen on anyone walking across its holdings.[28] Trespass is a criminal offence in Scotland; it's just that only certain types of people trespass, certain types of movement and activity count as trespassing. Threats to public order can still be prosecuted, for example.

Questions about trespass and use of land have always been about drawing lines to decide what counts as permissible movement, allowable use, or transgressive settlement. It's no coincidence that the first Trespass Act in Scotland came into force in 1865 after the Highland Clearances. As poor men and women were evicted from their homes and off the land, any attempt to lodge or to settle was now an act of trespass. Impoverished migrants became a threatening form of mobility. While it's likely most forms of wild camping are covered by the 2003 Act, you can still be prosecuted in Scotland for trespass, and it is marginal communities such as Travellers who are most likely to fall on the wrong side of the law. Today's rights of way still remain rooted in particular ideas of freedom and particular definitions of the notion of staying and going.[29]

I thought of all those ways in which we lose freedom without the opportunity to walk to places. It's not just losing the ability to hike, to bag a Munro, or complete a long trail, or, indeed, get to a destination. Restrictions erase the chance that we might walk in a way which is about haphazard discovery or play, meandering to glitter beaches or into creepy abandoned lodges.

In the Corrour bothy book in June 1930, an anonymous visitor recorded a snippet of poetry. 'For go I may, but come I must.' It's actually a misquote of Gerald Gould's poem, 'Wander-thirst':

> And come I may, but go I must, and if men ask you why,
> You may put the blame on the stars and the Sun and the white road and the sky![30]

I like that this verse is about the idea of wander-thirst, not wander-lust. It suggests a visceral, bodily connection with the act of walking but not one that is about devouring in greedy need, rather that without walking and movement, the body might simply perish and waste away.

Without the ability to roam, to wander, to meander or to amble, it is not just access, a legal right to be in a place, that is lost but the deeply embodied connection between place and movement and the ability to walk in ways that resist modernity's pull to speed, goals, order and rigidity. Sociologist Hartmut Rosa talks about the way in which on foot 'we perceive space in all its immediate qualities, we feel, smell, hear, and see it'. As roads get laid and space is manipulated in ways which make everything fast, immediate and obvious, the focus on getting from A to B as quickly as possible changes how we view a place. As Rosa writes, 'We no longer roam through it; we single-mindedly cut across it.'[31]

What I remember most about the walk with Debbie was the time for talk and diversion, exploration, and laughter. We wanted to reach the bothy before dark, but we did so in a way we chose.

I am aware I can walk in ways that many others cannot. Walking is an act of agency, but we cannot always control how and where we walk. And yet in the steps we take there's that exciting possibility of freedom, of destination. Walking for me has often been a hopeful act, even when you don't know where you are going exactly, and I am hopeful too for a future where more of us can playfully roam and wander as Debbie and I did in sunny valleys and on shining sand.

SEVEN | KEARVAIG

A Wilderness Away From It All

Kearvaig is not the end of a journey but a beginning. The bothy is nestled into a picture-perfect bay at the northern tip of Scotland on Cape Wrath, so far north you are nearer to the Arctic Circle than London. It's the end of earth to walk upon, as due north there's no land mass between here and the icy polar continent. But as one path ends, so another begins. Cape Wrath is the starting point for ancient sea roads which led down to the south and the Rathad chun a'Bhaltaic, which stretched across the Baltic to the northern Polish coast and Russia.[1] Without knowing it, I have stood at the other end of that road on archive trips to the Vistula Delta, pausing for a moment on the northern shore at Gdańsk in December and staring out to the blue-green of the Baltic. By these ice waters, I thumbed a fiery nugget of amber, fossilised pine resin known as the gold of the north. For hundreds of years amber made its way across these seas, traded as a precious luxury to be set into jewellery and finery. On a crannog in Loch Glashan in Argyll, an eighth-century bronze brooch was found set with amber that had travelled along the sea roads. It's where Cape Wrath gets its name, from the Old Norse word for 'turning point', *hvarf*, and not from the Old English, *wroth*.[2] A point at which paths meet, roads turn, worlds collide.

When I disembark from the ferry that crosses the Kyle of Durness from the little jetty, it's a still, sticky August day. The air is thick with midges, which cling to my sweat-covered skin as I wind my way up the hill away from the sea and across the inactive firing ranges. It's not a difficult walk. After all there's a shuttle bus that runs from the ferry to lighthouse and back again, so the road has got to be good enough to allow a rickety 16-seater passage. But it's forbidding, fairly long, and a little dull at times.

If Cape Wrath is the last Scottish wilderness, as the sign for the ferry from Keodale Pier outside Durness claims, it's a funny kind of wilderness. Not long after you start the walk to the bothy, you pass signs reminding you that you are stepping onto an active MoD training site. It's not firing time when I arrive. The air is quiet, the ranges still, the red flags lowered. Yet the high moors have that strange emptiness of a landscape that is there to simulate the tough places of endurance, the only place in Europe that can play host to simultaneous land, air and sea military-training exercises for British troops, but also any NATO nations. This is not a wilderness of untouched beauty but harsh and bleak, littered with the remnants of firing practice.

I stop for a quick sausage roll before passing on to the part of the walk marked DANGER ZONE on the map. It's an environment drowning in little lochans, ground covered in russet grass and purple heather, from which rise dumpy peaks coated in rainclouds like fluffy icing. Nudging at the loose rocks and mud with the toe of my boot, as I sit on a particularly unpicturesque scrap of land topped by a cairn, I see something glinting in the earth. A bullet, a blank, its end tapered into a star-shaped crease that looks like a candle holder. My lunch spot has good views, so no surprise it's been used as a rifle-firing position. Tucking the bullet into my waterproof, I decide I will take it back to sit alongside the other strange mementos of my trips, such as bones, groatie buckies, and jars of glitter sand. The cold, rusted relic, which has a pleasing weight and curved sharpness in my hand, seems a fitting reminder of this spot's particular aesthetic: empty but not abandoned, tough but with its strange beauty.

A note pinned to the board in Kearvaig bothy.

* * *

Wilderness is one of the most fraught terms in nature writing and conservation, an idea that originated out of the constructs of civilisation and barbarity, and at times of conquest and colonial expansion. The *terra incognita* of sixteenth-century maps was succeeded by imaginings of the Wild West or the Outback. The great American wilderness became a fantasy of blank space on which conquerors, settlers and pioneers inscribed narratives about acquisition, extraction and adventure. Humanity and the wild were pitted against one another as opposites. But as William Cronon has critically written, if nature can only be true when it is wild, then there is no place for the human in this landscape. In a worldview he finds troubling, wilderness must be untouched and unadulterated, for only then can we experience it as a sublime revelation of the otherness of the non-human world. There's something that remains appealing about the transformative ecstasy of the wilderness, but it's problematic for all sorts of reasons. It tends to suggest we cannot really be in nature in any meaningful way, because if we are, we will spoil what is pristine. It also ignores long histories of use and settlement. It sets up primitive simplicity as some prelapsarian ideal that both sentimentalises and others past lives and indigenous peoples (until they too fall from grace).[3] Wilderness implies that nature and truth can only be found in the long trek to nowhere.

Wilderness has become something we seek as if to rough the edges of our ordered world, particularly in the West and the Global North. It's as if we demand something from the landscape as we go out into it; we search for a wildness that we think we have lost. But in so doing we skirt over the scattered bullets, the ruins of habitation, the rusted vehicles, and the hills emptied of wolves hunted to extinction by human hands. We run away from modernity and humanity even as they are presences that have shaped places like Cape Wrath, realities that we must live with wherever we are in the world.

Under NatureScot definitions, however, the idea of this place being wild is neither problematic nor controversial. Cape Wrath is one of forty-two named Wild Land Areas (WLA), a series of locations listed under the nationally important but non-statutory designation developed in 2014. Remoteness, emptiness, solitude, sanctuary, risk, and lack of human artefacts make it deserving of WLA status. A 2015 report notes, that though few, the concentration of human remains at Cape Wrath supposedly 'diminish the wild land qualities'.[4] From my vantage point, I look at old firing targets and military structures. To me, these make it seem a little wilder.

Belly full of pork-and-apple pastry, I continue up the road and pass Inshore bothy. Once the low-slung building, a former shepherd's house and barn, used to be an open space but now it is used by the military. I peer inside. Orderly plastic chairs, a working clock, a neat, fitted kitchen. Rather different from the welcome I am expecting at Kearvaig. As the path winds up into the hills, I can hear and smell the sea but not see it, and I am bored of the track that brushes through purple ling and low peaks.

The featureless heath can play tricks on the eyes when the simple vegetation and lack of features make it seem as if the expanse of horizon never ends. The rain has held off mostly, but it's hot and murky, and grey clouds gather behind me.

The road ahead is foreboding but not because this is untamed. It's the markers of human presence which unsettle. Passing over the bridge, two red, white and black signs loom out of the heavy air. *Width restriction 7 foot. Weight 7.5 tonnes*. They are the same you get on any road in the UK, but here they are set against oil-dark pools, where any monster might lurk, surrounded by decaying, malting bog cotton that signals fast-approaching autumn. Peat hags lurch out of the water. The eroded tussocky stacks hunch over as if they are trolls waiting to be roused.

The track continues to the lighthouse, constructed in 1828 to illuminate the dangerous coast for approaching vessels, but the path to the bothy peels away to the right. The raging sea calls, and I turn off, but not before passing an abandoned minibus. The grille of the front is flaking, the seatbelts frayed and loose, and the floor is littered with a mix of cans and empty drinking vessels. For a moment I think I see a message in a bottle, only to realise that it's a can of Red Stripe stuffed inside a broken wine bottle, a Jam Shed red. And everywhere there are spiders, orb weavers who sit in the middle of their intricately spun silk. Webs stretch from peeling windows to plastic dashboard, across the gear stick and roofless carcass of the vehicle. Some are small, some monstrous, and they all wait patiently for the midges to fly into a sticky trap. The bus is theirs now, a Shelob's lair of rusted abandonment.

There was something about the juxtaposition of chaotic metal junk and neat arachnid precision that made this seem like a crazy, deserted theme park, a twisted weirdness of industry and nature. In documenting the unseen weapon ranges of Scotland, photographer Alex Boyd described these as 'lunar landscapes', littered with wreckage and debris, supporting biodiversity but also contaminated and contorted. His project 'Tir an Airm' (Land of the Military), is a startling evocation of the rusting, bewitching relics from the bombing ranges of Cape Wrath to infantry-training areas of Kirkcudbright. Pocked, crater-covered slopes, abandoned training dummies lying as if dead, and thistle-choked tanks are monuments to military endeavours over the last century, left on moors, grassland and clifftops.[5] No one has purposely preserved these as sites where nature and man-made structures live side by side, but it reminded me of an experimental nature park in Germany, Landschaftspark Duisburg-Nord on the site of old coal- and steelworks. The designer, Peter Latz, did not attempt to beat back physical processes or erosion nor rid the site of industrial structures. He did not want restoration or 're-cultivation' but rather recognised 'their destroyed nature and topography' to allow the 'existing forms of demolition and exhaustion' to remain within the landscape.[6]

The weaving spiders on the bus aren't rare but their presence hints that alongside the guns and the rust there's a diverse and increasingly threatened non-human world of caterpillars and birds, heathers and grasses. Large parts of Cape Wrath have SSSI (Site of Special Scientific

Interest), SAC (Special Area of Conservation) and SPA (Special Protected Area) status. Not all the active firing ranges, but stretches of land along the coast are designated as sites of ecological, geological and scientific importance. There are numerous precious specific habitats on these 'vegetated sea cliffs', the technical description for the protected SAC regions. The coastal grasslands and heaths support a rich range of species such as the montane dwarf willow (*Salix herbacea)*, while the ledges of the gneiss cliffs are important nesting sites for all manner of seabirds: northern fulmar, kittiwakes, guillemots, puffin and even skua. One recent fortunate visitor who wrote in the Kearvaig bothy book has recorded sightings of many of these birds, as well as twites, merlins and ringed plovers. He is lucky. Numbers of all the seabirds, except the guillemots, have been declining since the turn of the century. Black-legged kittiwake Apparently Occupied Nests (AON) have declined by 65 per cent since 2000.[7] Perhaps this scarcity and rarity, too, can make somewhere feel wild. In some senses, when we think about degradation and conservation, the word 'wild' has come to imply not so much pristine nature, but scarce nature, things at the edges of existence. It's the pockets of what once was and could be again if we were to restore ecosystems in some form of Edenic recovery.

The risk factors to the coastal habitats are both usual and unusual ones. Grazing from sheep and deer but also naval shell damage top the list: 120 training days take place every year here, and part of the manoeuvres include naval gunfire practice. An Garbh-eilean, an island just off to the east of Kearvaig Bay, is one of the main targets. When it's firing time, you might see the eerie green light from HMS *Sutherland*'s para illum star shell illuminate the coast, as the 4.5-inch gun fires 180 rounds (120 in the day shoot, 60 overnight).[8] A recent NatureScot report states that shelling continues to have 'deleterious consequences' for the habitats.[9] The birds are fewer each year, though it's not just the shelling that's the problem but the impacts of fishing and climate change resulting in decreasing food sources. But the emptiness necessitated by the firing range produces its own kind of protections as well as threats for the wildlife here. Jarring notions of human and non-human wilderness sit side by side, MoD land and SSSI. There's an odd parallel between these types of 'exclusion landscapes', as historian Peter Galison puts it, between the idea of waste and wilderness.[10] Paradoxically, sites of disposal, decay or, here, of military training, sites that are fenced, ringed and cut off, create their own strange wild embargo.

Rewilding seeks wildness in the past and in the restoration of lost places, but the 'wild' future of the decaying bus will perhaps see nature and culture side by side as metal becomes weathered and plants smother broken glass. In such places, as geographer Caitlin DeSilvey writes '"restoration" and "preservation" sit awkwardly' in a vision for the future.[11]

Picking up my bag after a handful of wine gums, I leave the spiders to their machinations and turn down the track.

At last, the view opens out onto the sea and the building. The bothy itself is around 13 km south of the stormy peninsula, where the buses trundle up to Cape Wrath lighthouse and the Ozone Café. White walls welcome me, picked out against a calm, blue sea. I push open the door, hang up my waterproof, and fling down my bag. No one there yet, it seems.

As is so often the case, next to the bothy are the outlines of other buildings that once stood here too. There's a blackhouse, possibly used until after World War II, and a complex of walls, once a working farm, but which was cleared of people in the nineteenth century.[12]

Sutherland, the large expanse of the historic county that encompasses most of the northwest of the Highlands, has a feeling of emptiness, but it is also haunted by shadows and ghosts of settlement, displacement and violence. It is infamous in the history of the Clearances, despite being atypical in many ways. The scale and devastation of the forced removals here have become etched onto the collective memory and are evident in the absences written into the landscape. From the late eighteenth and early nineteenth century in some of the earliest Clearances and some of the most brutal, Elizabeth Sutherland Leveson-Gower, the Countess of Sutherland, and her husband, George Leveson-Gower, Viscount Trentham, removed around 15,000 people from the fertile straths, wide valleys, out to the coast. Sheep replaced people and the people went to the harsh eastern seaboard, with limited smallholdings of no more than three acres (1.2 hectares). There was not enough good land to eke out a living, but that was the point. Treat 'em mean and keep 'em keen was the brutal motto. Property managers hoped that people would turn to fishing to make ends meet, but without the skills or the necessary infrastructure of port towns to do so, this was hard labour. Attempts were made to ensure people could readjust. The planned village of Helmsdale, with its new harbour, was designed to ease the resettlement of the men and women coming from the Strath of Kildonan but there was little thought given to how the poor farmers might become fishermen. So brutal and infamous were the Sutherland Clearances, embodied by 'agricultural expert' Patrick Sellar, who showed no mercy even to the sick, the aged and pregnant women, that it is sometimes hard to see beyond or behind this to the landscape and people that existed before.[13]

Before light fades and the rain comes in, I inspect the ruins, surrounded by nettles and brambles, and try to imagine what life might have been like here for those who suffered during the Clearances. There is a feeling of desertion standing in the ruin but not exactly the sense that it is an unpeopled place. There exists a sense of the wild, as historian and author David Gange puts it, that comes from 'being amid the remnants of human action' entangled with weather and place. Little remains of the farmhouse, but it's clear this was a substantial holding: a few rooms and walled enclosures for livestock, the blackhouse to the west linked once by a footbridge over the burn. Rhubarb grows in the corner, once assumed to be cultivated but more likely wild, still a reminder that the land here could provide and was not barren and inhospitable.

The place-name books made to accompany the OS maps of the nineteenth century, that huge cartographic exercise that has shaped our view of the British landscape ever since as a terrain of contours and lines, has a page dedicated to Kearvaig. The neatly drawn table of names, sources and informants lists the bay and a building, originally transcribed with the Gaelic rendering *Bàgh Chearbhaig*, the meaning not yet known to the compilers. Later additions in red made in 1894 anglicise the title. Now it is Kearvaig Bay, and the accompanying notes describe what will be the bothy, the shepherd's house, one storey, still occupied and maintained at the grace of the Duke of Sutherland.[14] It was inhabited by the McCallum family, who had lived there even before the lighthouse existed on Cape Wrath. What had happened to the larger farm is unclear. If I had visited Kearvaig bothy a few years ago, I might have seen a message inscribed on the walls of the building from Mrs R. W. Nicoll, 1966, the granddaughter of Robert McCallum named in the OS map source lists. She wrote:

> Visited by R W Nicoll on the 11th September 1966 whose father Edward John McCallum was born here on the 9th August 1862 and her Grandfather before him, Robert McCallum who was here before the lighthouse was built. My Grandfather Robert McCallum had the farm at Sheigra before it was broken up in 1912 where I was born.
>
> – Mrs R W Nicoll

The graffiti has been covered up with recent renovations.[15] The fading presence of these places and names, then rediscovered and reinscribed, only to be scrubbed out once more, gives Kearvaig a ghostly feel. It's a place inhabited by the spectres of different pasts, strange, sometimes eerie, but not a remote refuge untouched by humans.

I pored over all the maps of the region, the OS surveys, archaeological expeditions and cartographic outlines that trace the coast, and looked for Kearvaig and Cape Wrath. The building was substantial enough to appear on maps even in the eighteenth century, on Alexander Bryce's detailed cartographic rendering of the coast ca. 1744.[16] It's a map which for the first time has made intelligible the complicated interweaving of the rocks and sea and captured the shape of the place. Bryce was chiefly interested in shipwrecks, tides and seas, hence the focus on the coast and rocks. His endeavours were not popular with the locals. Smuggling and searching wrecks provided income, and mapping the coast would threaten both. I imagine him going out, armed, inappropriately dressed (I'm not sure why), with paper, pen and survey equipment, beating people back as he races to chart every detail.

As cartographic records so often are, the Bryce map is a beautiful thing. I picked out my walking route and ran my finger along the line of the coast, retracing my steps along the black lines on the off-white background. There's the deep gash of the Kyle of Durness, and shielding the water as you walk along the coast is the promontory of Faraid Head or 'Farout', as it is on the map.

* * *

I stand on the beach and look out at the mass of rocks and the sea stacks that spring from the water, impossibly complicated, pieced together in a game of dark tectonic Jenga. Inside the bothy there's a guide to the climbing routes of the various pitches and I think about how the hands and feet of scramblers have known the surface in a different way from the walkers and the kayakers, but all carrying with them their own cartographies of place, of climbing face, rock arch or footpath.

Early maps of the north of Scotland, before Bryce, hazarded guesses at its nooks and crannies. I was intrigued by the way these cartographic descriptions, through absence, inaccuracy and impression, captured not only outlines of land and sea but the sensation of place. It's a hard spot to get a handle on unless you live on the cliffs' contours, sail them, ascend them, or smuggle booty in the caves. Earlier cartographers knew that the land ended here, and the sea began, but the tip of the 'last boundary of mainland Scotland' was hazy fantasy. The Romans thought it was like a wedge-shaped axe, and in the second century CE, the Alexandrian mathematician Ptolemy imagined projections that twisted the coast to the east. By the time Joan Blaeu compiled his *Atlas novus* in the mid-seventeenth century, the contours are more recognisable. Faro Hea/Faraid Head is there, stretching out inevitably to the Arctic. Alongside is the Latin name invented by Ptolemy, Tarvedrum or Tarvisium, a name which he conjured to describe the end of the island. Blaeu noted, 'Tarvus in British has the meaning "ending", with which we too shall put an end to this book.'[17]

With manuscript charts made in the sixteenth century, Timothy Pont inked faint and thin lines of jagged cliffs, empty space, the gashes of sea lochs, and the rising mounds of mountains. In his annotations, we find side by side 'black flies . . . seene souking me[n]s blood', 'Many Wolfs' and 'sea fowles' off the coast. Across Caithness, he writes 'Extreem Wilderness', although his is a wilderness filled with living things. Perhaps my favourite map, though, is the simple sketch of Ben Hee to Faraid Head. There's no Cape Wrath, the fact it is unmapped underscoring the idea of the unknown, and the unknowability of places. It's a few lines, a sharp point and a blank expanse of a page that stands in for the vastness of the ocean.[18] Here at the northern tip, you can almost hear Seamus Heaney's 'ocean-deafened voices . . . lifted again in epiphany and violence'.[19] Maybe wildness comes from that desire to understand the boundary between land and sea, to read the point of turning, the vanishing horizon where land and sea fray.

I walk along the beach, which remained unmapped until Bryce. He identified Cape Wrath as a promontory that stretched out into the Atlantic, surrounded by ragged rocks. You stand on the edge of the sand, the shoreline shifting with the moon and the wind, and look out to the horizon. The cold blue swell crashes over boulders, waters pulled from the frigid Arctic, swirling together as oceans collide beneath towering stacks of gneiss. Sea and sky merge into a hazy edge-place. At the margins of my vision is Kearvaig Stack, also known as the Cathedral, two pillars of sandstone eroded away to look like the wings of a fallen angel. Evening light shines through the gaps in the rock, which is white with the guano of sea birds who have crafted an avian city. It's August. The days are still long. The light is that of a northern summer. I imagine what it might be like to stand atop the stack, for all the world resembling Tolkien's Amon Hen, the Seat of Seeing. I can only get as close as the slippy flat rocks at the edge of the bay and look out to the water and the cargo ships passing one another on slow journeys in the dying day. The text that accompanies Blaeu's Atlas notes: 'Here the summer days are very long and there is scarcely any night. For those sailing directly from here towards the North Pole, no land can be found.'[20]

Before I settle in for the night, I pick around for treasures, meandering along the slick stones of the burn. Strange, weird treasures of the sea and the land. There's a shotgun shell, what I think is the mast of a ship sticking out of the ground like the carcass of a beached whale. The mother lode is a map encrusted in sand, still in its plastic case. I am sure it once belonged to kayakers. They have noted the tides and times, adjustments and waves. I hope they were OK without it, and I imagine them pulled out to sea without their OS Explorer to guide them, instead having to read the swell and the white ruffs of water.

You need to know the tides here. Bryce's map warns that if there's ebb, and the wind comes from the west, or when there's flood and wind from the east, ships have to avoid Cape Wrath.[21] The danger is clear. The legend on the map marks blind rocks, the rocks which are covered over in spring tides, and the dangerous currents that pull ships to the seabed. In the danger and the beauty, the whole place has the feel of an enchanted kingdom, maybe a cursed world. In between the slabs of sedimentary rock that form expansive gates to Kearvaig Bay, goblin-green pools of tidal water collect. Raucous gulls pick at the sand near the cairns of bone and feather that house the remains of more unfortunate comrades battered by storms. A pair huddle conspiratorially, perhaps squawking murder to one another, and soon they will return to their black roost on the escarpments of Stac Clò Kearvaig.

Time for food and fire, I decide, and return to the bothy. Despite the ruggedness, the company of birds, the sea and the deer mean it's not solitude exactly that characterises this building. And I see I won't have the bothy to myself anyway, as a couple of figures rock up in fairly quick succession. Not that I mind. The company is nice because this can be a bitter, perilous, lonely place.

I am 39 when I visit. The same age as Margaret Davies, who spent the winter here in 2002. It's a tragic story, one I am familiar with long before I come. She made the journey in alone, miles along the coastal tracks. She brought food. She came to write and to think and sketch. But she would not walk out like I would. A desperate tale, the exact details unclear, but on a December morning two shepherds, Alistair Sutherland and Hamish Campbell, found her wrapped in a cardigan and sleeping bag, cold, lacking food. She was airlifted to Stornoway hospital but could not be saved.[22]

My mum is understandably worried when I go to Kearvaig, worried but also excited. She's read about it in books and an old family friend Jeremy has told her about it from his own youthful adventures. But still she pleads, don't go alone. It's summer, I assure her, the weather is fine, I have loads of food and an emergency beacon. I will text as soon as I can. It's all OK, and it is. The bothy is warm and comforting, there's company and a fire.

There's Paddy, a young lad who has come up to test his Scout-leading skills in the wilds of Sutherland, and next to him there's Andy who's just out on a jolly from down south. They chat in front of the fire, as you do, Andy and I offering our goodies - cheese, gin, chorizo - to Paddy who is doing it on iron rations.

'Where have you come up from?', Andy asks.

Paddy reveals that it's Devon way. It turns out that both were on the same bus up from Plymouth to Bristol airport, and Andy had even taken a snap of Paddy as proof to friends he was on the right connection. A small world for a wilderness.

We sit by the fire. It's warm, cosy, and the weather outside has started to turn as the sea gives out the low grumble of building rage. It would be traditional, of course, to burn peat, blackening the walls and air with the smoky fuel. Blaeu noted the expanses of 'turfs, or black bituminous earth, formed into blocks and hardened by sun and wind'.[23] Peat is still sold and burned, though setting fire to these precious carbon stores in a time of climate breakdown feels like an act of brutal self-immolation. But it still flavours whisky and heats some homes in this part of the world. Local businesses cut and sell it to keep people warm. It is easy, it seems to me, to agree that the excessive muirburns for grouse shooting are destructive and reckless, but eliminating a low-cost fuel in rural Highland homes and transforming traditional distilling practices may be harder to change.

Paddy's route is a tough one. He has come in from Sandwood Bay and, unlike me, isn't taking the easy way back with the ferry but tramping six hours round the edge of the Kyle before heading north again to Durness. I wonder what he got out of this trip alone – no signal, little food, his head down on long treks. Not in a bad way, it is just clear that he has a slightly different way of enjoying the landscape from me, where it seems to be more about the endurance of the walk than the history or the wildlife.

People in bothies often speak about getting away from it all. Paddy's hard journey reminded me of that demand for wilderness to necessitate suffering. I thought again about Margaret Davies and the difficult, lonely path she had taken, or of Chris McCandless, who died after months spent living alone in a deserted Alaskan bus, his life and death made famous by Jon Krakauer's book.[24] When you get away from it all, at the end of the Cape Wrath Trail, for many it's a narrative of suffering as much as ecstasy. There's ecstasy in the suffering too, and we ask wilderness to purge us somehow, through a spiritual experience of transcendence. Perhaps this is the legacy of purgative religious sojourn, such as those who travelled barefoot to shrines and holy places. Henry II, distraught and ashamed after his part in the murder of his friend Thomas Becket, was whipped as he walked unshod from St Dunstan's Church to Canterbury Cathedral in 1174. But there's a persistent idea that true encounters with the wild have to involve hardship of some kind; danger, peril, a hangover from the 'great white explorer' trope that involved young men going off into the wild in the hope of finding wonder and themselves along the way. Perhaps it's just the pure thrill that comes with bareknuckle adventures. Yet it's a dangerous idea. We demand too much of the landscape, we impose on it our own cartographies of want and need, ask it to be something other than the urban lives we lead, just as the old mapmakers did.

I get it. That desire to get away from it all. There are plenty of us who revel in the lack of phone signal and the absence of screens (if only for a little while). The call of the wild and the lure of the simple life runs through nature and travel writing like an unbreakable thread, and it's all over the pages of bothy books. Wendell Berry's iconic verses on wilderness speak of the peace of simple things, and the darkness, and the 'dumb life of roots'. But he suggests, too, that the search is difficult, impossible almost in the modern world 'lighted by burning men'.[25]

Clichéd as it has become, rather than isolated emptiness in big, extreme places, I prefer the idea of the wilderness right in front of us, not just 'out there'. There's a wildness that poet and essayist Gary Snyder writes about that includes city pigeons, arachnids tucked up in nooks or crickets that kept him company as he worked on Pacific oil tankers.

> Exquisite complex beings in their energy webs inhabiting the fertile corners of the urban world in accord with the rules of wild systems . . .[26]

Ideas of wilderness and the sublime and beauty might also include rusty buses, ruined places, and industry.

When I take the usual trip out for a wee before settling down for the night, I see the dark and light of a late-summer sky. Sunlight clings to the clouds like a backlit movie set. A silver eye searching a screen, the intermittent glare of the flashing lighthouse mingles with starlight and sea-light. It's not crystal clear tonight, only a few stars are visible, but right above is the Great Bear's tail, the tip of Ursa Major. The sixteenth-century Italian polymath Gerolamo Cardano supposedly claimed that as she whisked her tail towards the sun, she scattered empires below on the earth.[27]

I wake up in the morning to wind and rain, and it's a wet walk back, hot still, and damp. I hope the bus might catch me up but of course it doesn't, and I arrive at the ferry at the same time that it rattles into the lay-by. Chatting to Malcolm, the straight-up ferryman who rages at the tourists unable to navigate the roads, he explains it's been a difficult summer. The North Coast 500, a scenic road route launched in 2015, which starts at Inverness for a 830 km circular trip, has brought lots of camper vans, but they sit inside their cabins and plastic kitchens eating Tesco-bought food, and not spending any money. Tough times, he observes.

After hopping off the ferry and grabbing some food, I am on the winding drive back home, but I choose not to head due south and instead divert round the coast to see the places outlined on the maps of Pont and Bryce as wolves with hills, shipwrecked coasts and places of extremes. Wolves still seem to embody wildness with their howl, their size, and their absence from the UK's shores. There were once many wolves, who filled the hills here and attacked the flocks. In the early modern period, hunts were permitted three times a year, targeting adults and cubs. It was successful from the point of the view of the herds and humans, as the savageness of wolves was banished.[28]

Now, though, it's a very different kind of landscape from that lupine hunting ground. Driving through the Caithness countryside is a barrage of dreamlike, jarring images. There's industry, farming, power stations, castles, cemeteries, wind turbines, big skies, hanging cloud, and expansive moor. It's a misty day, so the shapes and forms loom out of the mist like fantastical conjurings.

As I approach Thurso, hazy blue-grey skies, edged with the dark clouds of rain, swirl like the inside of a crystal ball. On the margin of the coast, a Lego-block outline of industrial structures rises out of the *haar*, the sea mist. It's Dounreay, the decommissioned nuclear power station. It was built in the 1950s, as two facilities - the Nuclear Power Development Establishment (NPDE) for civil reactors and the Vulcan Naval Reactor Test Establishment (NRTE), which tested military submarine reactors. What had once been a farming region became a bizarre radioactive reproduction ground. The idea was that Dounreay would 'breed' manufactured plutonium from natural uranium. Fissionable plutonium would replace uranium as fuel for the reactor and so keep generating power in a form of nuclear eternity. In the end the plant was open less than forty years, as nuclear testing was wound down.[29]

There were parallels here of past and present stories of power, labour and industry, and of decisions made by higher authorities that shaped ordinary lives. Contrary to the depopulation trend in the Highlands and the narratives of emptiness that predominate in this part of Scotland, the creation of the 'Nuclear North' brought people to the area to work. The closure of the plant left people without jobs, and at a Select Committee held in 2002 after decommissioning, scientist David Craig warned that without future thinking and investment, it would 'become a "retirement home" for those who do not want to or cannot leave . . . existing businesses will decline, house prices will depreciate, and the area will become the equivalent of a "ghost-town"'.[30]

I think of the older stories of places cleared, people moved and livelihoods ruined. Clearances emptied settlements, nuclear energy brought in people and work, but similar dialogues seemed to prevail about inscribing onto the landscape ideas about use, productivity, emptiness and industry. Caithness, away from the south and with low industrial development, was chosen specifically, seen still as a 'place apart' in many ways as the nuclear project was developed. Colleagues from London apparently talked about it as if it was 'just south of the North Pole'. The construction of the untamed wilderness of the north hadn't gone away.[31]

I stop briefly in Thurso for snacks and fuel. Everywhere there's abandonment alongside living. Huge wind turbines wheel in the grey skies; beneath them are dilapidated houses but also working farms. This is Halsary Windfarm, Tesco's green-energy investment project. In this white, metal forest, once more I feel that this is a weird and rugged place, with looming towers, industry and also ruin, but it's not the traditional wilderness of the sublime. Perhaps it's the sublime of photographer Richard Misrach's *Petrochemical America*, documenting the environmental abuse along an industrialised section of the Mississippi River, or philosopher Timothy Morton's dark ecology.[32] Morton argues that negativity, ugliness and irony must all be part of an honest form of ecological thought, not privileging humanity or beauty, nor placing humans outside the world as commentators who make pronouncements. Morton uses the example of the Russian Artic town of Nikel, the focus for a four-year art and research project in 2014, to suggest the political and ethical implications of this approach. He explores the melancholy of the broken landscape and livelihoods in this mining and smelting area, the death, but also the warmth and care, even comedy. Dark ecology considers intertwined living worlds, and by thinking about the 'truth of death', suggests we might arrive at a different way of conceptualising futures, responsibility, social forms and our relationship to the non-human. As Morton writes, perhaps we should store plutonium not in deep vaults but in full view, in safe structures, where we can take care of it.

> You, the human, made the plutonium, or you the human can understand what it is – therefore you are responsible.

This is a new ecological politics. It incorporates both hope and despair, explores the agency of non-human forces and focuses on co-becoming, which is the way in which all humans and non-humans emerge through relationships and connections.[33] It is also perhaps a way of thinking about wilderness and wildness that allows the 'neutron- and isotope-minded' remains of Caithness, the military remnants and the ruined houses to exist alongside the whining kittiwakes and the crashing seas.[34]

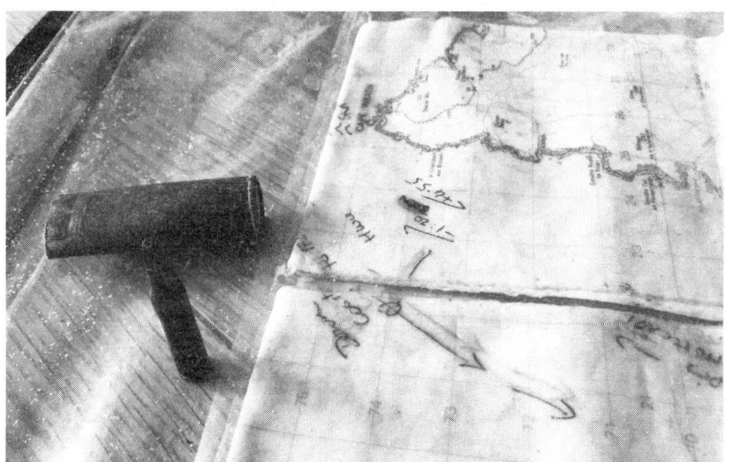

Momentos of a bullet, shell casing and the map from my travels.

I always bring back mementos, and this time my trophies are a strange collection. The bullet. The shotgun shell. The drowned map. And of course, a crab claw, always a crab claw.

That's not to say there weren't plenty of other bits of the living, geological world I could have added too. A huge deer skull. Minute shells. Lovely rocks. All mixed up together in an entangled story of journeys and sea and sky and wild, a dark ecological cabinet of curiosities to match the weirdness of Cape Wrath's uncanny beauty.

EIGHT | PENRHOS ISAF

Human Traces

There's gold in them hills. The hills and mountains of North Wales near Penrhos Isaf bothy, to be precise. People have mined the rock here for many hundreds of years, at least as far back as the Romans and probably much further. Evidence of prehistoric British gold work from the Bronze Age and earlier has been found across the UK, from shattered sun discs discovered on Orkney, probably hammered out of Irish gold, to the elaborate aureate cape found in Mold, a small town in Wales not far from Theatr Clwyd.[1] I went there often as a kid to see Christmas shows with my drama school.

Penrhos Isaf bothy looks a bit like a fairy-tale cottage in the forest, where a stepmother or wicked witch cooks up poison apples or tempting candy, but it's at the heart of a historic industrial landscape. This was a place where gold but also copper was wrenched from the mountain's innards. If I am hoping to use my trip to the bothy to make my fortune, my hopes are soon dashed. As I cross a stone bridge that spans the Afon Wen, a small river flowing into the Mawddach's winding expanse, there is a warning sign, complete with an illustration, reminding me that gold panning is not permitted. Fortunately, I am more interested in the tumbling waters and dappled light of the forests, all of it taking me back to childhood holidays in Wales, than I am in any prospecting. But the signs are there for good reason. The promises of wealth and buried treasure have burrowed into peoples' imaginations and driven them to delve into the mountains for rich resources. The hunt for rare Welsh gold goes back hundreds of years, and people still sift the waters in the hope of finding gleaming specks hidden in the silty mud.

When there was discussion of reopening the Dolgellau mines, a *Daily Mail* headline from 1930 told of 'Candlelit visions of wealth'. The *Evening Standard* went with 'El Dorado in Wales?'[2] Humans have shaped this landscape in pursuit of treasure, hollowing out shafts, cutting timber, extracting minerals. As I traipse up to the bothy, through dark woods managed by the forestry operations of Natural Resources Wales, my path follows the entangled threads of human, geological and living pasts. Traces of our presence, destructive and creative, are everywhere. We might think of bothies as buildings in wilder, remoter locations than the post-human worlds of abandoned fairgrounds or crumbling apartment blocks, but everywhere is post-human in one way or another. Layers of human presence, good, ill and indifferent, deposited over millennia.

Drawing from the Penrhos Isaf bothy book.

Penrhos Isaf is a good first solo bothy trip to a traditional bothy. It is pretty close to my home, not too isolated, and comfortable. Like Greensykes, it also has an outdoor compositing toilet and generous sleeping arrangements. To be honest, I am also glad of the emotional space. Anxious about being single, I forced myself into the macabre carousel of dating apps despite not really being ready. I know they work for some people, but it always makes me feel like lonely people getting lonelier. The incessant demand to be engaging and enticing is unbearable. A little thing, perhaps, but going to a bothy alone feels like reclaiming myself.

I went to Eyri so often as a child I got a T-shirt that said 'I climbed Snowdon the hard way'. Returning stirs happy memories of family hikes and holiday cottages filled with board games, laughter and the occasional argument. I manage, of course, to choose the only rainy day in the month, but the gleaming slate and dripping ferns are still achingly familiar. It is the smell of the bracken more than anything that transports me back, that woody, earthy aroma of autumn, even when it's summer.

After an afternoon in Dolgellau, with tea and Welsh cakes, as well as a trip to the excellent second-hand bookshop to pick up some Edward Thomas and Rainer Maria Rilke, I start my walk to the bothy in drizzly mist. I check and recheck I have all I need, determined to make a good job of this. Out I stride, pacing in step with my younger self, little Kat, who was always climbing trees, mucking about in rock pools, or running away from home on an adventure to the wild unknowns of the end of the garden. She liked to be alone too.

Yet doing a bothy by myself is always a slightly nerve-wracking prospect, as I don't know who will be there and there is no back-up if I make a mistake. Penrhos Isaf shouldn't feel intimidating. It's an easy walk, close to habitation, and I chide myself. I start to wonder if the disquiet I feel is precisely because this is a landscape full of human activity. It feels different from the remoteness of an island or

Highland bothy. I don't think I am likely to encounter anyone up to no good, but it crosses my mind that it is probably more likely in a building near popular tracks and trails than somewhere on the far edge of a small island. I can't quite work out whether I want to find the bothy empty or full, and I have my tent and a pitch booked just in case it turns out to be heaving with revellers.

The walk to Penrhos Isaf starts at the ruins of Cymer Abbey. Like her grander, richer sister Tintern, Wordsworth's 'wild, secluded scene', the former abbey is now just crumbling walls and empty arched windows.[3] The abbey might have been devoted to the quiet learning of Cistercian monks, but they weren't uninterested in the lucrative positioning of their surroundings. In 1209 they were granted a charter by Prince Llywelyn ab Iorwerth that gave them the right to dig for minerals. The monks were permitted to take 'stones of whatever kind, metals and treasures'. It's unclear just how much metallurgy the brothers undertook, but there were forges in nearby Trawsfynydd and Llanfachreth, and they were in good company in their industrial enterprises. Tintern smelted lead for silver within its outer court and the abbey of Strata Florida in Ceredigion had a great lead mine in Cwmystwyth.[4] Cymer was never an opulent foundation but had wealth enough. Hundreds of years later, in 1890, two men prospecting for gold found treasure, a silver-gilt chalice and pattern buried somewhere on the slopes of Cwm Mynach. The precious objects were probably concealed by the abbey around 1536, when Henry VIII dissolved religious houses great and small and acquired their wealth in the name of reform.[5]

Winding away from the ruins, up the slopes of the valley, I pass through forests in dripping rain. The husks of the industrial past more recent than monastic mines lie decaying in the lush woods, left over from nineteenth- and twentieth-century operations. Warnings remind you that the adits (horizontal or gently sloping passages into the mines) and shafts are dangerous. Symbols indicate that a path is forbidden. Silent mills lurk on the banks like vultures. Near the Rhaeadr Mawddach waterfall, north of the bothy, are the barred gates to the old mining operations. The ready supply of running water always made this a good place to mine, as noisy stamp mills, powered by gushing streams, were needed to break down the ore to powder. Stonebreakers pounded away at the rocks so that minerals such as gold and copper could be extracted.

Sign on the way to the bothy warning against gold panning.

After following the well-marked roads, then the forestry track through the heart of the woods, and after making the final steep scramble up the hillside, I arrive at around 4.30 pm, rather wet, and a little grumpy. My fears of overcrowding are unfounded: I have it all to myself, and it's a generously sized bothy. There's a large main living area with a stove, several smaller downstairs rooms and two cosy sleeping lofts. No phone signal and no people at all, with heavy rain probably preventing any further visitors. I have a wave of mild panic about what to do without company or a phone. It is probably the scenario I wanted more, but it is still strange, a little disconcerting. The disconnect with the wider world doesn't give me an immediate release from the worry of obligations but makes me imagine all of the important pings people are surely sending to me, all going undelivered into the ether. Well, the books I have brought with me from my Dolgellau outing - three for one night away, pretty standard - can be my company instead. Flicking through the Thomas, I scanned the lines of his poem, 'The Shieling', written just before he went off to fight in World War I.

> It stands alone
> Up in a land of stone
> All worn like ancient stairs,
> A land of rocks and trees
> Nourished on wind and stone.[6]

I sit on the plastic chair in front of the stove, book in hand. The walls are rough, whitewashed stone and through the window I can see the crowding pines and darkening sky.

There's no sound but the rustle of my pages and the slow drip of rain on stone and leaf.

Solitary in the woods, Penrhos Isaf bothy was built as a nineteenth-century farmhouse, perhaps dating back to as early as 1800, though there was a farmstead here from at least the late 1500s. It was worked until 1965 by Willem Foulkes, and for a bothy it's really rather grand, with spacious accommodation, an enclosed front garden and a woodshed to the back, complete with an outdoor toilet down the path. I am pretty sure I could work up a good advert for *Country Living*. Its comfort certainly appeals to numerous Duke of Edinburgh expeditions.

In my advert I might also mention the abundant natural resources in the vicinity, and this is precisely what marketers did in a sale catalogue in 1873.

> . . . Lots 4 and 5 [Pen Rhos Ucha and Pen Rhos Issa] lie . . . upon the same strata as the Glasdir copper mine, one of the most lucrative speculations in North Wales; surface trials have been made on these lots and in each case considerable indications of copper, lead, etc have been discovered . . . [7]

As recently as 2022, when the Johnson family put up their large holding in the area for sale, the headlines proclaimed you could buy an estate with your own gold-mine for just under £4 million.[8] Land laced with riches. A tasty prospect, it would seem.

Gold has inhabited our imaginings of the British land-scape for hundreds of years, drawing people to its hills.

When the nineteenth-century gold rush exploded worldwide, accounts abounded of gold's history and how best to prospect. The reputation of the British Isles as a source of treasure was long established in literature and legend, according to one commentator, A. T. Vanderbilt, writing in 1888. From the Irish chronicle, the *Annals of the Four Masters*, that recorded tales of fine ornaments wrought of gold and silver in the year 2816 after creation (roughly 950 BCE), to claims that Phoenician merchants were really on the search for auriferous rocks as well as tin when they came to the British Isles, he conjures a picture of the riches hidden beneath the mountains.[9] The Romans traced lines of quartz in Dolaucothi studded with gold, and in 1790 John Glover painted a group of men panning for gold in the waters of the River Mawddach.[10] But it was only with the nineteenth century that the mountains were exploited on a large scale.

Modern interest in Welsh gold was reignited in 1844 when Arthur Dean presented a paper to the British Association for the Advancement of Science, stating he had discovered 'rich gold ores' in the Cwmheisian mines near Dolgellau. When Dean was called in to inspect the jigs at the lead mines, bouncing troughs that separate ores, his eye was caught by gleaming specks in the galena (lead ore).[11] This was not news to locals, but his claims were taken up for investigation by other professionals and interested parties. John Calvert, an Australian mineral surveyor, reviewed the state of gold mining, and Professor Ramsay produced a paper for the prestigious Geological Society in 1854. Ramsay's report is filled with chummy references to one Mr Byers who, the academic is keen to point out, had told him of the gold back in the 1830s. All of this backed up Dean's assertions. Old place names, too, confirmed their suspicions. On the banks of the Afon Wen you could find old ruins and rubbish tips that were the remains of an old settlement where ores were probably once worked and melted. The name Merddyn Coch 'r aur, so Ramsay noted, means 'the ruins of red gold'.[12]

Coinciding with the Californian rush, there was a minor flurry of activity in Wales in 1853 and then further discoveries in the 1860s led to more vigorous explorations. Yet despite the promises, these initial forays were small and short-lived. Some made money - in 1854 a single piece of gold worth £25 was found and in 1865 the Clogau mine yielded dividends of £22,575 - but many did not. Welsh gold was a trickster playing hide-and-seek. As one Welsh miner said, it was like looking for a sixpence in the biggest Christmas cake in the world.[13] You never knew how much gold was going to turn up, as gold in the Dolgellau belt is subject to high-nugget effect: uneven distribution of sizeable pockets makes it seem as if the ground is full of the stuff if you are lucky enough to find one, or barren if your search hits just wide of the mark. In the hope of finding the Welsh mother lode, T. A. Readwin & Co opened the Gwynfynydd mine in 1863. However, costs were high, and two years later the venture ceased.[14]

The mid-century rush fizzled out, but hope was rekindled by the arrival of William Pritchard Morgan, a solicitor-turned-mining investor who had made his name in Australia. Originally hired by Readwin to help with the infrastructure, he took over the mine in 1887. Determined, ruthless at times, a risk-taker, he immediately struck lucky and hit upon the Chidlaw Lode, which contained over 200,000g of gold. The Welsh Gold King, as he is now known, got rich, and though he ultimately sold the mine and it closed, he never quite gave up the dream of finding another pocket of unimaginable wealth.[15]

Rich men's fortunes were transformed, won or lost, in the search for treasure. But so were the ordinary lives of the people who lived in the Mawddach valley. The census records for the little farm at Penrhos Isaf tell of this transformation. While men and women still worked the land, they began to take in lodgers who were miners, working long days in the mills or shafts.[16]

I scan the bothy book and write my note. (I think it said, 'Writing a book, so should probably write in the book'. Not very imaginative.) Entries for Penrhos Isaf are often a playful reminder of the allure of treasure. 'We explored the area looking for gold!' exclaimed one DofE group from Gloucestershire in 1983. It was Mandy's birthday. They saw gleaming nuggets, they joked, a fitting birthday present.[17] If they really had found any, they would have been wealthy young people. Welsh gold is the rarest gold in the world and much prized. It's even got royal connections. Appropriately enough, as I wrote this chapter, news flashes of the UK coronation flicked up on my phone. With little interest in the proceedings, I saw the photos of a bored Louis and gently smiling Charles. He and Camilla's wedding rings are made of pure Welsh gold, in a tradition going back a hundred years for coronation and wedding regalia for British queens and kings, princes and princesses. Even Meghan Markle's wedding ring was fashioned from the stuff. Though the mines have shut, the royal family have a massive ingot for future weddings gifted to Queen Elizabeth on her birthday in 1986. Needless to say, the DofE-ers could not compare.[18]

Gold was deposited in rocks around Penrhos Isaf sometime from the Upper Cambrian to the Devonian era, 500 to 400 million years ago. Heated deep in the Earth's crust, it flowed into the white quartz veins, softer than the crystalline mineral, and found the holes and spaces where it solidified. Its appearance in the crust is a piece of cosmic luck. Deep in the Earth's core there are precious metals but the gold that can be mined is the result of the lucky collision of asteroids 200 million years after Earth formed.[19]

After drying off a little from the rain, I settle into the rhythm of what you do in a bothy: laying out my kit, sweeping and tidying a little, arranging my sleeping gear before the light goes. I pull out my iPhone to check the time, which is of course unusually quiet. Black mirror shining back at me, it's odd to think it's a wonder of human technology but also possesses fragments of elemental forces. The miniscule amount of gold inside is a tiny reminder of stellar nucleosynthesis. Aztecs called gold the excrement of a sun god.[20] It's not so far from the truth. All the gold that ever was or is or will be on Earth, was formed in cataclysmic collisions before our solar system was even born. Gold on Earth, like all heavy metals, was produced by explosive supernova when the universe was young. Standing on the vertiginous precipice of deep time, gold gleams at the bottom of the rift.

It's just most of us don't think of our phones that way, of the dust of ancient stars hidden in a plastic and glass case. It obscures, too, the 'shadow places' of its production.[21] For such a beautiful thing gold, like diamonds, has an ugly history that belies its glittering grandeur. Welsh gold might seem romantic, intertwined with stories of princesses and dragons, but it's inextricably linked to imperial and colonial pasts of extraction, violence and land grabs. Both Pritchard Morgan and the surveyor Calvert made their reputations in Australia as European nations were expanding their presence here. This was a time when gold rushes gripped the world, just one dimension of the scramble for resources by nations and settler colonial communities as they swept away indigenous peoples. In 1873 the USA officially adopted the gold standard. Power and wealth were measured against a nation's ability literally to prove the worth of their weight in gold. While banks of reserves were amassed and gold sovereigns were issued, stamped with the images of haughty rulers, the people who dug up gold were exploited and brutalised. In the past it was either working class men and women or slave labour that provided the manpower for these endeavours. Today it is little better with people, including children, working in appalling conditions.[22] The non-human world suffers just as much, and the landscape is forever scarred by the ugly wounds and gashes left by mining.

As soon as I began researching, I started getting social media ads for sustainable gold mining. Google was listening.

But the reality is that extraction of the precious metal is a dirty industry. Large scale gold extraction is generally considered to be one of the most environmentally damaging processes in the world. It causes toxic run off, it is responsible for degrading soil, as well as deforestation, and making one wedding ring can cause 20 tonnes of wastewater. Surface mining in particular leaves the land dead, eerie.[23]

Welsh gold was always mined slightly differently. There were never large open pits because the gold occurs in nuggets. Like a dog following a scent you hunt veins of quartz to lodes of gold, grind and then sift. Essentially large-scale panning, but still disruptive and damaging. It's hard to get a clear steer on exactly what the effects were of gold mining in Wales, because it all happened decades before environmental impact reports and monitoring were standard. Yet even at the beginning of the twentieth century commentators were conscious of the damage that might be done to the landscape as debates continued over whether mines should reopen. In 1918, the UK government report on mineral resources, compiled by the newly created Department for the Development of Mineral Resources in the United Kingdom, stated that the benefit had to be carefully weighed up against the 'disfigurement of the countryside'.[24] *The Cambrian Daily* reported in 1934 that if the mines were to be reopened, they would devastate the forests which, as the official inquiry on Merioneth mining noted in 1930, had been denuded during the First World War. Hordes of timber were taken away to be laid down for railways or hauled across the sea to make the A-frames and duckboards of trenches. The landscapes in

Wales were only just recovering. Mining would mean that lush valleys would be 'lost to the nation'.[25]

But the mine did reopen. The rich Chidlaw Lode, that which had made Pritchard Morgan's fortune, was worked once more. In the end what forced its closure was not the lack of gold, but regulations that demanded the mine take responsibility for the impact it had on the environment. From 1991 the Water Regulation Act made it an offence to knowingly pollute, and from 1999 this included water run-off from abandoned mines. Yet even now Dolgellau may not have seen the end of mining. Alba Mineral Resources Plc bought the mine and in July 2023 ecological permits were issued. There are always environmental surveys of course, sustainability metrics assessed. Maybe new Welsh gold mining won't be as damaging as other forms of extraction but it's hard to marry the enthusiastic delving for wealth with the evocative images of Welsh mountains that grace the Alba Mineral Resources website.[26]

Gold: an innate part of the landscape, a trace of the impossibly ancient movements of the universe, something that came into being before humans were even conceivable. Yet it's profoundly entangled with humanity's fascination with things. We may not arouse the fearful beasts of caverns deep and dark but nonetheless something is awakened in the heart of the mountains. The lure of Welsh gold beckons once more.

After a rest, a sort and a read, I wander round the vicinity of the bothy. There are the ruined outlines of another building being choked by vegetation, and small grassy mounds that could be sleeping giants waiting to be roused. This is the discarded material from trial pits dug by those who lived in Penrhos Isaf in the hope of finding riches on the land, once more reclaimed by the moss and the ferns and the grasses.

Close by too is the copper heritage trail, in the woods just below the bothy. Gold was the big money draw but there's copper here also that was extracted from the middle of the nineteenth century onwards from the lush Mawddach valley and its environs. The Glasdir Copper Works 6 km north of Dolgellau have long since shut, the last such mine to wind down its operations in the UK when the machines fell silent in November 1914. In its final year, it processed 1,600 tonnes of copper ore, but it was abandoned, and the shafts left to fill with water.[27] Wandering down from the bothy, dew on the grass, sun striping the forest in light and the heather glowing purple, I inspected the silent wheels and crumbling platforms that jut out of the riverbanks. These decaying works look like something out of *Lord of the Rings* when Sauron rips out the trees of Isengard to make way for his metal-works.

The Mawddach valley is a reminder of the traces we leave, of what we have done to the landscape in the pursuit of things. Even if no more gold or copper or lithium or palladium is ever mined, the old mines are still a problem waiting to be solved. The gashes in the earth are the visible remains of mining, but you can't always see other impacts. Metal and slate mines were generally decommissioned before anyone knew what to do with the decaying husks, and the new legislation on water runoff for abandoned mines only applies to operations that were abandoned after 31 December 1999. Before that, no regulations. No rules. But even after the mines close, the wounds bleed. Dust and runoff continue to pollute water and air, and around a fifth of all river-quality issues in Wales are the result of mines. The extent of the problem across the UK is clear, with 315 bodies of water at risk from non-coal operations.[28] As we move to sources of cleaner energy, we can't just forget the dents we have made in the Earth. Even if governments shut all the mines in the world, communities must deal with the problems of erosion, pollution, contamination and flooding.[29]

As I make my evening meal, I realise I am out of water. Helpful notes in the bothy inform me there is a water course just over the forestry track road and I head out in the fading day into the dark forest. I am thirsty and gulp greedily, pretty certain it isn't too polluted by metals and confident my water purifier has taken out the worst of the nasty residues. But it's impossible to know. Toxic water, pure water. They look pretty much the same.

Even if we could simply address the damage done, the question of cleaning up the mines is not as simple as it might seem. These are not just places of destruction or damage. The old slag heaps and the unrestored ruins of buildings by Penrhos Isaf are covered with a lush green shroud, the spiny backbones of old walls now covered in moss. Growth has returned. The spoil tips and cuttings support lichen and bryophytes, the tunnel networks provide space for swarming bats, the damp adits shelter reptiles and amphibians. The relationship between damage, repair and renewal is a complicated one. Inadvertently we have created new havens for the living world, landscapes that may appear to be untouched nature but are shaped by traces of our lives.[30]

Cleaning up the old systems of shafts and tunnels will destroy heritage sites and dismantle environments to which new forms of life have adapted, some now designated SSSIs. Every site has different values to different groups - ecological, archaeological, social, economic - and questions about their futures are fraught. I have spoken often to my former colleague Lesley McFadyen, an archaeologist, working on a similar abandoned industrial site on the Ardeer peninsula. An old dynamite factory is covered in graffiti by the women who worked there, the sand heaps around the huts are alive with singing birds. As she puts it 'the built environment is decaying whilst ecological habitats thrive, and yet there is the constant possibility of further development that would put all of this at risk'.[31] There's a need to balance the needs of the future in places like this, a conversation to be had about who or what gets to leave traces, and what marks should remain of our presence.

People living near one old slate mine at Corris Uchaf have made their own decision about what should fill the cavernous absence left by defunct industry. Just south of Dolgellau is the 'Cavern of Lost Souls', a chamber filled up with cars dumped in a Jenga tower of waste. I pass the mine on my way back from Penrhos Isaf but think better of a solo caving expedition. As the obsolete vehicles have been piled in, paths have crumbled, entrances collapsed. No doubt lead and other toxic waste has mingled with the water. It's hard to see this as a place of much that's positive, though it captures the imagination of cavers and photographers. It's almost like an infection of abandonment.[32] Both slate mine and cars are redundant, superfluous objects and spaces, one valued as the heritage of the industrial past, one deemed waste. Perhaps it's a fitting space of desolation in an age where nature and culture collapse, an eerie monument to the fact that we leave trace upon trace, piling up the discarded stuff of our lives.

While it is not particularly cold, I am damp and the bothy is damp, so a fire seems advised. I have brought some kindling and am grateful for the logs left and chopped. In due turn, I saw my way through some hefty branches left in the outhouse at the back and pride myself on my solo cutting skills. Wood has long been a prized resource here. In the dark woodland, it's impossible to miss the stubbled chin of slopes felled for timber, wood carted away for any number of uses. These are not native trees, but firs planted for forestry operations over a hundred years ago. A case from the late sixteenth- and early seventeenth century pointed the finger at Hugh Nanney for despoiling the woods and accused him and others 'of having, of taking away and converting to their own use 30,000 oak trees growing on the Penrhos Common in Llanfacreth'.[33] Aside from the fraught arguments about common and private use, the case suggests how different the landscape might have been at this time. Industrial fast-growing Sitka spruce introduced in the twentieth century has now replaced older deciduous woodland here. The forests look nothing like they would have done a few hundred years ago, and there is no pure native woodland left in Wales.[34]

Out alone, a shed and tools to myself, I am discovering my own resourcefulness and am grateful to do so. As is always the case, the aim of bothying or camping is to make as little impact as possible. 'Leave No Trace' is the mantra of wild camping, bivouacking or bothy dwelling. It's a good, important one. You gather fallen wood (not too much of an issue here but definitely trickier elsewhere) and leave some for the next person. Although there's plenty at Penrhos Isaf, bothy etiquette is a nod to the reality that things are exhaustible. When you can't just order an Amazon next-day delivery, you must think about what you have and how you use it.

We all leave things behind. Whether we make tracks or carve paths into the mountain for mining, we all make marks of our presence, from individual hikers to industrial corporations. It's so easy to scar places with fires or waste or plastic debris. It's something you are conscious of in a bothy. You are reminded constantly at Penrhos Isaf that you can't light fires outside and not at all in dry season, when the forestry officials warn of the danger of destructive blazes. A party visiting in April 1984 were disappointed not to be able to cook toasty jacket potatoes in the stove but stuck to the guidance. It was a good thing they did. Annotations by a later visitor, an MBA work-party member, noted that they had seen five forest fires in the area that week.[35] I light the fire and glance out of the window as I wait for the stove to warm. Blackened stones and earth in the enclosed yard remind me that people do not always heed the warnings.

I realise I know exactly what I am doing with the wood I saw, but have no idea what will happen to the trees felled around me or, indeed, where the wood or paper or cardboard that arrives with that little FSC approval sign actually comes from. That's not to suggest shady dealings or bad intent, but we are divorced from the processes of production and consumption in everyday life, reassured by symbols that promise us that our buying habits are not too damaging. We've become used to the idea that every act of consumption leaves some trace in the world. What that means for how we remedy or respond to this is far from clear. Trees can regrow if we cut them down. In theory, at least. No guarantee that tree-planting schemes will grow the right ones in the right places, nor that we can keep pace with our exhaustive habits. But there will never be any more gold in the world than there is now. Like the lithium we mine for the new forms of energy that we hope will be our saviours, it will run out at some point.

After warming up by the fire, I quickly snuggle down to sleep. The dark crowns of the imposing Sitka close around about me in the bothy as the light fails, conspirators in some plot. You never want to leave the warmth of your sleeping bag once cosied in for the night for a wee, but I inevitably, often, mistime this dance of bedtime ritual.

Reluctantly I crawl out of the downy comfort to the outdoor toilet. Stepping into the wet, pine-scented air feels like the opening scene of an episode of *The X-Files* – one when they were still filming in British Columbia forests rather than L.A. deserts. Fortunately, no crazed murderers or little grey men await, just moths lured by my torch, and then a rather large spider.

Just as in Scotland, the dense pine, so evocative for many, is really another human trace, planted here by our hands for use in any number of construction projects. There's no easy division between nature and culture. Human industrial relics have become embedded in this landscape, and the idea of 'natural resources' is a convenient byword for whatever we deem a useful commodity taken from the land, a commodity that may have been brought here by human hands.

From notes left in the book to the tins or kindling you might stack for a future visitor, your existence makes a dent somehow. I like to think that's what being out in the living world like this in a bothy does, though, gives you a clearer taste of how your feet fall on the earth, how the breath of your existence ripples in the world. Bothiers are generally quite conscious of the traces they leave, the harm they do, at least on a small scale. Don't light fires, don't pollute streams that people will need for drinking.

On a larger scale, in bigger time frames, it is much harder to account for the traces we will leave. On any number of apps and websites, you can calculate your carbon footprint, while labels on goods proclaim they are carbon neutral. Yet like the mark you leave in a bothy, the idea we can spirit away the impact of our existence is a fantasy, the magical wish-fulfilment of children. Our transition to batteries and electric vehicles is not a sudden fix-all that ends extraction, and future mining works will continue as we dig for different resources that power them. This form of power requires graphite and lithium, materials which, too, must be mined. Graphite can be created synthetically but that's expensive and fossil-fuel intensive, so much is mined in China and Africa.[36] In addition to the Welsh gold, Alba Mineral Resources has a subsidiary called GreenRoc whose flagship project is the Amitsoq high-grade graphite mine in Greenland.

We can choose, to some extent, what mark we make, good or bad, but no matter what we do, we can't help leaving a trace. Humanity is now grappling with the problem of how to cover the tracks of our existence where we have already caused damage. As we bury rubbish or encase nuclear waste in deep tunnels, we try to account for our impact on the landscapes of the world yet to come. Maybe these will be littered with the bones of hydros and dams, or stuffed with the future fossils that David Farrier, author and professor of literature at the University of Edinburgh, describes, of forever plastics and silent skies.[37] The absence of living worlds destroyed is also a trace.

As we have to live in, on and with this world, we all must consider the effects we have. It's tricky, as we are on a path with futures that are hard to know or predict, for in many cases we cannot tell what the things we leave behind will do in hundreds or thousands of years.

Even more reason to tread carefully and to think about the positive traces we want to leave in the world. Leave no trace remains a good guide out in the wild, but perhaps we can do more. Organisations like Trashfree Trails remind us we have an ability to go out into the world and leave it perhaps a little better than we did before.[38] Whether it's picking up rubbish or spending money locally, or even sweeping the bothy a little cleaner, our footprint does not always have to be a heavy or destructive one.

In the shadows of darkening night, as I lie down to rest the natural and unnatural, real and imagined all become intertwined. I don't believe in ghosts, but there's a presence in the bothy nonetheless, the traces of past visitors and lives, from the handprint on the stone outside, to the drips of wax from the candles of those who have occupied the wooden platform before me. The faint glow of the fairy lights strung above the window gives me a glimmer of light as I nestle into my sleeping bag and continue my novel.

I put on a bit of folk music as I drift off. The gentle guitar mingles with the creaks of the house and hoots of owls, which then, suddenly, are drowned out. At first, I think it is an aircraft. The set of valleys between Dolgellau and Machynlleth are known as the Mach Loop, used for low-level military flight training. But it is far too late. Then I realise it is the wind and driving rain, so hard it strikes like bullets on the roof. Strangely comforting as I snuggle deeper.

Just as I am drifting off, I think I see a sliver of light illuminating the bars of the window. Maybe I am imagining it. It flashes again. The main door opens.

A fellow traveller who has arrived with his torch says a quick hello, then beds down in the other room. I thought I would be terrified in that scenario, but I am not. Initial fear soon gives way to somnolent content, I sleep a little easier with the parallel presence of another, in the thunder of the rain. It's a funny world, that of the bothies, where human and non-human traces intertwine in a way which is helpful, hopeful, confusing, surprising. I sleep deeply in this place of gold fantasies, hollowed mountains, industrial wastes, flourishing worlds.

In the morning I get up, flick through the book once more and leave my kindling for the next visitors. I don't see my companion, as I have woken early, and he is still sound asleep. A few items moved and a stove left tell me he stayed up long enough to make dinner.

I set off alone again, confident that the next solo trip will be easier. On the way back down from the bothy, I realise I have left a small bag of rubbish. I retrace my steps, pack it away and stuff it into my rucksack.

I tread lightly on the wet grass, the press of my walking boots just visible. Marks in the dew, footprints in the mud.

NINE | PEANMEANACH

Common Places

Private Land. Keep Out. No Entry. Trespassers Will Be Prosecuted. Anyone who spends a fair amount of time walking through the English countryside will have seen signs with the same or similar messages. But there's no keep-out sign here on the start of the path to Peanmeanach bothy. Not for walkers, anyway. As you cross the crumbling bridge that takes you over the railway tracks, a post-box-red board warns: *Not suitable for vehicular traffic.* No shit. It's a narrow, moss-covered path curving over the iron tracks and it definitely wouldn't support a car. But that's the only sign. No placard warning against trespass. No barbed wire. No trolls under the bridge. In Scotland, where the right to roam is the default position, signs that warn and protect the borders of landowners are less common. I cross over onto the Ardnish peninsula, hoisting my bag higher on my back, and start the walk to the bothy. You know a bothy is there waiting for you, free, unlocked, open for any travellers.

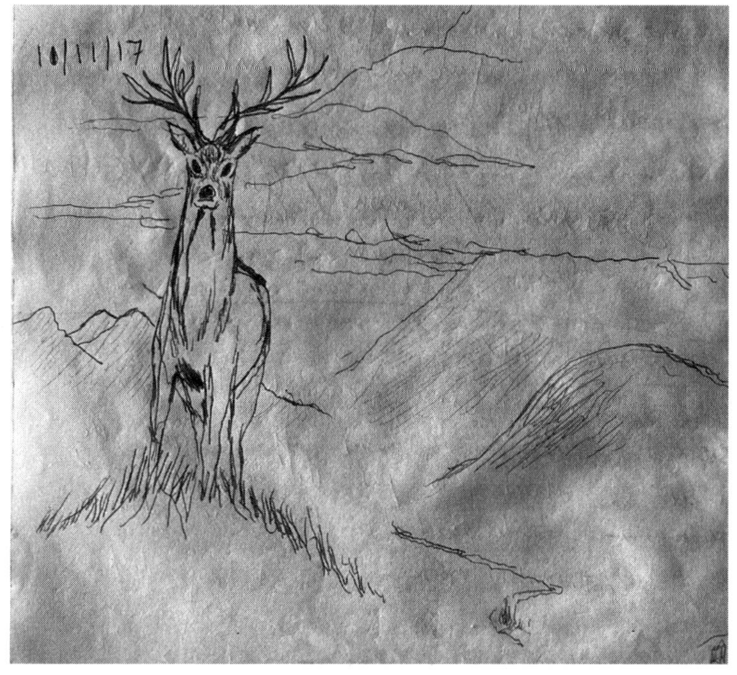

A sketch taken from Loch Chiarain bothy book.

It is the last two days of a trip to Scotland early on in my bothy adventures. I have planned a grand tour of the Highlands, culminating in the savage beauty of Cape Wrath. But things, as so often on a trip of this kind, don't go to plan. Road closures and torrential rain slow my progress on more than one occasion. Scouring maps and the *Bothy Bible* from my accommodation on Skye, I make and unmake plans as I search for one final stop. After rejecting Greensykes, close to the Tibetan monastery (too far away), and Ruigh Aiteachain in the Cairngorms (too well known), I find a possible alternative. The bothy at Peanmeanach, an isolated but well-maintained structure on the Ardnish peninsula, situated on the edge of the land which stretches out to the sea lochs of nan Uamh and Ailort. The name Ardnish is a fusion of Gaelic *airde* and Old Norse *nish*, both meaning point.[1] The doubling of meaning leaves you in no doubt that the character of this place is bound up with the protruding position of the headland.According to the *Bothy Bible*, the hike there is not too demanding, and the idea of this untamed outcrop is irresistible as I seek to delay the return to the world of work as long as possible.

Peanmeanach proves tricky to get to because navigation skills let me down. I park up off the fast main road at Polnish, grab my rucksack, and duck into the wall of greenery that winds along the kerb. Following the track down, I enter a place which at once seems a million miles away from the cars and the highway. Dappled light plays between the leaves, the trickle of water vibrates the air, birds and bees take up their chorus in the late light of day. The first markers on the route are easy enough to find, so I carry on up the side of the hill. As I pass through wooded slopes, accompanied by views of the glowing water of the loch, the path becomes narrower and more treacherous. Finally, it meanders away to nothing. A misstep on what is supposed to be an easy, if steep, track leaves me on the side of a sheer ridge on the northern edge of the peninsula. I hastily glance at my GPS app, which reveals that I have, indeed, taken a wrong turn and strayed from the path. Since the light is fading, rather than turn back, I choose to go up.

I clamber with all four limbs, up slippery soil and tufts of bracken, balancing the weight of my backpack like a drunk beetle. After reaching the summit and finding the path, I am sweaty, tired and a little lost, but press on. When I crest the top of the hill around the side of the peninsula, I am rewarded with an idyllic panorama from an older world. Under broken-light canopy of a birch woodland, bright green moss covers every inch of the rocks and branches. It's the kind of moss that looks like it has been growing for eternity, claiming the land for its own. As I emerge from the trees, a flat reed bed, marbled with tufts of heather, spreads before me and stretches to the isolated waterfront. The bothy breaks the sightline of an otherwise untouched view. It seems like a wild world outside time. I feel that if I touch the image too suddenly, it will shatter.

This is estate land, but it gives me the impression I have my own private wild spot, somewhere that belongs to no one, or perhaps to everyone. It's an illusion, of course, that the place is without a keeper. The land on which the bothy sits is owned by Peter Stewart-Sandeman, a market researcher who is now a full-time estate manager, inheriting land that his family bought in the 1970s.[2] But there is no immediate evidence of that as I approach the loch edge. Land ownership can be felt keenly in signs, fences and insignia, or it can be an absentee presence that imposes little physical mark of its existence. Our relationship with space varies according to the rules that govern it and the material markers of those rules. When I lived in Berlin for a while during my PhD, where jaywalking is a fineable offence, I quickly became accustomed to waiting for the striding green *Ampelmännchen*, even when the road was empty. Back in London, I found the habit hard to shake. Follow the rules. Wait for the signal. My relationship with the English countryside is similar. In empty fields, no wall or groundsman to be seen, like nineteenth-century poet John Clare in his poem 'Trespass', I feel anxious if I stray from the permitted path.

> I dreaded walking where there was no path
> And pressed with cautious tread the meadow swath,
> And always turned to look with wary eye,
> And always feared the farmer coming by[3]

The Ardnish estate belongs to someone. I am careful where I place my step, but I do not feel that watchful yet unseen gaze.

As I get closer to the bothy, I do notice eyes are watching me, not human eyes, but the stare of over thirty red deer, who seem intrigued by my presence. It is I, not they, who is the stranger here. The deer and the birds are secure at Peanmeanach that this is their terrain. It is a haven for a wide variety of species, increasingly uncommon elsewhere: skylark and pipits on the heath, woodland passerines in the trees, ringed plover, oystercatchers and sandpipers on the beach, and then, circling the skies above, birds of prey, maybe even a white-tailed eagle. I have intruded onto a place where the buzz of insects and the soft pounding of hooves are the only noises that fill the air. The glow of dawn and the gloaming hold you, your senses shift in response to the quiet chatter of slow solitude. The place ticks with the time of a different way of living.

The approach to Peanmeanach bothy.

Sweating profusely in the evening heat and after the long climb, I come upon the bothy. I set up camp close by, not planning to stay inside, as Covid remains a threat. But I push open the door, stepping in to see, and I am grateful for its coolness. It has two downstairs rooms and a large sleeping loft above. In one of the lower rooms, where there's a welcoming fireplace, there's a high platform etched with names and notes from many years of use. As I set about preparing dinner, another couple, who have kayaked in, pitch up and set up camp with their tent on the shore. I don't have the place entirely to myself any longer, but it still feels empty.

The alluring isolation has been felt by many before me, but this is not deserted or common land, nor has it always been as devoid of people as it is now. There have never been many people here, although the Highland Clearances drove more families to Ardnish. In 1841, the census listed forty-eight people in seven houses in Peanmeanach, yet this brief spike in population soon subsided.[4] Competition drove out people from a remote area that can only sustain small communities. The bothy was the last building at Peanmeanach to be occupied, the home of the mistress who ran the school in Polnish. Margaret MacDonald left in 1942 with her brother-in-law, Sandy, having watched as families drifted away as work dwindled, until there were no children left to teach.[5] Yet people still lived on Ardnish when Elizabeth Taylor, who would later become better known as Betty Heath, arrived to scout out the bothy in November 1967 to see if it might be suitable for the MBA. Impressed by the beauty of the peninsula that forms the enclosing seawall of Loch Ailort, she made investigations to see if it would be possible to save the crumbling building as a shelter. The roof was dilapidated, and anyone sleeping on the ground floor would be likely to receive a visit from roaming cattle. A jetty in the neighbouring bay looked a good spot for transporting the necessary materials across. A boat was still making the crossing to provide supplies to an old shepherd and his wife who lived in the last habitable building on Ardnish.[6] I settle down for the night, hearing no sounds but lapping waves beneath the moonlight.

The next morning, I wake to clear sun and idle down to the water to explore my surroundings. A tiny island just off the shore is in touching distance and tall dark ridges of rock surround the bay like fortified walls. Taylor was right: it is the perfect spot to anchor a small boat from any nearby launching point. Within hours I have gone a little feral. Stripped down to shorts and sports bra and with bare feet, I wander over the rocks in search of driftwood for the fire. Cresting the rocks on one side of the bay, I scan the outlines of ruined buildings that stand in a line next to the bothy. Tumbledown stone walls are the imprint of communities who once lived here. Memories of these people live in language and the landscape, and there are scars all over the land of disappeared pasts. We think of islands and peninsulas as shut-off spaces, but these places on the margin were once contact zones, crucial for trade and travel. Historian David Gange urges us to resist the narrative about the inevitability of the push to centralisation and integration, away from the 'frayed' borders of our coast. It was, he writes, 'just a blink of an eye since the Atlantic edge was these islands' centre'.[7]

The toppled stones are the remnants of only the most recent human habitation. This land is deeply layered with different pasts. Nearby Rùm has some of the oldest recorded human settlements in Scotland, remains dating back to 8000 BCE.[8] As I splash in the shallow water, I can just make out Eilean nan Gobhar, on whose rocky summit are the remnants of a vitrified hill fort, not as old as the Rùm settlements but still indicating there were people living here 1,500 years ago.[9] Whatever life was like for the communities who called this home, it would have changed when the Vikings came to Ardnish around 800 CE. With its sandy bay, Peanmeanach was a safe haven for their longboats. After a fireside snack, I stand on the sand, the waves washing away my footprints immediately, but the marks left by the Vikings are not so easily erased. They hauled their vessels onto the shore into a *naust*, or harbour, and the etched shape of the prow of the ships still cuts into the land, clearly visible in aerial photographs. Echoes of the Vikings are heard too in the name Peanmeanach, which roughly translates to 'penny middle land' and recalls the Norse system of land rents.[10]

The name is a reminder too that this place has long been settled, embedded in hierarchies of power and ownership. Once it was rented by farmers who paid dues to lords such as the Macdonalds of Benbecula, now it's the property of a businessman.[11] When the MBA first scouted out the property, Taylor knew that they would have to negotiate with the owner to try and save the more habitable end of the cottage. A further entry in April 1969 noted restoration was underway, but privately. It was feared the bothy would no longer be available, but from 1975 Peanmeanach became an MBA shelter.[12] Behind the ideal of shelter for everyone is the reality of land owned privately by someone.

Negotiations, however, did not always go to plan when the MBA were on the hunt for bothies. In a particularly misguided effort to establish a bothy on Eigg, Bernard and Betty Heath swooped in and started busily making ready to convert Grulin in 1970. The old shepherd's house, the last roofed building from the cleared township of Grulin, sits in the shadow of the peak of An Sgùrr.[13] B&B were impressed, they said in their notes, with the 'FINE BOTHY' in a 'spectacular situation' and put up the MBA badge, little emblematic placards that mark out a bothy as an official

MBA project. But it turned out that while a verbal agreement had been made with the factor (the person who manages a property or estate for an owner in Scotland) that it could be used as a shelter from the rain, this did not mean permission had been granted to make it an official MBA bothy. B&B had to give up their MBA badges as a result, for fear they could not be trusted, and the event was referred to as the 'Grulin fiasco'.[14] The MBA have always had to negotiate with landowners and estates to get permission to use bothies, and despite laws which allow access to walk and camp in the Scottish countryside, a few wealthy landowners still dominate land ownership in Scotland. Eighty-seven owners alone have possession of 1.7 million hectares.[15]

Bothies are not on common land, but sometimes on the most exclusive swaths of territories. If you fancy climbing the glacial amphitheatre of Lochnagar, for example, you can stay in Gelder Shiel, one of the royal bothies on the Balmoral Estate. Wrangling over access with landowners is the norm when it comes to bothies, and the balance is always finely managed, the freedom of bothy culture limited by the land on which the buildings happen to lie. Going to certain bothies in shooting season is prohibited. Forestry operations limit access to others. You have to be careful up at Kearvaig to time your trip around firing times. The land beyond the cocoon of the bothy, a little island of temporary dwelling rights and openness, is still enmeshed in a web of ownership that bears witness to the realities of commercial enterprise, private property and exclusion. Permission granted can be revoked too.

* * *

During my final hours on the shores of Peanmeanach, I fall into conversation with two men who have made the journey to the secluded spot. Unlike me, they have found the path and don't look exhausted from a vertiginous scramble. They have come, they tell me, for one last sojourn to a place that they love but which would soon be off limits.

'The estate's taking back the bothy,' says the taller and thinner of the two men.

'Might be making it into a hunting lodge or something fancier for tourists,' the other explains. Although the right to roam means that the peninsula will always be available to hikers, the bothy will be shut and the land round it restricted under rights of curtilage. My gut reaction when I realise that I cannot go back to Peanmeanach is dismay at a landowner making money from something that had once been free.

As the two men predicted, the old cottage is now a holiday rental. It is still properly off-grid, with no vehicle access, no electricity, and no cleaner to tidy up after you, but it is now a bookable bothy, not open to larger, casual groups. The rate's very cheap, as the Ardnish Estate has decided to run it on a not-for-profit basis. At peak times the property has a price tag of only £59 for the whole building. The reclamation of the bothy is not a simple story of profiteering and privatisation. But its closure cuts to the heart of messy debates about access, ownership and use. There's a delicate balance to strike between the competing needs of providing access, respecting the land, limiting overuse, and leaving space for the environment.

Estate owner Stewart-Sandeman claims Peanmeanach bothy was a victim of its own success. Its picture-perfect location drew in too many visitors, too many of the wrong sort, who held parties and contravened the code of responsibility.[16] In a particularly topical, attention-grabbing headline, the *Daily Record* blamed 'Covidiots' who piled in for parties.[17] Peanmeanach is not the only bothy over which there are arguments about increasing numbers. An Cladach on Islay has also recently shut its doors.[18] Spats over irresponsible bothy use have always been common. Some of the pages in bothy books are covered with tales of drunken revelry, sometimes spiced up with various drugs. In a form of self-censoring policing, some of these stories are scrubbed out by later visitors, editors and archivists. A particularly vivid entry in Tunskeen from the summer of 2000 was happy about the alcohol and cannabis brought with them, less happy about the lack of 'pussy and Ecstasy'. A subsequent bothier (in equally strong language), struck through the lines and added to the margin, 'Don't need your type here you fucked up dickhead.'[19] Most exchanges aren't quite this heated, and arguments are more commonly about toilet spots being too close to the building, or mud and dirt on the floor.

I have never personally seen stag parties or excessive revelry, and there's probably a degree of posturing in bothy-book entries. Crude characterisations are an easy target for newspapers, which love to whip up a moral frenzy rooted in class prejudices about the behaviour of ordinary people. Age comes into this too, and generational conflict is nothing new. When young people took to the hills, seeking out bothies and howffs in the 1930s, an older generation of ramblers disapproved of this changing of the guard. Hiking was seen as disruptive and noisy, compared to peaceful, respectful rambling. In 1937 philosopher Cyril Joad wrote of the 'Hordes of hikers cackling insanely in the woods, or singing raucous songs' and lamented the appearance of 'fat girls in shorts, youths in gaudy ties and plus-fours' who left piles of rubbish in the woods.[20] I find it amusing how these complaints against the pioneers of hiking, bothying and howffs echo the concerns of some people now. Perhaps the friction between young and old never really changes too much. But bothy use has become a particularly fraught question in recent years, and the fact that bothies are now more popular than ever, exacerbated by the rise of the staycation during Covid, is a source of tension.

But just as it's easy to categorise every landowner as a profiteering businessman, it's hard not to feel that some reports about bothy visitors are overexaggerated. Not everyone who visits a bothy is well behaved, respects the code and looks out for the natural world around them. Litter is left, fires are started where they shouldn't be, green wood is burned. However, simple demonisations, on either side, obscure the more important issues at stake. The debate over bothies mirrors concerns elsewhere, not just about private and public land, but the damage done by the footprint of human activity. Too many people ruining beauty spots, the danger of increased footfall on land, the commercialisation of the wilderness, and the squeeze of space in the balance between people and nature.

We crave space in a world where it seems inaccessible

to so many. Places for people to enjoy nature seem increasingly closed off in a shrunken world of possibilities. The majority of us live in cities, and concerns about urbanisation and the impact of lack of green spaces on our mental health is now well documented, echoing arguments heard over 100 years ago, when rights to roam were first discussed in Scotland. In 1908, Liberal MP Sir Charles Trevelyan supported the bill for greater freedom, stating that 'sixty years ago, when their fathers were free to wander all over the wild places of England and Scotland, only thirty five per cent of the population lived in towns; now seventy five per cent lived in towns'.[21] More and more land has been closed off. This was felt even more keenly during Covid, when our worlds became smaller, more contained, enclosed within the four walls of houses and flats that were a place for sleeping, working, playing, educating, loving, arguing, socialising. Dispiriting pictures during the first Covid summer showed queues for the peak of Snowdon, or crowds round the Lakes.[22] But it is little wonder people sought the outdoors for refuge and that the lure of the Peak District or the Highlands was irresistible.

The fact that bothies are free is only part of the attraction. It's also that they are in locations that seem to promise escape at a time of increasing restriction. One of the critiques of the new type of visitor is that they come for just the destination, not for real shelter. This seems to me a false distinction. Corrour was once a stalkers' hut, but it hasn't been for a long time. Bothy books suggest that for as long as bothies have been used by hiking groups from the 1920s, only sometimes have they been about genuine emergency shelter for a lost wanderer. Rambling and refuge, both as leisure activities, go hand in hand. It is, after all, this idea of the bothy which has allowed a community to evolve. The concerns of people who have used and respected bothies for many years is understandable. But there's some irony to the complaints about the *Bothy Bible* by newspapers or estate owners. Peanmeanach recently made a *Guardian* top-10 list of the coolest places to stay in Scotland and was featured in a glossy *Financial Times* piece.[23] It's hardly any wonder these places seem attractive when people seek out somewhere to escape.

None of that diminishes our responsibility to the communities of which we are a part, or to the environment. One frequent complaint at Peanmeanach was the burning of green wood, trees sometimes chopped down just for the fire. Our need for space can crowd out nature, and the environment is suffering from the increased impact of human life, as we build, walk and consume. Casual acts can cause unseen damage. Treading on bluebells can destroy the colonies of delicate flowers that have taken years to establish. Fires caused by a dropped cigarette rage through forests with more ferocity than natural ones, like those in California. Repeated stepping on already muddy ground leads to further erosion, scarring the landscape with ugly gashes. The damage that tourism can do to the environment is a real and pressing concern all over the world. Perhaps in places like the Lakes and in Scotland we are now simply seeing this closer to home.

In an era of globalisation where we have been used to shipping out the impacts of tourism elsewhere, the effects have been shaded, hidden. The places that suffer as we drop in to visit are like philosopher and ecofeminist Val Plumwood's 'shadow places', which feed a consumer culture yet are places that we know little about or fail to take responsibility for.[24] But especially after Covid, tourist impacts on the British landscape are seen in the harsh light of day. The story here is a parallel, if distinct one. Peanmeanach's story reveals the realities of pressure on land not just from overpopulation but from the way we have decided to divvy it up, and the types of relationships we encourage people to have with environments. It's not just a question of visitors, but who visits, how many and what's deemed acceptable or responsible behaviour. Peanmeanach is not a story of simple saints and villains, greedy landowners or irresponsible partygoers. It's a story about what draws people to open spaces, what pressures there are on land, what understandings of landscape we give people, and what education may be needed to encourage positive bonds between people and place.

In his objection to the Mountains Bill in 1908, the Conservative MP for Barkston Ash, George Richard Lane-Fox, complained that opening up access was a bad idea. The later 1st Baron Bingley said:

> Members must know what that was likely to lead to, having regard to what they knew of the failings of tourists in many parts of the country. They knew what was seen in the way of forest burning, names cut in trees, plants taken up and destroyed, horns blowing, and cornets playing.[25]

It's an assumption that hasn't quite gone away that the majority of the ordinary population simply don't know how to look after the land. Places should be reserved for only limited numbers, for certain people. Lane-Fox's comments don't sound so different from modern-day complaints about too many visitors to beauty spots. But instead of telling people they are the wrong type of visitor, perhaps narratives should focus on producing positive forms of connection with place. Environmental damage is at least partly a failure in education. The Scottish Land Reform Act has been accompanied by a campaign of education on care for landscapes. Responsibility and care of place may be essential but are unlikely to develop, so some argue, if we shut off common spaces and people never get to experience nature in the first place. The Right to Roam campaign in England suggests that the careful balance of rights and responsibilities in nature can only be achieved with access, so that: 'Nature is no longer relegated to occasional visits, but instead becomes part of people's daily routine, woven into their lives.'[26]

The debate comes down to key questions, as historian Andy Wightman has argued, of what and who land is for.[27] Do we measure, control, limit, or free up use? Some may argue it is there for revenue, others for common recreation, for walking, hiking or hunting. Certain groups may want areas reserved for wildlife and conservation, others for people. And there's debate how much land should be available as a common good, a common resource. Peanmeanach was never part of the commons in the sense that it was not owned collectively, but it was available for common use, common enjoyment, in a country where access to land for recreation is understood in progressive terms. Yet it's a story that also reveals that the lines between public access and private use are still unclear, and the question of how we inculcate responsibility still up for debate. How we see the land shapes how we use it, and, conversely, our perceptions of these places shift as they become more closed off and restricted. Common land is a deeply political question, since debates about the commons are also debates about power and rights. Dispossession is the mark of lack of privilege and repossession of common land has often been part of a campaign against privilege, a tradition associated with radical and egalitarian politics. In the English Civil War, the Diggers took over land to farm communally on St George's Hill, Surrey in 1649. In 1524, German peasants rose up in revolt, demanding restored access to common resources from fish to forests, meadows to mines.[28] Calls for common access continue to this day, as environmental and land-reform movements campaign to resist forms of modern enclosure in the form of corporate enterprise or large private estates.[29]

The arguments for enclosure and privatisation, arguments against common land, echo the refrains of the debate about bothies, and exemplify the tensions over use. Outsiders don't know how to respect the place, overuse ruins it, enclosure protects it. It's a well-worn argument. American ecologist Garrett Hardin's famous essay on the tragedy of the commons has become a byword for arguments against common use. It's a game-theory model for understanding attitudes to resources. Players shoot out in a zero-sum contest. As rational beings, Hardin argues, they are all in it for as good a deal as they can get, so the result of unregulated use of the commons will only be degradation.[30] So, what to do with common land or resources? If you are a libertarian, like economist Milton Friedman, you privatise. He believed that the US should fund parks with paying entry points looked after by privatisation.[31] This guarantees their protection. Not everyone agrees. Counter to the zero-sum logics of Hardin, political scientist Elinor Ostrom argued that individuals and communities could manage their own collective resources. She produced one of the most robust arguments for an economic theory of collective sustainability.[32]

I'd agree with Ostrom, but it's worth remembering that the case for money is not all about greed. Paying for things has two potential results. First, if you pay, you arguably have more responsibility and, secondly, it puts money back into communities who need it. Tourism matters for people in the Highlands and Islands to live, to work. I thought of my trips to bothies where I wasn't having much impact on the land but also perhaps not contributing to the local economy. Some have suggested that the solution is a small fee in line with hut systems in Norway or New Zealand, which would contribute to upkeep and make bothying more sustainable.[33] It's on this economic basis that green and eco-tourism has been sold, that it seems to promise to fulfil social, environmental and ecological goals of sustaining ecosystems and local communities, protecting wildernesses and cultures, while also generating money. Trees for Life's rewilding projects, for example, illustrate how some commercialisation of environmental activities might go hand in hand with the protection of Gaelic heritage and landscapes. Further afield, we could point to any number of initiatives such as Biosphere Expeditions' conservation holidays or WeWilder's locally built rewilding campus in the foothills of Romania's Țarcu Mountains. Alongside explicitly ecological aims, tourism of this nature is focused on the needs of local communities and the impact on the people and cultures of the region, whether that's using indigenous skills or knowledge, or channelling resources back into the local area. Money might be a powerful instrument in the green economy to bring about change and shape behaviours.

On the local level, it's nice to feel that your money may go to good places. Yet there are questions about whether global and grand claims made for green tourism ring true. Money may not always flow into local communities or conservation projects, and marketisation often leads to or reinforces structural inequalities. And only a few can pay for some of the more pricey sustainable or ecotourism options. They tend to be expensive and may only become more so if travel costs soar and biodiversity declines. Ecotourism may be simply perpetuating some of the social divides that exist when accessing nature, and these are legitimate arguments against asking people to book and pay for bothies.

Many people would say anyway that it's not a bothy if it's not free. Bothies aren't on common land, but they have become a form of collective resource. You could argue that what's happened with bothies proves Hardin's argument about the degradation of the commons. Rational self-interest means people took advantage of a space open for all to use. I think it tells a rather different story. For the most part, bothies seem to demonstrate the opposite, as something which is held and used for the common good, respected by its community, open to all. Sustaining this in a world of squeezed spaces is the challenge, but there are models for more sustainable, cooperative and open use of land. As Ostrom argues, this type of arrangement works best when there's clear local benefit, cooperative rule-making and -keeping, graded sanctions, low-cost dispute resolution and nested responsibility, where accountability for governance is spread across tiered, multiple layers.[34] The MBA promotes many of these values. And we should encourage social, cooperative behaviour wherever possible, through education and dialogue. We all have an individual responsibility to each other and to our landscapes, as environmental philosopher Aldo Leopold argues, but we also operate in communities.[35] The histories of MBA bothies, with their volunteer work parties and hodgepodge collectives, or the evolution of more recent forms of community action, such as Bothy Project, demonstrate that the idea of bothies can also offer a hopeful future pathway. Reinvigorating the local economy, respecting the local community, preserving places for public access, for people, but in balance with nature, and fostering educated communities of care.

Fundamentally, I feel it would be very sad if bothies

were no longer open and free at the point of use. I have gone to luxury versions of off-grid huts, but my stays here have not been cheap, and even the comparatively small fee for Peanmeanach makes a difference. The unique ecosystem of shelters, much beloved, seems something worth preserving. And anyway, bothies may be free when you use them, but it was a suggestion that might sit at odds with many MBA members, Geoff Allan says when I talk to him. You don't pay to stay, but bothies are maintained through both the membership dues of individuals and also their time. Collective resources are put in, shared and redistributed in a way Ostrom might well approve of.

I return to Clare's poem as I think back to Peanmeanach, where he talks of being free, encircled only by the sky.

Unbounded freedom ruled the wandering scene
Nor fence of ownership crept in between
To hide the prospect of the following eye
Its only bondage was the circling sky

That's how I feel, standing with toes in warm sand, salty water drying in white lines on my body, sunlight catching the crests of the water to form diamond peaks. It is partly an illusion, that sense of wilderness, and I certainly won't feel like that at Peanmeanach again. I can't go back to Peanmeanach bothy to visit as a wayfarer. It's closed to the casual guest. As I left, I wrote in the bothy book, inscribing a farewell. The trip to Peanmeanach was more special because I was one of the last people to see the old school mistress's house before it closed as an open bothy.

It's a tangled tale about access to land, the demands of tourism, the squeeze of space, and rights and responsibilities. Just as we should be aware of our responsibility to the land, we should be cautious of narratives that quietly turn back long histories of freedom, often working-class freedoms for space and leisure. There's an urgent need for common open spaces, of access to nature and places of retreat, recreation, encounter and freedom that are not just reserved for a few. Spaces which are openly accessible have shrunk, even as Covid has shown that we need more places that count as the commons, not fewer. Perhaps that's why bothies are so popular, as that's what they seem to represent: common land. There are real concerns about the pressure on places and landscape, and the diminishing values of responsibility and accountability that can come with the anonymity of mass travel, the lack of connection visitors may feel. But perhaps learning to deal with these conflicts, learning how to respect others, respect places, rub along in shared space, promote education and cooperation is what we need to do and what access to commons offers. Losing places where we can do that, places like bothies, means we lose those chances of creating a different relationship with the land, shared experiences and chance encounters.

I wish I could go back to Peanmeanach bothy as it was that sunny September. But I can't, and I will only stay now if I book and pay.

There's another reason too I can't return to that moment of spontaneity in the sun, not in the same way.

Because I haven't been quite honest about my time here. I wasn't alone, I was with a partner with whom I thought I would be forging a new life as all the possibilities opened up again. But it didn't turn out that way. In the end, as our lives went separate ways, he didn't want to be in this book. I won't tell his story, though I would tell him, as he often bid others, 'Fare forward.' Now the absence of recollection even fades on the page.

Yet perhaps it's also the knowledge that I can't return that makes the memory of this so potent, a memory of freedom and connection in the clear warmth of midday sun. It's a little like waking from a dream you only half remember. In the fragility of these moments, we sometimes grasp a sense of what's worth preserving or worth taking forward for the future. When I look back, it's not just nostalgia or loss I feel, but a powerful sense of what mattered here, what we can save, and what we can create.

TEN | PAPA WESTRAY

Back in Time

I came across the old photo when I was sorting through some boxes in my parents' house during the fuzzy isolation of lockdown. We had been on a family holiday in Wales when I was about 10, visiting a mine near Snowdon - I don't remember which one but, probably Llechwedd - and part of the fun of the day was to dress up as a nineteenth-century working family. Looking back now, that was pretty odd. The mines were places of hard labour, and there we were, playing make-believe in a romanticised vision of the past. It's a perfect snapshot of a happy childhood. My brother's beaming cheeky grin, my dad's impressive twirling moustache. The fact that the photo is a Polaroid is even more perfect. It's already got the patina of a bleached wash, no need for any Instagram filter to conjure up the illusion of faded time. I handle it reverently, savouring the sweetness of childish things now put away.

Everyone's nostalgic for something. Your first love. A favourite holiday spot. A landscape that moves the soul now ripped apart by roads or houses. The song of a bird whose voice becomes rarer with each passing year. There are all sorts of shadows we try to grasp, things to which we know we can never quite return.

A lot of bothying feels like trying to reach back to the past in search of something that's disappeared, simpler ways of life and connection to the environment. But when you think about the reality of going to live in lonely, damp stone dwellings, it seems a strange thing to be nostalgic for. In the Bothy museum on Papa Westray in Orkney, you get a sense of the hard lives that were the reality for people living in such buildings.

The Bothy museum is a very small museum on a small island. Right at the centre of Papa Westray, it is housed in one of the old buildings that's still attached to the working farm at the heart of the island. It's a tiny little thing, not a museum of modern bothying, but two rooms telling a visitor what it might have been like to live and labour on the farm in the past. It's obviously not a bothy you can stay in, but I was delighted to have discovered a Bothy museum at all.

The hinges are rusted, the latch heavy. Pushing open the heavy wooden door, the damp, chill air hits you as it seems to seep from the thick walls that are rough and cold to the touch. Little light creeps in through the small windows, small, of course, because they were designed to minimise heat loss from poorly insulated dwellings. At first glance it's not a scene that would seem to evoke happy, nostalgic feelings, but nonetheless it's the stripped-back, basic life that evokes a warm glow for a lot of bothiers. No electricity, no heating, a simpler way of being. But while we may long for this for a few days, most of us wouldn't really want to go and live in a bothy all the time. It's easy to feel nostalgic when you are only experiencing that life for a snapshot in time.

Exterior of the Bothy museum.

Nostalgia is an early modern word. Johannes Hofer, an Alsatian doctor, first came up with the phrase in 1688, putting together two Greek words - *nostos* (home-coming, so famed from Odysseus's fantastical journey back to Ithaca from Troy) and *algos* (pain) – to diagnose the sickness that seemed to plague people who were separated from their home. For the countless migrants and exiles of early modern Europe, the sorrowful ache for return in the face of displacement was a malady triggered by the sound of Scottish bagpipes or Swiss cow bells.[1]

Now understood as an emotion, not an illness, we might tend to perceive nostalgia as a particularly modern phenomenon produced by the sense of a world out of pace with itself. As individuals, we generally think about nostalgia for moments in our personal lives, for the golden days of youth, perhaps, but it also has a macro, generational meaning. Nations, communities and cultures can feel it too. The shifts of industrialisation, capitalism, globalisation and climate change have left us hurtling towards an unknown destination in ways that disrupt our sense of past and present.[2] In the current moment of ecological rupture, there is a keen sense of loss and nostalgia for the living worlds and landscapes we are losing.

Nostalgia traces 'lines of rupture', as American historian Peter Fritzsche put it, when people feel 'a nagging, unmasterable presence of absence'. He was talking about the problems of modernity post-1789.[3] But people have probably always felt nostalgic, even when no word existed to name the feeling. The shape of our nostalgic visions changes, but the desire is a universal phenomenon that emerges from a sense of dislocation in time and space.

The whole Orkney trip is about looking back, thinking about a sense of something lost that could not quite be regained. It is supposed to be a mix of museum visiting and archival work for the book, returning to the documents that I love, and then exploring the wonder of the islands off the north coast of Scotland.

It is a weird time. A little unsettled. Covid restrictions have been lifted but are not quite gone. The world unsure if it is sad or hopeful or simply anxious. New paths opening up but as yet unclear. I was one of those lucky people for whom lockdown had been frustrating, worrying, at times lonely but also a strangely welcome caesura from the troubles that had plagued me, a pregnant pause of promise. I was a little wistful for the time when social obligations were lifted and when the person I wanted to be next, a younger version of myself pulled out of the rubble, was still a hopeful sketch in outline. Limbo gone, I had to deal with the reality that I was in my late thirties and that the choices I had made had closed off paths. I was unsure now if I would ever have children, for one thing. Christmas ever since the divorce had a strange melancholy, and it was the last Christmas with my then husband that really confirmed my suspicions that the marriage was over. What had been such a happy time as a child, surrounded by my three siblings, varying numbers of dogs and cats, and my parents' easy comfort, became a painful reminder that things were not going to work out as I had planned and, perhaps, I would never know the comfort of the large family that

I had grown up with. It wasn't even something that I definitely knew I wanted, and so much of my independence I welcomed, as I had the freedom to plan my life as I wished. But I also looked at my friends in long relationships, starting families, welcoming babies into the world, and there was a grief for a life that was at least a possibility a few years ago.

I plan to get loads of archival work done in Dundee on the way up to Orkney, but I am (as so often happens at the end of a busy term) really ill. Not Covid but the other horrible flu going around, meaning that I see little else but the inside of my hotel room, a tonne of *Bridgerton*, *Outlander* and the final season of *The Last Kingdom*. I tell myself the last two are definitely research for the next leg of my journey up to Orkney, and that the Netflix binge is a calculated exercise in thinking about how we romanticise, narrativise and idealise our pasts. I half-believe it, though after two days I have had enough 'research' and I am longing to be striding around the Scottish landscapes myself.

Fortunately, though still shaky, I am recovered enough to enjoy Orkney. The ferry over is restorative, invigorating, a passage to another place. I spend as long as possible on the deck in the wind and sun, the golden glow sinking behind us as the ship carves through the water, its foamy trails of overturned sea forming ephemeral paths. We arrive in the dark. The harbour glare glitters in the black water and the outline shape of the Mainland's gentle rise and fall is picked out by coruscating lights.

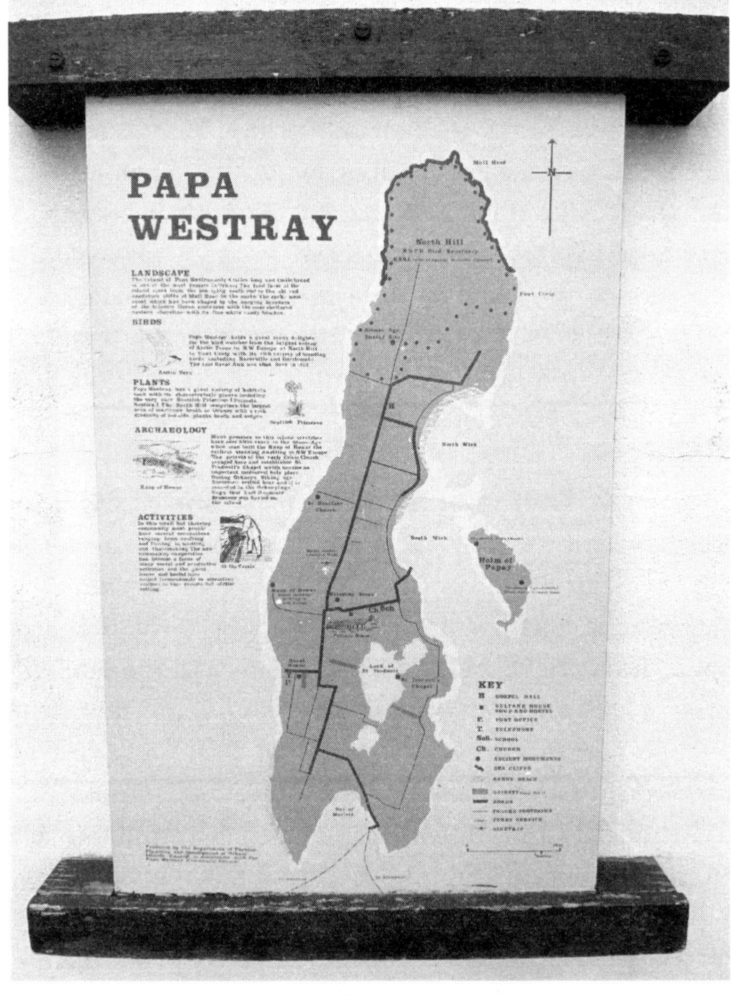

A map of the island near the airport.

Papa Westray, or Papay, as it was long known and is still called by locals, is north of the Mainland, only 6.5 km long, a low-lying diamond of land that scythes between the Atlantic and the North Sea. It's small enough that you can walk round it in a day, though it's just pipped to the post of the claim of the northernmost island of Orkney by North Ronaldsay. Papay, from the Norse word for priests, refers to the monks who made their lives in these windswept places. It's a mantle shared with Papadil on the Isle of Rùm and the ruins on Kilda, and many other locations. Papar, Pabbay or Papil sites, those places whose names incorporate the word *papar* (priest), referring to Celtic priests in the northern and western islands of Scotland, were located on rich lands once connected by busy sea routes.[4] Next morning, my first attempt to get the flight across to Papay starts in glorious sun as I leave my B&B in Kirkwall, but this has turned to low-hanging mist by the time I get to the airport. The infamous Orkney *haar* has stymied us. I and the only other passenger, the teacher for the school with six pupils, will have to wait. Next day rises clear, bright, beautiful. As the tiny fixed-propellor plane glides across the green-blue water, wheeling round to make the runway, I get a sense of the proportions of Papay. It looks like a leaf barely floating on the surface of the sea, and at its northern point the Atlantic and the North Sea meet, a churning line of colliding currents.

A short stroll from the airport where the windsock is blowing merrily in the spring breeze, cheerful orange-red, is Holland Farm, a large and active holding in the centre of the island. Papay has long been famed for good soils and rich seas, and it was once praised for 'containing some of the best pasture and arable lands in the whole country'.[5] Some hyperbole, perhaps, but while Orkney's land may look harsh, it is fertile and productive. Even the sea provides pasture. North Ronaldsay is home to the famous seaweed-eating sheep whose gamey meat graces expensive dinner tables around the world.[6] In the absence of written records, the Neolithic remains, the ruins of an Iron Age roundhouse and the wealth of the important church of St Boniface attest to the lure of the productive island that also guarded the main sea routes to Shetland and beyond.[7] Blaeu's beautiful seventeenth-century map of Orkney, on which Papay is a small smear with a church, depicts seas busy with ships. Rudd fish hang from the title inset, gleaming silver bodies, pink fins and tails.[8]

Holland Farm's name is Old Norse, suggesting a holding going back to the days of Viking settlement, but by the time it starts appearing on maps in the eighteenth and nineteenth centuries, it was the property of the prosperous Traill family. Thomas Traill purchased the property in 1637, and the family worked the land for 250 years, 'improving' (they claimed) agricultural techniques that had remained largely unchanged for centuries. By the end of the nineteenth century in 1886, in the same year that the Crofters' Act issued its landmark ruling to protect the rights of crofters, the farm had fallen into debt and the Traills were forced to put it up for sale. But farming continued and the estate cycled through tenancies, until it was bought by the Rendall family in 1967.[9] Two hundred years earlier, in 1750, Murdoch MacKenzie's fine-lined cartographic outline of the islands noted the farm at the centre; the only homestead marked on the island, though the church is visible.[10] Then, as now, the working heart of an island.

As I approach the farm, I see the yokes of former ploughs and old cartwheels, painted red, which are arranged artistically on the outside of one of the farm buildings, and a small sign points me to the tiny bothy museum. Inside these four walls lived the unmarried young men who worked the farm. Up until World War II, there were still around ten farmhands, young men of around 14 to 15 years of age, who all bunked up in the bothy after a long, hard day of labour with only a small kist or chest for possessions and a few stools.[11]

Interior of the Bothy museum.

I enter and look round the various displays and faded photographs, trying to imagine what it must have been like to live in here for long stretches with other farmhands. Inside are all manner of objects detailing the past lives of the islanders and the working rhythm of the farm. A hay-knife to slice the bundled stacks like sponge cake, tattie chappers (a potato masher), a ploutkirn for milk, quilted blankets and long johns. It's one of those intriguing micro museums, similar to other small heritage sites I have come across on my travels, such as the former black-house on Eigg, now known as the Cleadale Crofting Museum. It's piled up with the assorted paraphernalia of past lives. These places gather together evocations of times gone by, a jumble of objects that symbolise the daily experiences of former decades.

Alongside learning about the history of the farm, you can also buy homemade souvenirs, odds and ends such as jams and knitted goods. There's no cashier here. Like the Eigg blackhouse, the Papa Westray bothy museum is free and unlocked, in the same spirit as a mountain bothy, reliant on trust and goodwill that you will leave things as they are and shut the door behind you. Simply leave money for the postcards or gifts as you depart. I only had a tiny bit of change, so I dropped it into the box and took nothing with me, not wanting to abuse any trust.

When Hofer coined the term, nostalgia was understood as a diagnosable malaise that struck when people missed places, but it's come to mean longing for a time that's past, looking back to years gone as a golden age. Certain places have a power to stir that uncanny sense of being in a different time, and to take us back to the past or away from the present moment, even if the memory has been distorted over time. Who hasn't got something in their garage or in boxes under the bed that once seemed deeply uncool and unfashionable but now has a nostalgic retro chic. Among the same photo collection as the family mining-holiday snap, I find one of me in a neon, scratchy shell suit of the 1980s. Even this seems to have a certain renewed appeal, though I am not sure it's a look I can pull off any more. Through this rosy-tinted reimagining, what was uncomfortable or unpopular is transformed. We do this with experiences as well as things. It's like seeing a childhood toy and wishing yourself back to the worry-free days of those years, when of course even then you carried all the childish concerns that make us fret when we are little. In my own life, I sometimes shake myself out of the illusion that I have missed chances or given up on things that could have worked. While in a different universe I might have met someone younger, bought a house, had children, perhaps; this was also the life I had run from with my ex-husband, and children in the damaging relationship after would have felt like an ending of things, not a beginning. I have so much love and joy and adventure in my life, I remind myself – there is no point mourning a dream that never was.

Don't get me wrong, lots of people visiting mountain shelters or writing in bothy books seem completely unconcerned with the past. They are using bothies to move through the present, bagging Munros or otherwise whiling the weekends away, challenging themselves with long hikes. But even when not expressed in so many words, I think there is always a feeling of visitors grasping at something fading, something intangible. Sometimes it's simply the compulsion to scrawl down in the bothy book their experiences, adding new layers to the folds of history there – laying their memories out for strangers who might flick past them in the future. There is a slowness to the communication here, a gentle archiving, which feels in some ways opposite to the immediacy of posts we put on social media for our friends to see. There are scribbled notes or casual conversations that talk of a trip in youth that sparked the love of bothies, the longing for a particular vision of the landscape, the old mountains, high peaks, the rugged places and written recollections of times past. Grainy photographs in the MBA newsletters or the images of work parties often included in bothy books recall the early days of bothying. Photography here often seems particularly wistful. It freezes a moment in time, pinned like a butterfly to a board. As art historian John Berger writes, 'The camera isolated momentary appearances and in so doing destroyed the idea that images were timeless.'[12] In a photograph we sense a moment of time past, lost time, a fleeting absence.

I have wondered, though, as I have cooked on stoves, purified water and lit candles, why do we find such joy in looking back to a time when running water, electric lights and a gas hob were not even possible. For many there is a certain nostalgic romance in the simplicity. Part of what appeals in bothying is the way that time seems to tick over in a strange way. You are seemingly pulled out of the hectic rhythm of life and the ever-quickening beat of modernity. There's no clock in a bothy. It's not that you don't know the time – you may have your watch or your phone – but for most people, the demands of the world begin to operate differently. Or at least that's the aspiration. You are released for a moment from what the historian E. P. Thompson labelled the capitalist time and work-discipline of the modern world.[13] Perhaps, you think, this simple world of the bothy was what life was like before all the technology and social media and work emails got in the way. Particularly in more recent entries in bothy books, people write about stepping away from modernity by a return to simple ways of life. A visitor to Guirdil wrote that it was nice to find a place 'where time keeps standing still'.[14] Perhaps French sociologist Pierre Bourdieu was right that people grasp for a rural ideal where 'no one dreams of mastering, using up, or saving' time.[15] You make things with your hands that have been franchised out now to machines and institutions. You return to the rhythms of the body, of the weather, the light, the dark.

There seems to be a powerful ache for what scholar Michael Bunce calls the 'old symbolic imagery' of imagined rural idylls, from the twee, cosy comfort of English pastoral landscapes to Highland crofters' cottages to the prairies of America.[16] It's also often imagined, constructed out of rosy memories that may not even be ours. As you hold a handmade pot or handcrafted sweater, it's easy to romanticise this as something purer, made of love, not hardship. Craft items bought on country holidays, the character of bothy trips, or Highland tours with stags and whisky all feed off idealised notions of rural life. From its inception, tourism became inextricably linked, at least in the Western world, with notions of place and landscape, divisions of rural and urban, as nature 'out there' became a thing to be revered but also an attraction to be visited. As I travelled up and down on trains from Bath to London I saw, every day, GWR's spate of adverts that are a nostalgic nod to the romantic age of railway and the desire to travel out to rural escapes. It's basically the Famous Five in pastoral pastel places. Rural, as an imaginary concept, has come to embody a distance from the city as centre. Most of us, me included, may have posted a filtered picture, or purchased something like a cuddly-toy 'Highland coo' that's a reminder of a supposedly romantic retreat to the wilds.

But in hankering after the simple, cosy rural life, we risk simply idealising the harsh reality of the past, playing dress-up like my family did as mine workers. As sociologist John Urry puts it, 'the pure and innocent eye is a myth'.[17] We can be romantic because we observe from the privileged position of not having to live the lives we are nostalgic for. Damp, cold and dark, the bothies, crofts or ghillies' cottages were not idyllic wilderness retreats. As one former farm worker puts it:

> The bothy is an old dirty-looking thatched house, joined on to the end of a cow byre . . . At the end of the house is the fire-place, about which there is generally a large heap of ashes. The bothy is very often in a terrible state of filth.[18]

Nostalgia may exist for what never was. The buildings that make bothies for hikers are not a relic of some happy pre-industrial past when people gathered round fires, sang folk songs and lived in harmony. It's not even true that staying somewhere without electricity is the equivalent of stepping back in time. The Ardnish peninsula, home to Peanmeanach bothy, has never had electricity. 'Modernity' is not a concrete thing but a category of thinking that has emerged from ideas about past, present and future, though it seems to be such a truism that most people never question it. It seems to mean living in the now and all the trappings that come with it, on the road always to progress and improvement. But French philosopher Bruno Latour argues, we have never been modern, for there was no great revolution that saw science free us from the constraints of nature and separate us from pre-moderns. 'Western innovations' are not 'a vast saga of radical rupture'.[19] There are many modernities, many pasts.

Despite being a small island, Papa Westray is a place humming with life, although it is now much quieter than it used to be. It once had 40 small farms and 350 inhabitants, down now to only 50 people. The same is true of many Scottish islands, and is a reminder that past and modernity don't always mean what we expect. Not everywhere in the world is becoming more populous and more concentrated. Bothies were once working buildings, and Guirdil bothy on Rùm and Peanmeanach, for example, were buildings among a number of small homesteads, not places of isolated glory. Some bothies were emptied as a result of the Clearances, others the victim of the poverty, famine and economic shifts of the later nineteenth and twentieth centuries, and the ruins beside restored shelters are often a terrible footprint of violence and deprivation.

But the appearance of ruins and empty cottages can give an illusory sense of the pasts of these places as always wild and lonely. The tourist vision of the rural landscape, as author Rebecca Smith writes, forgets these were and are places of labour.[20] Imagining the Highlands and Islands as wilderness is an act of erasure, a form of nostalgia we should guard against, though for the most part bothiers and the MBA are pretty good at recording the local histories of the places they restore.

Orkney itself was largely spared the Clearances, although Rousay was subjected to forced evacuations by none other than Sir George William Traill of the family who owned Papa Westray. While the land on Papay was 'improved', there were not the mass evictions that characterised other parts of the Highlands and Islands, and the farm and the farmhands' bothy never fell into disuse.[21] Perhaps the museum's walls would never have felt quite as remote as somewhere such as Maol-bhuidhe or Uisinis bothy on Uist. Or perhaps that's just a perspective shaped by histories of use and disuse, and if all Orkney had been cleared, Papay's bothy museum would feel as isolated as her sister bothies.

Nostalgia often seems overly sentimental in this desire for disappeared pasts. In its gentler form, this whimsical longing for a Golden Age might be harmless, amusing. It makes me think of Woody Allen's time-hopping movie *Midnight in Paris*. The Golden Age keeps receding as every era idolises the one that came before. But nostalgia can be a regressive call to tradition which aims to stymie positive change. Demands to 'Make Britain Great Again'. A time when men were men, women knew their place.

Whatever it might be, appeals to narrow nationalist and populist ideas can make a political tool of nostalgia.

Yet nostalgia isn't just about looking back, and it doesn't have to be reactionary. It's a Janus-faced being, one foot in the past, one eye on the future. It might also be a way of thinking about what's fractured in our world. Nostalgia for simplicity and a stripped-back life that escapes some of the demands of the modern world may be no bad thing. It is a way of reflecting critically on what surrounds us and expresses the ache for something different in the world that is yet to come.

After the museum, I walk west to the edge of Papay to take in the other sites of the island. The Orkney tapestry, as Orcadian author George Mackay Brown put it, is woven thick with many threads, from Neolithic farms to Viking graves, from ancient rocks to calling sea birds.[22]

For most people, the bothy museum wouldn't be the main draw of Papay. A short stroll from the farmhouse is another, much older farmhouse, the Knap of Howar. The stone walls resounded with the chatter of life over 5,000 years ago, and it's the oldest surviving such building in Northern Europe. Two houses built into the earth would have sat in pastureland surrounded by freshwater pools, dunes separating the settlement from the coast, cows and sheep grazing on the grass.[23] This all sounds a familiar pastoral scene, but the cattle, only recently domesticated, would have looked less like modern cows and more like the giant aurochs, now extinct, that used to roam the Earth and that could be up to 180 cm tall.

The Knap is the thing most people come for. That and the birds. I know my archaeologist colleagues would shudder at this, but the evocative remains of the pre-Christian world almost seem as if they had always been there. Stone walls sunken into green turf seem to grow out of the landscape, survivals of a time that is so far distant it appears timeless. Ruins and crumbling remnants are particularly powerful stimulants of nostalgia, perhaps because they remind us of the impermanence and the disposability of the modern world. As literary scholar Andreas Huyssen writes, 'the chance for things to age and to become ruin has diminished in the age of turbo capitalism'.[24] An imaginary of ruins, whether it's bothies, Neolithic farms or even destroyed landscapes, may be needed to combat the idea of neoliberal progress. Maybe what we are nostalgic for in the presence of ruin is the decaying but still present memory of a deeper time.

As I wander down, I can see I am not the only person visiting that day. A small group hails me as I approach and I fall into conversation after signing the visitors' book left by the tiny school on Papa Westray, a little like a version of a bothy book. I introduce myself to the group - one a resident of the island, the others friends visiting - joining their impromptu guided tour. We chat as we amble up the coast, and in the strange coincidence of travelling encounters, one is a doctor who has known my father as a GP in Shropshire. Past and present become interwoven, a strange magic at work.

It is funny to have that sudden link with my own history. I was born in Shropshire and spent my whole life there until I moved away for university and work. We lived in the same family home for all my childhood, idyllic in many ways, with a large garden and endless places to play or get lost. One of my great regrets as my marriage broke down was that I had no time or energy to return before my parents sold the house and relocated. No goodbye to the prickly bush where I investigated the finds of a day in the garden, to the weeping cherry I hid under, to the warm greenhouse where I read all summer, and to the walls of books that my mum has always collected.

We enter the dark chill of St Boniface's church. It's one of the few survivals of pre-reformation Christianity, alongside the magnificent cathedral of St Magnus on the Mainland, known as the Light of the North. My new friends treat me to a spontaneous performance of hymns that takes me back to schoolday assembly singing. I don't remember now the exact tune, but the strains of melodies that have no devotional import for me personally wash over us in a beauty of cascading sounds.

Just before we part ways, we walk past the crumbling shelves at the edge of the island where you can see the middens, old rubbish pits for domestic waste, both Neolithic and Iron Age. Skeletal fragments and shells stick out in a mosaic of earth. Lying loose, broken free by wind and water, is the discarded bone waste of some feathered meal, eaten centuries ago. I pick it up. If this were a gift shop, I would buy a plastic Knap of Howar or a foam grave, a cheery remnant of my trip. I thumb the cool, ridged spine of a long-dead seabird and pop it into my pocket. There is something brutal, strange in carrying a skeleton memento of such a vibrant place, a little like deer antlers or animal-skin rugs that romanticise death.

Like a gatherer of shells strewn on the beach, nostalgia too is a collector, gathering up the scattered fragments of a supposed pre-industrial world such as folk songs or fairy tales. The Brothers Grimm, the nineteenth-century German collectors of tales, talked about the search for these relics in the edges of places, like kitchen stoves or in hedgerows.[25] Perhaps they would have really liked bothies as a hunting ground. They, and men like them, were the product of a collecting passion that emerged after the French Revolution when it was thought this past was gone for ever.

Alone again, I wander up the west coast of the island, past the low, flat rocks of Dull Flag, like paving stones arranged on the shore, and the numerous geos, cliff gullies etched out by relentless waves. At the top end of the island is the RSPB reserve of North Hill. The expanses of maritime heath resound with the call of kittiwakes, a particularly pretty gull with black-tipped wings. Their delicate dark eyes and small yellow bills give them a friendly appearance, unlike the angry hawkishness of a herring gull, while their chatter sounds like playing school children. Following the path up along the sea's edge, I notice a few great skua, the pirates of the sea, who sit hunched, waiting to steal eggs or dive-bomb invaders. They have dark brown wings, speckled with white, and curved, short, vicious black beaks. Aggressive and notoriously unafraid of humans, they will make a beeline if you get too close. The poster in the RSPB hut tells me to be on the lookout. Beware of the 'bonxies', as they are also known, a title probably derived from an old Norse word meaning 'dumpy'. It's an apt name for their huddled forms, I think, as I eye them suspiciously. In his *Fauna Orcadensis* of 1813, Reverend George Low described being attacked with 'great fury' and he lamented that his gun 'did not startle them in the least, rather seemed to enrage them the more'.[26] Reading his account, I am cheering on the bonxies from the sidelines.

The Traills were not able to enclose all this area of the island for 'improvement', as it was resisted by the locals as common grazing land, and it has remained a wild place of birds and sea and sky.[27] The cliffs are rich in life but also haunted by the spectres of vanished beings. In 1813, on the steps of Fowl Craig, one half of what was probably the last breeding pair of great auks on British shores was shot. These large, flightless birds could grow up to about 85 cm tall and had heavy, hooked beaks. Their bellies were white, their backs black, and in between the eye and the beak was a recognisable white oval patch.[28] They were long prized as a food source and were of symbolic cultural importance for many communities, but as egg collectors sought to gather up rare specimens, their numbers declined. The King, the male, was shot by local man, William Foulis, for a collector called William Bullock, and it was Miss Traill who handed over the preserved corpse to him. The Queen, the female, was sadly stoned to death as she sat on her nest.[29]

With bitter irony, Reverend Low with his gun commented, in the same year that the King was killed, that he had often enquired about the great auk but had not found it here. No one would have known that the auks on Papa Westray were the last breeding pair when the male was shot, but the bird's death sentence had been signed. There were a few more sightings of great auks round British waters, and the bird was probably finally extinct worldwide by the mid 1840s.[30] Now all that's left is a monument on the rocks and a display in the Stromness Museum, fading in a case, a monument perhaps to 'unrepeatable and irreversible time'.[31] The reality of extinction is a hard stop on the possibilities of nostalgia.

Back on the Mainland the next day, I cycle across the main island on a chunky bike I have hired, through gentle rolling hills with sheep and clear lochs, and always the backdrop of curlews. Like nightingales and turtle doves, vanishing birds, the curlews' keening cry seems to recall an older time. We often find comfort in this. Unlike the auk, they have not yet been destroyed and their sound seems to be the echo of a time when there was more abundance and flourishing in the natural world.

Going right back to Greek myths, bucolic longing is deeply embedded in Western consciousness. Halcyon days are an old trope of nostalgia, suggesting buzzing wildflower meadows and thronged skies, summer, calm days, youth, times past. It's also an old Greek myth of loss and longing. The Greek gods took pity on two desperate lovers, Alcyone and Ceyx, when he is killed by a thunderbolt from Zeus, and she plunges off a cliff in despair. But by divine intervention they are turned into kingfishers, an emerald-jewelled flash of feather and beak. The *Alkionides Meres*, or halcyon days, were not long summer nights but the days after the winter solstice when it was calm enough for Alcyone to lay her eggs. The halcyon birds still the seas in the poems known as the Idylls of Theocritus, paeans to the rural imagination from the third century BCE.[32] Kingfishers still bear her name. In taxonomic categories, their family name is *Alcedinidae*.

Old myths, but it's striking how often nostalgia remains intertwined with landscapes and beyond-human worlds. It is, perhaps, why so many people pore over sites of ruin reclaimed by nature. Even without awareness of the biodiverse worlds these 'islands of abandonment' might support, subconsciously perhaps they call to mind the return of a paradise. As cultural theorist Svetlana Boym writes, quoting writer Viktor Shklovsky, it's the idea that the city has gone pastoral.[33]

Perhaps people feel nostalgia for the living world particularly keenly now as we face environmental and climate breakdown. We look back to times when there were more animals, denser trees, noisier birds, and we fear that the future will be barren, dry, dead. Like the Brothers Grimm, people look for the remnants of disappearing worlds at the edges and at the margins, except it's not the pre-industrial world of folk imagination we search for but the endlings of species or rare ecosystems. I think of the lonely death of the last male northern white rhino in the world only a few years ago. It was an iconic reminder of loss, but decline is happening closer to the home in the UK. MacKenzie's map of old Orkney notes the abundance of fish and seas full of life, albeit life that was already being harvested in increasingly resource-intensive ways. On the top, he marks that this is where ling and cod can be found. In the margins of the map, they are there, at a time when the ling would have been caught by hook and line to be dried out. But now ling, lonely fish that live in the dark worlds of benthic waters, have been pulled from the deep by trawlers and are declining rapidly.[34]

There's even a name for the strange new kind of nostalgia or sense of grief we feel in an era of environmental change – solastalgia. The word does not describe absence from a homeland or the past but rather tries to capture a sense of loss in real time as the place which is still your home is destroyed around you. Glenn Albrecht coined the term when he visited Upper Hunter in New South Wales in the hope of finding rainforest, fantails and bowerbirds only to see open-pit coal mining. In this moment of pain, he created this neologism to describe 'the homesickness you have at home'. We need new emotions for a world in change. Nostalgia, development and environmental destruction often go hand in hand, and solastalgia aims to capture something with which vocabularies in other languages are already grappling – uncanniness and unease at the rapid pace of change. But perhaps the positive thing about solastalgia is that it does not see these fractures as irreversible.[35] Even though we will not avert all disaster, as singer-songwriter and author Mallachy Tallack writes, 'there is hope to be found amid this fear'.[36] We cannot conjure back the great auk, but we may be able to rebuild our relationships with place.

Precarity may be the 'condition of our time', as anthropologist Anna Tsing argues. But if so, nostalgia or, indeed, solastalgia might be essential as we try to live in a world of 'capitalist ruination' and think beyond simple cycles of progress and ruin. To end the story with decay, she argues, is to abandon hope. We must learn to live with the patchy landscapes of past and present, human and non-human.[37] It's a way, too, of thinking about the messy entanglements of time and existence in an era of precarity and extinction.

I come back from Orkney with the bits and bobs that I always gather and that make me think fondly of the trip. A groatie buckie (a lucky cowrie) and some miniscule shells that form the patterned bedspread of the Bay of Birsay. The seabird spine. The sound of curlews, which I can still hear ringing in my ears. The smell of the bothy museum. Senses of a time and place and the scattered remembrances.

We are all bound in these processes of collecting pasts, presents and futures. Individually and collectively, we all have our own halcyon days and golden eras. We all have to guard against the slip into a form of nostalgia that obscures, hides, excludes, overwrites. French author and philosopher Albert Camus warned against the nostalgia for unity, impossible and pointless, since it is a desire to make reasonable a world which is not reasonable.[38]

The allure of a bothy building in the towering mountains, alone in the wilderness, set beside ruins, perhaps, is complicated and fraught with problems for all these reasons, since bothiers may too be implicated in an act of erasure or of glorifying old, simple idylls. Yet nostalgia is not always the enemy, the stuffy spectre of regressive pasts. It can make us create, hope, see forward even as we look back. Nostalgia does not have to be melancholic longing for a past permanently absent and destroyed. And we are right to be nostalgic and to grieve the loss of certain landscapes, the loss of connection to the beyond-human world, of freedoms, and of time. Feeling grief and loss is important and inevitable as 'loss renders visible the contours of the thing mourned'.[39] The desire to get out, to vote with our feet, to live more simply, to reset the rhythms of time and to mourn the loss of living worlds may be no bad thing.

In the bothy book for Penrhos Isaf a visitor in 1985 has written of their hopes for the future – it's like the 'I Have a Dream' speech but for bothies. He writes that he can envision a time

> When such places are numerous, a network throughout the mountains where those who sigh to enjoy the hills and woods simply can.
>
> Of a time when most ruins in the hills are rebuilt.[40]

It's a striking vision for the future because it dreams not simply about growth or progress, but a return in some way to a time when people and landscape were connected. It's about ruin but also restoration, and bothies, after all, don't freeze the past. Bothiers rebuild and inhabit places in new ways. Ruins surround many bothies, but they themselves aren't ruins. They are patchy places of entangled worlds, human and beyond-human, authentic and yet invented, ruined and restored.

Maybe seen in all its fractured and problematic realities, then, there is something fitting about bothy nostalgia. A cottage shaped by the processes of improvement and capitalism, falling into ruin, only to be reclaimed in a different way. These are places at the margins that suggest a different temporality of being that is neither wholly past, present or future.

As I return to the mainland of Scotland on the ferry, I sit eating a breakfast of muesli and orange juice and gaze out through the scratched glass. A lone figure stands there, a young man having a cigarette and I take up my camera. Through the haze of the window and the soft morning light, the image that emerges is like a sepia snapshot of a soldier sent off to war or a lover parted. A mirage of imagination and things past. But the sun rises over the dock in Aberdeen and brings with it too the promise of the future. A new day to start afresh.

ELEVEN | ATHNAMULLOCH

Wilded Landscapes

'There's a piece of me there, and there's a piece of the place deep within my body.'

That's how one of my students, Lynn from Minneapolis, talks about her visit to Athnamulloch bothy in Glen Affric. We are having a short debrief of our week visiting this flagship environmental project in the sunny seminar room at the new Dundreggan Rewilding Centre, owned by Trees for Life. I ask the students how it felt, what did they expect, how has the experience made them think differently, if at all. Like nearly all of the other students on the trip, Lynn has never been to the Highlands, though she has spent plenty of time in the backcountry of Wisconsin. The wooded slopes and mirror-glass waters of Loch Affric are not a bad way to start.

I had chosen Athnamulloch for a field trip/holiday/research outing with the MA students at my university, students to whom I would soon be bidding farewell as I left academia. After the exhaustion of Covid and endless demands with restructures, cuts and strikes, academia no longer felt happy, and I was two months away from accepting the severance that my university had been eager to give, to avoid compulsory redundancies in favour of voluntary ones. It felt like a good place to say goodbye to my old life and hello to my new one, even if I didn't quite know what it would look like yet. Something involving bothies.

I knew Athnamulloch bothy would be a little more comfortable than a normal bothy, as it's a bookable space that has been kitted out for work parties and conservation groups. I wanted to see how Trees for Life, an iconic rewilding organisation, had transformed this landscape over the last thirty years. Trees for Life was born in 1989, when Alan Watson Featherstone started to persuade landowners in the Highlands to support his goal of reforestation, allowing him to plant seedlings or protect saplings. Since the early 1990s, the rewilding charity have been clawing back ground for the ancient Caledonian Forest that once covered the Highlands, planting and protecting over a million trees in pockets across these glens, and in 2008 they bought the 4,047-hectare Dundreggan estate.[1]

Only scraps of the ancient tree cover that once extended to 2,600 km cling on in the Highlands, 1 per cent of what was there. Humans have felled and cleared it for timber and for farming, while deer and grazing animals have nibbled at saplings, unchecked by large predators, which have now disappeared from the UK.[2] Trees for Life aims to restore trees and with them the vibrant ecosystems that have vanished. In what is often described as the most beautiful glen in Scotland, the former shieling-turned-cottage of Athnamulloch is now a base from which the charity runs conservation weeks, work parties for planting, and eco-educational trips.

Nothing about rewilding is uncontroversial. It triggers debates about land use, which environmental baselines should be deployed when restoring living landscapes, who gets to make decisions about environments, jobs, community, and the balance of human and non-human worlds. There are contested pasts and futures.[3] Precisely because of its controversial beauty, I couldn't wait to see what my MA students made of it. I wanted to know how they would see the Highlands, how the landscape of recovering trees and returning wildlife might inspire them, what they made of the controversies and conflicts.

Something deeper was also at work, which I couldn't quite grasp as I made plans for the trip in the months before, and finally made the decision to leave academia. On the treadmill of relationships and work, I hadn't realised I was worn out. Neoliberal marketisation had drained the job of joy, so my colleagues and I ended up feeling like dispensable cogs in a marketing machine. Birkbeck, the institution where I worked, was losing out in an arena that had removed caps for student numbers as they went to universities with bigger names and greater capacity. At the same time, we felt we were in a draining battle of constantly trying to prove the worth of subjects like the humanities. I had tired of the demands of admin, the lack of mental health support for students and staff. We were dealing with hundreds of pleas for mitigation each year, distressing cases, some extreme, with nothing really to offer. I could move institution, I thought, but to do so in academia so often means starting again. When I finally turned down the massive grant that we are all supposed to want in that career because I knew the project management - on top of the 70-hour weeks - would break me, I realised I could not stay. Terrifying, exhilarating, I was ready for a new start. But I have always loved teaching. I wanted to share a part of the new adventures that were taking me away from these people who I had seen evolve and flourish as academics, thinkers and writers, perhaps for them to understand my decisions.

A painting on the wall of Athnamulloch bothy.

First stop is Inverness Youth Hostel. An unlikely gaggle of seven 23 to 50-something year olds, piling into bunk beds, we chatted about what to expect. Birkbeck has an unusual student body, some of the most determined, inspiring and courageous people I could ever hope to meet. It was and still is a radical institution, founded in 1823 and designed to cater for working men and women in London.[4] All the degrees can be taken in the evening and part-time if needed, so you get professionals and retirees, caregivers and career-changers, experts in their fields and even an 82-year-old widower. So, as is usual for a Birkbeck MA group, my party is not the usual collection of nervous 21-year-olds. I am sad to be leaving them - more than they know, perhaps - especially sad at the cracks that have appeared in Birkbeck's facade. It is a glorious, exciting farewell, a time for new growth and beginnings but also endings. Among all the debates over rewilding, the trip also feels like a place of hope, renewal, promise.

The excitement is tangible, as well as a few nerves. Mel has lived in London for a while but has been inspired by my work to move to Glasgow, and she is keen to get out hiking to see what might await her. Incredible views, I promise, but I cannot guarantee the sun. I have issued everyone lists for what to bring, what not to do, and what threats to look out for. I have warned them of the dangers of ticks and Lyme disease after walking through long grass in deer territory. Over drinks in the pub, conversations turn to the technicalities of tick removal, should it become necessary. Alasdair is from Scotland, though he has lived and worked in London for years, and so we designate him as the expert. There's some concern over the horrors of midge attacks or how to purify water. But, most of all, people want to get out into the forest and up close to the mountains.

Next morning, after a filling breakfast at the Morrisons'

cafe, we drive down. We go past the western shore of Loch Ness and Nessieland, debating whether Nessie is 'she' or 'he' – she, we conclude, but it's a close vote – then up the single-track road to the head of the loch. We park up, arrange bags, and prepare to set off. Like fighter jets locking onto a target, midges attack immediately, but spirits remain high.

Before we departed, I asked the group to imagine what they thought of the Highlands. Some talked of the 'green and rocky landscape with pinks and purples' that appears 'sometimes with a lilt and sometimes with a snarl'. Others wrote about a place of 'brutal beauty and majesty, unforgiving'. I wanted to prod at these statements a little bit, question romantic expectations, overturn assumptions, but there's no denying that the landscape of Glen Affric is pretty damn beautiful.

Oohs and *aahs* accompany our walk from the very first step, comparisons with *Harry Potter* and/or *Lord of the Rings* abound. Albeit the Tolkien trilogies weren't filmed in Scotland, yet these cinematic reference points were the new guys on the block shaping imaginations of the Highlands over traditional Romantic renderings in watercolour or word. Stopping halfway into the 8 km walk, we admire the north bank of the glen, munching on an eclectic mix of custard tarts, chorizo and crisps – everyone had been under instructions to be responsible for their own midday fare. Glorious sun warms us as we sit chatting, and the hills are stitched together with the silver thread of glistening burns. Five minutes later it's driving rain. Welcome to Scotland.

A somewhat soggy second half of the walk does not dampen spirits, and at around 2 pm we tumble into the bothy after a hunt for the key and a wrestle with the code box. 'Luxury' is my first thought, certainly compared to what I am used to. This isn't a bothy in the MBA sense, as it's not free and open, and it's too well equipped. There are cushions, mattresses, games and not one, but three wood-burning stoves stocked with wood and kindling. It takes a while to get the gas going, and there are no running taps, so we still have to collect drinking water from the burn to boil. But it's the perfect combination of simplicity and comfort for a trip with a large group unaccustomed to bothies in their full-on, unadulterated, hardcore form.

Athnamulloch bothy is at least 150 years old, a stalking cottage once used by the estate, as was Alltbeithe, which is further along the Affric Kintail way, the route that runs from Drumnadrochit to Morvich.[5] That building is now a youth hostel. Across the river from Athnamulloch is Strawberry Cottage, owned by the An Teallach Mountaineering Club. All this land was once the property of Clan Chisholm and Clan Fraser of Lovat from the fifteenth to nineteenth centuries, until it became a Victorian hunting estate turned over to shooting and stalking.[6] Its hunting days done, Athnamulloch is now at the heart of debates over pasts and futures in this part of the Highlands. Since 1991, volunteers from Trees for Life have been using their bothy as a base from which to plant saplings. Here a few remnants of the Caledonian pines were still clinging on. Some gnarled, ancient granny pines have survived felling, and in the peat bog there are stumps of 4,000-year-old monsters. Trees for Life was set up to nurse the Great Wood of Caledonia back to life, planting Scots pine but also other native species such as willows, birch and aspen to 'help rewild one of Scotland's great natural areas'. Athnamulloch has been witness to these efforts to restore and revive struggling eco-systems, and in 2016, after a huge fund-raising effort and money from the Commonwealth Games Legacy Programmes, the renovated bothy was reopened for volunteers and visits.[7]

The bothy's interior is full of reminders of how this landscape is used to teach and instruct, a place for getting out and experiencing the glen. Maps and drawings cover the walls and are stacked on the shelves, there's an incredibly well-worn OS Explorer 414 (Glen Shiel and Kintail Forest), marked with a few pencil lines, including an x marks the spot for an old elm tree, and a whole reference library of bird, weather, tree and fungi books. An easy calm settles over the group. They tend the fire and fetch water and are happy to walk further in the knowledge that a cosy bothy will be waiting.

'I want some more trees,' says Mel.

Appropriate, bearing in mind our location, so we wander out to the beach and jetty with a little fishing hut near the bothy, along the wooded valley, where birch, aspen and willow flourish at the edges. It's a different landscape from my recent trips to the scraped, bare Cairngorms. Anyone that knows me knows that I do like to tell people what's what. Though no real expert, I know a fair bit and love pointing out different wildflowers or identifying birds.

We passed the small hut on the way, thinking it was abandoned, realising on closer inspection the turf roof was entirely intentional. I presumed this was an add-on for the Trees for Life set-up, but some research when I got home uncovered this was the property of the North Affric estate, owned by billionaire David Matthews, Pippa Middleton's father-in-law, and where private parties come to fish and barbecue if they are booking the baronial-style palace of Affric Lodge. I have visions of *Succession*-style retreats, swathed in secrecy and private guards. Private shooting and fishing parties feel a stark contrast to the eco-volunteering that's supported by Athnamulloch, though each in its way provides an idea about futures for the landscape. It's certainly a reminder that the land here is still in the hands of only a few powerful owners, some national bodies like Forestry and Land Scotland and the National Trust for Scotland, but also private individuals. There's no one there when we visit the fishermen's hut. We are free to play about on the jetty, and joke and pose in the afternoon sun.

We return tired but happy and settle into the tasks of the bothy. Similar but different from the more stripped-back MBA bothy; Lynn tends to the fire, Jana, Katie and Fearn get water, Mel cooks up a delicious curry, Alasdair generally keeps an eye on the group. It feels like some strange, glorious family Christmas as we play Bananagrams in front of the flames, or read books nestled in corners. I am glad and grateful to share that sense of security with them I have so often felt in a bothy, as well as that knowledge that just beyond the door is a wilder world from the streets of home. The influence of the landscape outside creeps inside as some of the group study reference books on birds or fungi, and despite the threat of midges, dart outside to see the mountains and the mist.

Mel returns to the bothy. Photo by Alasdair McNeill.

There's that thing that bothies offer everywhere, a place from which to view the living world from an enclosed space and to venture out. After dinner, just as I am nestling down for the night, light fading, Jana summons me. Deer have approached the bothy, hesitating tens of metres away, just across the meadows of the valley. Deer, of course, are often unwanted here and numbers are controlled. The iconic monarch of the glen no longer reigns supreme, and numbers ideally should be limited to two or three per square km, certainly under five, for the good of other living things. Anything over that is damaging to the woodlands, and over eight also endangers peat through trampling and grazing. The average intensity of deer in the Highlands is ten per square km.[8] A strange tension undercut this rendezvous: a wild beast that was also farmed and curated for sport, seen as an enemy to rewilding, but also a moment, for my students, of encounter with the largest mammal that remains on our shores. The deer have the curious, slightly startled look that deer always have. They stare; my students stare back entranced.

Morning mist surrounds us when I wake, but as I peer out of the window, I see the bright blue that's waiting to burst through. Mountain outlines glower in the haze. It's going to be hot, and the sun is refracted in the air, slowly burning up the clouds, hovering like an otherworldly being. Soon enough the day becomes clear and we prepare to set off, once our tasks of care are done for the group that will come next. Considerable enthusiasm is shown for chopping the wood, less so for raking the composting toilet, but Jana steps up like a trooper.

The return walk is along the north bank of the glen, and I know it will be a little more challenging, though I tactfully say it's pretty much the same distance. That's technically true but it's not just distance that matters – it's also the quality of the path. Everyone is full of confidence to stride out after a night's rest in the bothy. Walking after finding a settled spot for the night from which to explore is not quite the same as going out for a day hike. It resets the rhythms of expectation in a different way. We wind up and down rocky and sometimes marshy terrain, not too tricky but challenging enough in midday sun. And there are fords. I have forgotten the fords.

The first ford takes time to negotiate. Lynn and I bound confidently across, but the others are a little more hesitant. With a combination of encouraging smiles, hands proffered and route guidance, we all make it across without wet feet.

By ford three, we are old hands. Good thing, too, as it's unexpected. We approach Allt Coire Leachavie, ready to cross the rope bridge, but the way is shut. Ominous chains and a board bar our route, a sign points down the valley - *FORD*, it commands. No fear. It's a mere hop across and we congratulate ourselves with a break in the sun by the water. The horseflies and midges, once a threat, are now dismissed with a casual glance of the hand, and they hum agitatedly in the heat.

The broken bridge at Allt Coire Leachavie.

I can almost see the familiarity and connection with the landscape evolving before my eyes, a slow tuning to the natural world around us. Mel picks up the keening call of a buzzard, pointing it out eagerly to the others, and when we stop for water, the sheer delight at the cool refreshment of a Highland burn is apparent.

'Is it safe?' they ask.

I am pretty sure it is, fast flowing, straight off the mountain, not a dead sheep in sight, so we all gratefully take a drink. Just at the right moment respite is provided by the mountains. It was a special moment, Jana tells me later, a deeply embodied link with the place and what it provides, and a playing out of their trust in me.

Even with refreshing fords, it's a scorching day, and everyone's relieved when we see the cars. Piling in, we speed off down the side of Loch Ness to Dundreggan. This is the brains of the Trees for Life operation, the place where seeds are grown, and plants nurtured. The estate was bought in 2008 for £1.65 million and ever since blocks of planting have been undertaken to try and restore the old-growth forest here and promote the recovery of rare species.[9] We are keen to explore, but lunch comes first, and we wolf down delicious salads and cakes, refuelled for the afternoon. I am glad that we have been able to meet up with Denise, another student. A health worry meant she couldn't join us for the walk, but the group feels more complete with her there.

We embark on the introductory tour, with Kat Murphy, the visitor experience manager, and we start in the nursery.

Shoes disinfected, she shows us how the native trees are nurtured and grown, some to be planted here and others sold. Particularly enchanting are the aspen, perhaps the rarest of all native trees, with fluttering, trembling leaves that rustle like tiny bells when the wind blows. Legend says that there are voices to be heard in the susurration of the leaves, the whisper of ancestors. These are forests where the dead seek refuge. Place a leaf under your tongue and it will give you the gift of eloquent speech, so other tales claim. Christian myth was not so generous to the trembling tree. An old Gaelic saying runs: 'Malison be on thee, O Aspen cursed, on thee was crucified the king of kings.' This is the damned aspen, excoriated for providing the wood that made Christ's cross, and doomed to tremble forever in shame and horror. Further blame is heaped on the tree since, of all those that grew, it proudly refused to bow as Christ was led to Calvary. It was also on an aspen tree that Judas strung up a rope and hanged himself, according to some legends.[10] Interesting how the tree, not the people, shoulder the blame.

Aspen now has been forced to the margins of existence and it is favoured by deer, whose numbers must be controlled at Dundreggan. Kat shows us where they are growing the trembling saplings in the protected greenhouses, away from the nibbling teeth, and trying to get them to flower. Apparently, they have to stress the trees, sometimes by cutting off branches or removing bark, almost to the point at which the life systems of the tree are endangered. The response is to rush to reproduce and flower. Trees are then taken from the nursery and put into the ground to try to simulate and recreate the landscapes of the past.[11]

The need to make the trees anxious, to imitate threat, made me think of a phrase artist and poet Alec Finlay used to describe his time as 'humandwolf' for Project Wolf, which was run at Dundreggan. 'Fear must be returned to the hill.' In this experiment, people imitated the wolves, appearing at dusk and dawn to frighten the deer. Instead of hunting and shooting, these 'humandwolves' imitated the patterns and movements of the apex predators, scaring the deer by scent and sound.[12] Death and terror and blood are an inevitable part of the relationships between living and non-living worlds, but in the absence of real wolves, this project played with an ethical creative experiment of human presence in the land. Conservation and ecological responsibility mean facing the realities of death as well as life.

Sika deer hide from us as we walk because the deer, of course, do fear humans. However, hunting is not a true relationship between predator and prey, but rather a manufactured bloody hierarchy of sport, where scarcity is absent and success guaranteed. There may be human wolves but there are no large predators any more, and wolves have long been absent from our shores. No one quite knows when the last wolf went extinct, sometime in the eighteenth century perhaps, but it is a ghost now that haunts language and place names.[13]

There's talk of bringing back the wolves to the hills, and other rewilding projects in Europe have succeeded. But it's more controversial in the UK, where space is more limited. Farmers complain of the threats to livestock, and people fear them. Even lynx seem unlikely, unless someone goes renegade, as they did with beavers, and just releases them into the wild.[14] Trees for Life, however, have initiated the 'Lynx to Scotland' project in an effort to open dialogue about bringing lynx back to the Highlands.[15] Twenty-two Scottish wild cats were successfully introduced to the Cairngorms in the summer of 2023, smaller and less threatening than wolves or lynx.[16] They were once abundant, too, in Glen Affric, but suffered at the hand of trappers, landowners, and later, vehicles. In 1895, Scottish ornithologists John Alexander Harvie-Brown and Thomas E. Buckley wrote of one seen alive in a cage in a courtyard in Glen Affric and skins hanging in gamekeepers' museums. The keeper at Athnamulloch reported in 1893 that 'few wild cats were still to be found in the lower part of the glen'.[17]

Now the deer have become the predators, seeking out the delicate aspen, and the balance has been overturned. Trees for Life and other organisations are doing their best to shift the scales back in the favour of the trees. But it's hard. The deer are persistent, and aspen is particularly attractive to all herbivores. While it doesn't normally seed in Scotland, it does reproduce in colonial shoots, producing ramets that spawn from the trunk, offshoots from one great mother tree. Once a colony is gone, it is hard to replace, its spreading connected network unrooted, displaced.

I ask Kat, how do they know what to plant and where, what are their sources (such a historian), how do they chart old growth? It's tricky, she acknowledges. There are old maps, but the OS surveys only go back to the mid-nineteenth century, and estate maps from the eighteenth century can be detailed, but survival is patchy. A fire destroyed all the estate records for Dundreggan anyway. Even further back, maps mark the mounds of peaks, the dividing lines of excise districts, parishes and roads, but do not detail the terrain and territory. Often, they are relying on plant and growth indicators, sometimes place names too. Kat says that their ecologist can read the landscape and its environmental past like I would read an archival record. Bracken, for example, is often a sign of old growth, but its proliferation is also the symptom of a problem.[18] When there was more tree cover, some of this bracken would have died back but now it's everywhere, perfect camouflage for the shy deer as well as their tick friends.

Being historians and archaeologists, we are interested, too, in the human history. There's some place for that here. The use of Gaelic across the site, a decision made after local community consultation, tells of entangled human and non-human lives, and every sign around the centre leads in Gaelic with a translation and phonetic sounding. Names and places everywhere tell of the past. Up the hill from the nursery is a small mound called An t-Sithean Mullach, the Fairy Hill - there's a fair few of these around, and this one is associated with the legends that circled around the dun fairies, the wee folk of the region.[19] Time operates differently for the magical beings who inhabit this other world; it runs more slowly or more quickly, racing ahead or stilling to an eternity. Numerous versions exist of legends where people have returned from their realm to find that time has slipped by, and years have elapsed.

Once upon a time, the two fiddlers of Tomnahurich, turned away from every door in Inverness, played unknowingly for the wee folk at a feast. When the night was over, they realised a century had passed as they made merry under the fairy hill of Tomnahurich. They returned home. They entered their church. The sermon started and they turned to dust.[20] Kat recounts the story to the group on the top of the fairy hill, next to an old oak, and the tale's evocation of the slipperiness of time, the overlapping levels of past and present, seemed an appropriate metaphor for thinking about rewilding estates like Dundreggan that attempt to conjure a disappearing past.

Alongside the remnants encoded in language, there are physical remains, less obvious, less clearly seen perhaps in the wooded glens and peatland moors, but revealing a patchwork of pasts. Kat points to the path we will walk tomorrow, to the high heather uplands. It passes alongside a hidden burn on whose banks there is an illicit still, a place where illegal spirits were made with clean burning juniper when regulations on the trade in liquor came in from the 1780s. To protect English and southern Scottish distilleries, new legislation was brought in. Highland distillers above what was known as the Highland Line had to pay a hefty £1 per gallon of still capacity to get a licence. Spirit production in the Highlands was forced underground by these draconian measures.[21] The same maps that only give the vaguest suggestion of what the landscape might have looked like make sure to mark out the boundaries of these new regulations. An 1804 engraving traces the Highland Distillery Line in a bold yellow arc.[22] The illicit site at Dundreggan was one of many where men and women sought to outsmart the authorities. Not always successfully. In 1832, two excise officers from Inverness 'discovered a bothie or distillery hut in actual operation', before being set upon by the bootleggers.[23] It made me consider how bothies had been used for more than shelter and herding, and summer shielings, it seemed, often became sites for distillation, possibly because they were in fairly isolated or at least hidden places.[24]

One of the complaints levelled at rewilding is the way in which it seeks to go back to some indiscriminate and possibly imagined point in the past. It runs the risk of erasing other layers of history, often human histories, by restoring the land to an imagined uncultivated, wild state. This land has been worked and used for many hundreds of years, and to restore a pristine untouched environment is impossible. Higher up on the Dundreggan estate are crumbling walls of ruined shielings, and near our accommodation, there's the mound of an old motte castle, probably associated with extension of royal power in the twelfth and thirteenth centuries.[25] But there are much older pasts here too. Not too far north is the chambered cairn of Corrimony, with its standing stones, a Bronze Age site for burial.[26] I wondered what place there was for these pasts too in the vision of the landscape that was envisaged at Dundreggan. This valley was inhabited right up until the defeat of the Jacobites in the eighteenth century (the supporters who wanted to see James Stuart and then later Bonnie Prince Charlie on the throne rather than the Hanoverians), and the Clearances that came after. We are not far from Culloden, the site of Charles Edward Stuart's brutal defeat in 1746. I point it out to the students on the drive down, and Bonnie Prince Charlie stopped off to hide in a howff in Glenmoriston, Ceannacroc, as it happens, not too far from where the illicit still was set up.[27] As English troops came through, they slaughtered or captured those who had fought with him, shipping them off to the colonies. Rewilding restores the land and the trees, living pasts, but it's not in the business of restoring all of these pasts.

Back at the centre after our introductory talk, we are filled with stories, facts and knowledge. However, there are uneasier realities here. Chatting to Kat, we talked about how rewilding so often gets portrayed in the media. The new clearances. A new form of colonial enclosure. The prioritising of nature over people. Rewilding landlords have also been called 'green lairds' who ride roughshod over the local interests of the community. As Fraser MacDonald, lecturer in historical geography at the University of Edinburgh, points out, when 'only 432 people own half of private rural land, rewilding can happen easily enough without local support'. It's not that people don't understand the dangers of biodiversity loss and climate change, he writes, but that they are sceptical that this represents any real change away from the patterns of land ownership that have long prevailed in Scotland. Once more it's 'a landlord with a passion for charismatic wildlife and landscapes'.[28] Seen from the perspective of maps, lines and borders, there are painful parallels between the demarcation of space decided by only a few, whether that's for whisky taxes, sheep farming or rewilding.

Maps are one thing. On the ground it's rather different, the reality much more complex. Different lives and realities rub against each other. There's still a crofter who grazes their flocks on the hills, a landscape for whom this remains a farmed, worked place. Concerns are legitimate that these pasts and presents of working-class rural lives will be edged out in idea and practice. But as we spent time in the bothy and with the staff of the Dundreggan Rewilding Estate, the criticisms of ignoring interests and merely replicating the romanticisation of the land in a new tradition of exclusion seemed unfair. These are good people doing good things, trying to build livelihoods. I did not get the impression from Dundreggan that these were absentee overlords taking over a place at all. Hard work had gone into building bridges.

We chat to the people in the café inside the Dundreggan Visitor Centre, some who have moved up to the area, others local. Alasdair has a particular flair for talking to people and getting life histories after a career in Foreign Office diplomacy. There are jobs here and opportunities. They are hiring, and I joke about taking up a role. The café is a warm place, full of community and life, but it's difficult for people to work here, as there's no public transport and accommodation is pretty limited on the shores of Loch Ness.

Bothy, café and rewilding classroom alike had become somewhere that provided a space for understanding different visions of the landscape and its futures, for new communities and connections. When we got back from the trip, Alasdair got chatting to family and friends in Tayvallich, where the estate has just been bought by Highlands Rewilding, owned and run by Jeremy Leggett. It turned out an old friend of Alasdair's mum had been to Athnmalloch years before, had worked with Alan Watson Featherstone and been part of the original rewilding campaign. He sends me some lovely photos of them all, laughing and making merry in the bothy after a day of planting. There was a lovely reciprocity in all this, a circle of growth.

MacDonald makes a crucial distinction - land and place are not the same, and he has been critical of Jeremy Leggett's words when he was talking about the water on one of the estates he is responsible for, which he described as 'my burns'. It's a criticism that is justified - language matters, but in fairness to Highlands Rewilding, the latest project in Tayvallich has been founded on a memorandum of understanding drawn up with the community and in partnership with a local charity called the Tayvallich Initiative.[29] Talking to the visitors and the staff at Dundreggan, as well as my students, looking at the careful interweaving of Gaelic in the centre and the telling of multiple stories about this place, I also got a different sense of the possibilities of rewilded landscapes even among these debates. There's no perfect solution, but Dundreggan stimulated ideas about agency and recovery.

The trip was not intended as a place of recovery, not for me, not for the students. It was a goodbye, an adventure, a research trip, a teaching event, but it evolved into something I could not have expected nor hoped for. For all the criticisms of rewilding projects, they are places of slow regeneration and of healing. They are places of vulnerability, for the landscape but also for people, or at least for us.

Some of these vulnerabilities became obvious as I walk and talk with the students. I am having a tough time at home, as are others. Such cares and worries would not be something I would share usually with those I teach. It breaks down the professional barriers that are necessary, but this is different. I am leaving the job, and here are people whom I trust, care about, whose company is soothing. As we walk and drive and cook, little details emerge about my life, theirs, the fears, the worries, the hopes. I am not one for the rather sickly stuff about rewilding yourself, but I was surprised how much this place of slow, gentle recovery for wildlife became that for us too.

On the second day, we go for our longer tour of the estate, up round Ceum an Fhraoich (the Heather Path). There's loads to catch our attention. Perfect scarlet toadstools nestle under ferns. The minute carnivorous sundews carpet the higher paths, where the heather and grass is spattered with tormentil, orchids and woundwort. As we walk round with Kat, she has a particular fondness for the lichen. It turns out her partner is a lichenologist, so perhaps no surprise, but she speaks with energy and love for the growths that cover every tree in blue-green blotches, like copper that's acquired the patina of exposed age. Old man's beard and pixie cups are everywhere; there's even a lichen called witch's hair – dark brown, straggly tendrils that drip from branches. Lichens, of course, are colonies of symbiotic partnerships between algae and fungi, whole ecosystems in miniature that rely on cooperation and collaboration. So, too, do all the remarkable fungi systems that spread throughout these wooded glens. Two names in particular stuck in my mind – tongues of fire and crown of thorns. This is a rust fungus, *Gymnosporangium clavariiforme*, that favours juniper. In later spring and early summer, in the wet in particular, it feathers out from the branches in succulent orange waves. When it fruits, the spores infect hawthorn and cause the growth of thorny fungal diadems, galls with tufts, that in turn release more spores that land on the juniper to start the cycle again. The fleshy tongues are also home to giant juniper aphids, farmed by wood ants that live in earthy fortresses below ground.[30]

Anna Tsing has written that 'mushrooms are well known as companions', existing in symbiosis at the unruly edges where they resist domestication and order.[31] In these earthy interactions of non-human forms, we all enjoyed learning about the tale of messy companionship that helped this forest thrive. As I don my appropriately themed corduroy mushroom dungarees that evening for dinner (and yes, they are as awesome as they sound) and as we play on the climbing frames, I imagine us all as friendly, disorderly companions in a story of learning and growing together. In the same way the trees are regenerating, I feel something shifting and regenerating, in me, in the students.

One of the crazy ideas I had when thinking about how to make the academic career work for me, that I have scrawled in my journal is: 'rewilding the curriculum'. I am not quite sure what I meant, but maybe it's not so crazy, and academia could learn something from Dundreggan. I know money and business still matters for Trees for Life, but in conservation terms, rewilding as an idea has dispensed with clear targets and goals in favour of the messy realities of growth and regeneration, a slow evolution of branch and leaf. I wish there were time for a gradual flourishing of learning and teaching in UK universities rather than the endless pursuit of targets driven by financial need.

I think of the jars that were left on the table for our final dinner by the café staff. They were those tiny pocket-sized jam pots you get in hotels, cleaned out and then collected by the café. They ask people to write little notes of hope and joy and leave them inside. People take one, read it, and then put it back for the next visitor to enjoy. I did one on the first day. I chose the Leonard Cohen lyrics from 'Anthem' about cracks and light and hope. Clichéd, I know, but I had always liked it and I remember it helping me and a mutual friend as we processed our divorces. My student Mel opened it. Her voice broke a little. And I was tearful also.

* * *

There's plenty of debate about the work of Trees for Life, and rewilding in general. I found few of the claims that these activities were the new clearances or that they de-peopled the lands to be fair criticisms of their work. On the contrary, this seemed a place still deeply entwined with human and natural stories. I loved that the bothy represented so much of that.

There are no easy answers, no straightforward ones. But the rewilding of Glen Affric and Dundreggan and what it offered has left a mark on my students. Jana, a talented musician and creative, is an adventurous, dynamic person whose energy has always inspired me, but she has for a long time lived in London and never really done anything like this. We'd got closer on the trip and talked about the ups and downs of managing love lives and careers as creative people. She talked to me after about the profound effect the experience had on her and about the dreams that she had, fever dreams of freedom and running away and wildness. She said she was now drawn to the danger and the elation of adventuring out on her own.

We had stepped into this place for a moment, but with all its fraught pasts and futures, it was somewhere for human and non-human connection. My students penned a leaving card for me which breaks my heart but also lets the light in. They thank me for friendship and intellectual companionship. With a quote taken from the walls of the centre, they wrote: 'In patches of disturbance, life can begin again.'

TWELVE | GUIRDIL

Fragile Futures

One of my favourite shots of summer was taken in the clear waters of the Atlantic on a warm September evening. Hoping my new waterproof phone case will withstand the waves, I am looking back to the wrinkly lump of Bloodstone Hill. The grass covers the cliffs, crumpled like a bed that's been slept in, and the setting sun makes the hills glow gold-green. Gashes in the side of the slopes are ancient river valleys, down which lava streams flowed hundreds of thousands of years ago, the top a crown of long-cooled molten rock. Nestled in the foreground in the curve of the bay is the bothy, Guirdil. Smoke rises from the chimney that Sian and I had lit before venturing out.

I met Sian on the final ford crossing to the bothy and neither of us could resist a swim in the chilly waters. We know the fire will be waiting for us when we get back, but we linger as long as possible, chasing those swirls of warmth that hover unseen below the surface, holding the glare of the late-summer sunshine.

Finally, we admit defeat and pick a painful path on round pebbles back to our clothes and food and fire. Inside the walls once more, we rustle up dinner and warm drinks. Guirdil is a place of drifting imagination. Inside the bothy is the washed-up detritus of the stuff we discard, all finding its way here after haphazard marine voyages. Crates, plastic bottles, buoys, netting. It's been piled up high in corners, either to clear the beach of waste or simply out of that impulse to gather. The sea's currents have been bringing things in to Guirdil bay for centuries. In the late eighteenth century, the English clergyman Edward Daniel Clarke was surprised to be served fine port wine from Lisbon by the islanders. Such luxuries were the reward for living on a shore exposed to waves and wind. The wine crates were 'the spoils of another part of the freight of some unfortunate vessel wrecked near the island'.[1] Sian and I don't have any port, but whisky and biscuits do us well enough to toast the bothy that we have all to ourselves. And as we sit by the warmth of the fire, the light chasing from red to orange to pink to midnight blue, the sea mirrors back the sky, framed perfectly by Guirdil's small muntined window.

It's a place shaped by the sea and water, rimmed by the Atlantic Ocean, with gales sweeping in off the sea that batter the bothy fifty days of the year. Most of this island that was not always an island is the remnant of an old volcano. The caldera in the centre filled up with layers of rock to form the peaks of Askival and Hallival, jagged teeth that dominate the skyline, and then gullies and corries were carved out by glaciers. As these melted and a great weight was lifted from the earth, the island rose, like a ship casting off ballast, and it has climbed further and further out of the sea over the last 6,000 years. On the southwest corner of Rùm, the raised beach at Harris is a reminder of a time when the sea level was much higher.[2] Many Scottish islands and much of the Highlands have been rising out of the water in this way by a process known as isostatic uplift.[3] Think of it like a trampoline emptied of bouncing children.

But now the edges of Rùm may be on the slide back into the water. We are still coming out of the last ice age, isostatic uplift is still inching land upwards in many places that were once ice-covered, and there's a slow, almost imperceptible, millennia-old race going on between the land and sea. Rùm has been winning, but the prospect of future gains in the Anthropocene looks uncertain. As mounds of ice tumble into oceans and glaciers melt in a warming world, the sea may be winning again. Eustatic change – that's the alterations that take place in the volume of seawater – are global, and rises in sea level are happening faster each year, often faster than the local rises of land that is still springing back. On the eastern and southern coasts of the UK, where land is sinking, the ravages of the sea are even worse. Rùm may still be rising but, like so many places on the edges, the decades to come for this sea-girt spot look unclear and dangerous in a world that's warming and drowning at unimaginable rates.

Guirdil and Bloodstone Hill as seen from the sea.

It's hard to match up the apocalyptic fear of global warming with the memory of the trip to Guirdil. It is pretty damn perfect as trips like that go. In a wet, miserable Scottish summer I manage to choose the three or four days of gleaming, hot sun, so warm that the walk back from the bothy reduces me to short shorts and a T-shirt. I channel what I think is Lara Croft but in reality comes off closer to pale beanstalk with backpack – but a girl can dream.

Travelling solo, I relish the freedom of the end of the summer. I determine to talk to everyone I can. On the Caledonian Sleeper, I wander for hot chocolate with a young man who is giving up his London life for a one-way ticket to Fort William. In the dining car we are invited to sit for a whisky with a passenger who has a cabin. (They are the only ones allowed to eat there. Got to keep the wheat from the chaff.) The train from Glasgow to Mallaig fills up with the unmistakable crowds of hikers, sightseers and backpackers, all *oohing* and *aahing* as we pass the Glenfinnan Viaduct, or as it's often now known, the Harry Potter bridge. A young American, Nick, has the *Bothy Bible* in hand, so it is not hard to guess his intentions. We share a few words on the train and then reconvene accidentally for a quick meal at the backpacking hostel in Mallaig.

After an evening in the little harbour town, which includes a joyous boat trip to see the seals and the dolphins and a swim at the Silver Sands of Morar in the evening sun, I rise for the ferry next day. The Small Isles ferries are, well, small, and I eye up my various companions. Excited children on the school trip of a lifetime, a few hikers, and Sian with a bike packed up with panniers and bags on every available bar. We won't exchange names until we meet again on the west coast cliffs, and for now we share only a quick smile, probably both wondering if we have the same destination in mind. I make friends with the school group as we spot minke whales and talk about the new sustainability subject that their teacher, Ross, has set up at the school. Lucky kids have just climbed Ben Nevis and are now off to see the Kilmory deer of Rùm. Temporarily all holed up together on the late 1990s vibe of a CalMac ferry, we disembark and go our separate ways.

The walk to the bothy starts from Kinloch, winding up through woodland of the valley and then across the middle of the island past heathers and rising peaks. It's a nature reserve but there's still evidence of the quarries that were worked up until the nineteenth century. Near the fork in the one road on the island that turns off to either Harris or Kilmory, the bothy path goes up the grassy hillside away from the gravelled track. As I climb up onto marshy banks, I spot a bike. My fellow ferry passenger. It is hardly cycling territory here, so no surprise she has cast it aside. After rising over the crest of the land between Minishal and Sgaorishal, the track descends into the boggy squelch of Glen Shellesder. It is warm and dry, and the river is not in spate, so aside from the occasional slightly wet foot, the various fords make easy crossing. A winter or stormy outing would be a different prospect. Tracing the route through the glen, the lure of the blue-green Atlantic seems to summon you on.

Hugging the coast on a muddy track, I encounter a soggy-socked Sian, who has just forded but got a little wet. I ask if she is headed for the bothy, though the answer seems obvious. She is on the home stretch of a Scottish bike-packing tour and we fall into easy conversation as we continue on our way, turning the corner of a curve of the cliffs to see the bothy building.

Guirdil is pretty old, dating back 180 years, though it's been restored over that time, like other bothies.[4] There was once a handful of homesteads clustered by the shore, all of which fell into disrepair as people were forced off the island in 1825–6.[5] The ruined outline of nearby buildings suggests what state Guirdil would have been in before the MBA got to work. It's a lonely spot, for no one lives near this bay anymore. Traces of much older settlements are evident across the island. Near one of the many fords of Glen Shellesder are the barely visible outlines of old shielings, post-medieval but of uncertain date.[6] Now they are little more than crumbled stone outlines, although a handy waypoint on the OS map. But not so long ago these were working buildings that would have hummed with life and fertility. There's been settlement, farming, even quarrying for thousands of years here, and Rùm is the oldest known place of human settlement in Scotland.[7]

When Reverend Clarke approached Rùm in 1787, he did so from the sea, landing at Guirdil. Dominating his view 'were high precipitate cliffs, almost perpendicular', green and covered in sheep that perched in the little outcrops, wearing away hollows for shelter. Behind this, he could see the summit of Oreval with 'a semi-circular, steep, craggy, and barren top . . . . At the bottom of this broken and irregular basin, a glen reaching to the sea, offered us a landing place.'[8] In addition to his clerical duties, Clarke was an avid traveller, mineralogist, collector and naturalist who journeyed around Europe. This time he was on a mission to gather stories of stones and landscapes. He was not that complimentary about the Hebridean islanders and the collection of huts that 'constitute what the natives term one of their villages'.[9] But his words offer a glimpse into the life of the small settlement here. The farmers worked the land and bloodstone was still being mined. It's not hard to see where the stone gets its name. The dark green chalcedony, flecked with the red of oxidised iron, drew nomadic hunter-gatherers 9,000 years ago as a substitute for flint.[10] Clarke talked with the local family and drank port. There was life and living here. Within a couple of decades these people would be gone, the whole island forcibly depopulated in the wave of nineteenth-century Clearances. In the ruin next to Guirdil, there's an old hearth choked by greenery; forever cold in a crumbling footprint of a house, it is all that remains of a family's home.

Sian and I make ourselves cosy in our home-from-home for the night. After gathering enough fallen branches and driftwood, with the fire lit and whisky in hand, we chatter happily. She tells me about the job interview she has just done from a youth hostel; I tell her in turn that I am here for work, and we share a few bothy and island stories, as you usually do. Nothing seems as important as the warmth of the flames and the cosy summon of my sleeping bag.

View from the window of Guirdil.

It is hard to see how this small spot, tucked out of the way and a temporary haven only to backpackers, could be entangled in the large forces shaping our world now. But even here, you can feel that destructive forces of consumption, emissions, pollution and technology are writing the future script. Give it another 100 years and the ruins and the remade walls of Guirdil might be underwater at the floods of high tide, traces of the small settlement steadily drowned by the rising seas which threaten coastal dwellings and island nations all over the world. Temperatures, water levels and landmass configurations have been constantly shifting for millennia. At one time the peaks of Rùm poked out of the glaciers as nunataks, and at others they were submerged.[11] But the age of the Anthropocene is an age of change that is more dramatic, more potentially catastrophic than the natural swings and roundabouts of the geological, climactic life of the planet. Whether it's the towering skyscrapers of New York or the stone walls of Guirdil, the reality that places are menaced by rising waters is just one dimension of life in the Anthropocene and the result of all the small and big decisions that we have made in the 250 years that we have been burning fossil fuels to power our world. Landscapes are shifting all the time, but it's the pace of change that is alarming, the sense of a future hurtling towards us with a force we cannot withstand.

Two things primarily cause rising waters. First, the more obvious, is the melting of glaciers, ice caps and ice sheets, which tips water into the seas, pushing up levels. Second is the warming itself, which means that the hotter water is full of particles whizzing about with greater velocity and occupying more space. The result, as temperatures have risen, is that average sea-level rises have reached between 3 and 4 mm a year (double the rate of the last century) and in worst-case scenarios this could rise to 20 mm a year by the end of the century.[12] Like temperature rises, this can seem marginal. After all, what's an extra half a degree or a few millimetres a year? But it doesn't take much. I thought back to a recent walk in the frozen Somerset countryside in early-spring sun. A frozen world was transformed in a matter of minutes by the breath of slightly warming air as the morning rose. Every day we see tipping points on minute scales that are now playing out on macro levels.

If you want, you can map estimates of the impact of rising sea levels via various models. At first, when you look at a map projecting the creep of water on Rùm, it's hard to see much difference, but as you zoom in, there's an ominous line, closing concentric circles edging the island. Rùm's Kilmory Bay, too, will flood. Its golden sands will be washed of deer prints and eddies of water. It won't be completely submerged, Atlantis-style, not yet anyway, but waters will creep steadily higher. These places seem isolated, eternal, ancient, immovable, but in reality are often some of the most vulnerable to rising seas. Of course, no one at Guirdil is going to need to be evacuated, but for the millions who live in coastal cities and towns, the coming decades will mean mass exodus.

It's hard to get a grasp on what this means in real terms from figures and numbers, even from the projection maps. Various projects, scientific and artistic, have tried to bring home the reality of rising waters. On one website you can slide-screen different scenarios based on different warming patterns. St Paul's Cathedral in London makes for grim viewing: a domed island with a 3° C increase, but still surrounded by lapping waves at 1.5° C.[13] When 1.2° C of warming is already built in, no matter what we do, it's a fearful prospect. The various options are not just doom-mongering. The reality is that we don't know what this future will look like. Uncertainty is a given since we can't tell exactly when we will pass the tipping point at which the huge ice sheets in Greenland and Iceland will start to melt, and precisely what this will mean. Recent research, however, suggests that rapid melt in west Antarctica is a given.[14] If the sheets were to disappear completely, this could represent a sea-level rise of up to 65 m in the long term, and if rises are significant, losses will be devastating.[15]

You can get some sense of just how high waters will get on the west coast of Scotland thanks to an eerie light show installation designed by Pekka Niittyvirta and Timo Aho, the project called 'Lines (57° 59' N, 7° 16'W)'. It was situated on low-lying Uist in the Outer Hebrides off the west coast of Scotland, around the Taigh Chearsabhagh Museum & Arts Centre in Lochmaddy, and used sensors and LED lights activated at high tide to provide a visual reference for where sea levels will reach in the future. An ominous white band ringed the museum, just under halfway up the wall, and glaring beams about a metre high reached across the grass. The light lines, beautiful yet menacing, showed where the water will be and how much will be underwater.[16]

If this feels fearful, apocalyptic, like the shadow projection of some horrific blockbuster yet to be made, that's sort of the point. These are meant to evoke concern, to make us care, to make us act before catastrophe happens. Maybe all this seems too distant in the future to imagine, but the east coast of the UK is already crumbling into the North Sea. In Scotland, the northern, low-lying parts of the Outer Hebrides, Orkney and Shetland are most vulnerable to these rises.[17] It's not hard to see why. Islands like Papa Westray seem to just barely crest the surface of the water. Just as Doggerland – now no more than part of the strange poetry of the Shipping Forecast – was once a fertile plain that connected the UK and Europe, so too the scattered islands of Orkney were once a single landmass. Rising waters have split it into the horsehead of Hrossey, the old Norse name for the Mainland, and her little sisters. Mesolithic dwellers were inundated, the scant physical evidence of their lives mostly under water. Now Skara Brae, the most famous settlement remains of the later Neolithic peoples who dwelt on Orkney, is under threat from a sea that gives and takes. At the other end of the UK, St Michael's Mount, possibly the last outcrop of the probably mythical ancient kingdom of Lyonesse, may become an island, for the causeway will sink for ever below tides.[18]

It's not only the rising waters that threaten the landscapes where bothies are. If Guirdil is slowly drowning, parts of the water round Cadderlie are suffocating. Midway through Loch Etive, the lake floor comes to a small crest and then drops precipitously. The Bonawe Sill peers over into a gully of 150 m where dark, deep water sits that suffers from periods of low circulation and so low oxygen levels. The mixing of sea and fresh water in the lake creates an imbalance of density, and deep salty marine waters sit below the less dense fresh currents that run into the loch and are mixed with the sea tides. However, overturning events see an exchange of the deep, isolated water. These occur when spring tides and drier spells, resulting in less freshwater runoff, mean that the salt water retains enough density to spill over the Sill and intermingle with the deeper, hypoxic water in the upper loch. But as temperatures rise and precipitation increases, these periods of overturning decrease, slowly depriving the deeper waters of the loch of oxygen and extinguishing its biodiversity.[19] In other places snows will melt and the bothies will remain but their character will change. By 2100 half the world's glaciers will be gone, even if we keep to the Paris threshold of 1.5° C. While we can't trust as science the individual stories that emerge about less snow on the peaks or warmer winters, these anecdotal collective and personal memories recall a time when the world was different. Baselines have shifted. Snow on the Cairngorms, for example, is declining apace and is 3 cm shallower now than it was in the winter of 1983–4.[20]

Sitting in my flat in Bath and writing this in a wet January, the rain was coming down and the Avon swelling. It's hard not to worry it's a result of climate change. There's something prophetic in a flood. From the Bible to Gilgamesh, from J. G. Ballard novels to Roland Emmerich films, floods inhabit world-destroying, apocalyptic imaginations everywhere. I will never forget the first time I saw

Albrecht Dürer's tiny watercolour sketch of a dream of a flood made in 1525. Sandy-coloured land lies in the foreground, a lake or sea behind painted in pale blue, and then a huge column of dark blue water that dominates the sky. Giant globules of rain descend as bleeding blue drips from the heavens.[21] It has the ominous feel and shape of a nuclear mushroom cloud 500 years before J. Robert Oppenheimer created the destroyer of worlds. Dürer's world was uncertain, shattering with the threat of religious and political violence as Luther's reformation split the western Catholic Church and peasants rose in rebellion. Times to come look unclear and fractured for us now too. I empathise with his dream of the flood and the menace it brings of obliteration. Like early modern prognostications, so many of us try to read the signs.

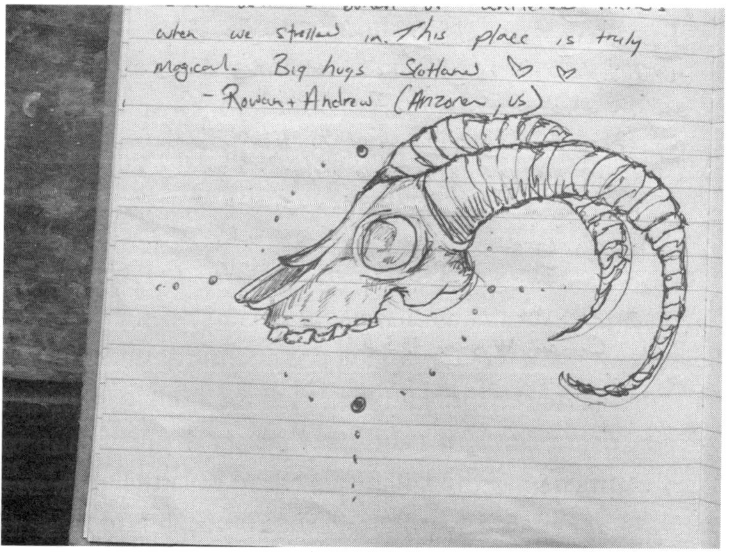

Sketch from the Guirdil bothy book.

* * *

As I prepare to leave Guirdil, I tidy up, pack away rubbish, sweep, fasten the door tight with the hooked latch to protect against the fierce winds that will batter the bothy in harsher months and set off. Sian left before me to collect her bike and I toy with the idea of scrambling up the side of Bloodstone Hill and taking the longer route back. Instead, I decide it will take too long, and want to try and head out to Kilmory on the other side of the island. The road out of the bothy is possibly even more idyllic than the walk in. The sky bluer, the sun warmer, the midges more voracious – the less fun part of any trip to Scotland in summer. Rùm midges are famed for being the worst in Europe, though they are pretty vicious across the Small Isles. Baithene, son of St Columba, considered it a trial of his devotion to let the Eigg midges settle on his face.[22]

I peer over the cliffs to an inaccessible small bay below the point at which the Shellesder Burn starts to run into the sea. Seals are basking and bathing. The rest of the day seems similarly blessed with abundant wildlife. No sea eagle, which was high on the list, but there are red deer and waders aplenty as I reconvene with the school trip and Sian at Kilmory Bay on the north of the island. We have taken up a casual invitation offered on the ferry to hear about the deer-monitoring project on the island. Deer far outnumber the human population on Rùm, 1,000 deer to around 40 people, but the 250 Kilmory deer are special. They are the subject of the longest large-mammal research study in the world, with every calf born in the spring tagged and mortality searches conducted in the winter.

With the schoolchildren, Sian and I sit on the grass in the sun and hear about the methods for deer track and trace. An incredibly complex matrilineal naming system means that every deer ever born into the project has a moniker and a family tree. The scientists have amassed a wealth of data on ageing, population patterns, behaviours and environments. Climate change is disrupting the deer, too. The timings of rutting and antler casting are changing, and females are calving earlier.[23] This isn't just a behavioural change. In a process known as phenotypic plasticity, the deer's genetics are actually evolving as the scientists watch. Whether this will be an adaptation that allows them to survive as temperatures rise, like Thor Hanson's description of Turks and Caicos lizards with large toepads to cling on in hurricanes, remains to be seen.[24]

After hearing the science, we get to inspect the physical remains. Inside the nearby sheds used by the project are row upon row of skulls and antlers collected from corpses, piled high on tables, and hanging from the eaves. We stare up in wonder at the Gothic ceiling of spikes and barbs, the remains of once-mighty stags dripping like stalactites. Given a couple to examine, the children hold huge bone branches above their heads like Halloween costumes.

That night, Sian and I decide to pitch by the beach at Kilmory, she on the grass, me opting for the sand, but we are low on reserves. She generously offers to bike all the way back to Kinloch to pick up food and wine, so I am left to myself for a couple of hours. Lying on the warm rocks, I watch through binoculars the deer and the sandpipers, oystercatchers and sanderlings picking at the beach. A head bobs up in the water and lazily I track the movement of what I think is another seal. It moves differently however, the dips more lithe, quicker, and more aggressive, and soon I realise it is an otter. Diving again and again for a tasty treat, it soon succeeds, carrying a large crab over to the rocks in the shallows. The crustacean's legs wheel hopelessly like out-of-control levers until the otter smashes it on the crags and scoops out the soft insides.

If you want wildlife, then Rùm is a good choice. Most of Rùm, apart from the inhabited borders of Loch Scresort, is a national nature reserve, becoming Scotland's second in 1957. From 1888 the island was owned by the Bullough family, nineteenth-century cotton magnates, who had bought it for their son and built the strange Neogothic incongruity that is Kinloch Castle. But in a changed economic world after World War II, they sold the estate to Scottish Natural Heritage. For a small island it has an immense variety of habitats, from unusual grasses, coloured by the metals in the soils, to lochans, from diverse heathers to machair dunes. The last copses were cleared sometime in the early nineteenth century, but woodland restoration has also been underway on Rùm since 1958.[25] The aim is to bring back native trees, although there are only pockets of forest now, mostly tracing the coast on the northeast of the island and following the valley of Kinloch River, and the number of deer on Rùm will make any recovery difficult. Once upon a time this may have been an island covered in wooded glades. It used to bear the name Rioghachd na Forraiste Fiadhaich (the Kingdom of the Wild Forest), though the word 'forest', of course, designated a place for deer hunting, not necessarily somewhere wooded.[26] But at one time this seemed to be a place where trees and deer thrived as a medieval sporting preserve.[27] Sitting as it does in a hyperoceanic climate, with minimal differences between the warmest and coldest months of the year, that sweeps in a band across the northwest of Scotland, Rùm may once have had swathes of the lost rainforests that used to cover a large part of the British Isles.[28]

The habitats of the island are protected areas and rightly so, but protection, SSSI status and conservation indices are also a marker of rarity, fragility and threat. Special because it's rare. It's not just human lives shaped by warming weather and rising seas: the Anthropocene is also synonymous with the ruination of landscapes, the eradication of species, biodiversity and habitat loss, and threats to all parts of the living world from diseases and destruction. People may not live at Guirdil, but non-human others face the rising seas and raging storms that are chipping away at the dunes and coastal landscapes. There's only a tiny fragment on mountainous Rùm, but plenty of the neighbouring islands are home to rare machair grasslands. Formed from shell-infused sand blown onto peaty soil, traditionally farmed by crofters in a way that is slow and attentive, the dunes are rich and biodiverse, producing a carpet of wildflowers in spring to rival any mountain meadow and drawing wildlife from corncrakes to bees. Over 70 per cent of this habitat is in Scotland, and it's rare, marginal and threatened. Alongside the dangers posed by new forms of agriculture and land management, the rising sea will also wreak havoc as it floods and erodes these fragile ecosystems.[29] Particular plants only grow in particular spots. Rùm is one of the few places where Atlantic sandwort thrives. Papa Westray is home to the Scottish primrose, a delicate purple primula that grows only on Orkney. Things will be lost for ever as the world warms.

Alongside the threats to habitat, living things face new challenges. As I crossed from the ferry to the land on arriving in Rùm, I walked through the disinfectant laid down. Avian flu had ripped through seabird populations on other islands and the deadly strain of the disease is largely the product of our intensive factory farming of poultry. There was fear that it would strike the Manx shearwater colony. If so, there was potential for it to decimate their global population, a third of which nest on Rùm. They are medium-sized seabirds, with glossy grey-black backs, bright white below and beady eyes, and their Latin name *Puffinus puffinus* is one of the most delightful taxonomic pairings. Betraying the way in which the geological past of the island is inextricably entailed with the living world, they burrow into the crumbling layers of igneous periodite on the peaks of the Rùm Cuillin.[30] I prayed they would make it out OK, the chicks would hatch. Fortunately, the nesting ground was nowhere near my route, but I was worried nonetheless I might do some damage. It was only months later, towards the end of the year, when I was relieved to hear that the Manx shearwaters had avoided the dreaded disease.

Small stories of danger and threat are everywhere if we care to look. Countless ongoing battles where sometimes nature wins and sometimes it loses. Dormice and dung beetles, for example, are threatened with extinction in the UK.[31] One's cute, the other a mini-monster, both tiny forms of life that it's easy to overlook. Some environmental ethicists have argued that people are often blind to the vulnerability of minute, ugly or unloved forms of life.[32] Some are so hard to measure, virtually invisible to us for most intents and purposes, that their extinction isn't a meaningful loss to many. After all, does it matter if certain things disappear from our world? Does it matter that in a few decades the purple primroses of Orkney might no longer bloom in May?

Sociologist Max Weber spoke of the disenchantment of the world that came with the Enlightenment's scientific rationalisation of explanation and the dismissal of spirituality.[33] Perhaps extinctions are part of the inevitable disenchantment that is the consequence of modernity and growth. Most people would agree we don't want an Earth that's uninhabitable because its resources are all gone and its seas boiling, but maybe it doesn't matter that some places will become uninhabitable or that certain animals will disappear. Certainly, people could and do say that those who are born in 50 or 100 or 150 years' time might never get to hear shearwaters, but this is not an existential threat to humanity. Anyway, future people can't miss or desire what they have never known. But we should grieve these losses, each and every one. As author Katherine Rundell writes in her devotional catalogue of threatened but wonderful species of the world, the non-human realm is full of things 'so startling that our capacity for wonder, huge as it is, can barely skim the edges of the truth'.[34] From spiders to tigers, inhabitants of the world beyond humans are the stuff of childhood stories, of myths, and of tales of flourishing. We must not resign ourselves to these disappearances, for losing them is like magic going out of the world.

The spell is not broken yet, though. Sian and I spend a luminous evening on the beach, Jupiter impossibly bright in the darkening sky, the Skye Cuillin rising on the opposite shore.

On the final day on Rùm, the weather turns. Despite heading our separate ways, Sian and I end up reconvening anyway. A punctured tyre slows her progress back to Kinloch and we have become easy in each other's company. We spend a damp few hours waiting for the ferry, scouring the shop for snacks, visiting the otter hide, and comparing notes on trips. Holed up in the hut by the campsite, we fill our veins with drops of alcohol-induced warmth, sipping some Rùm liqueur, and chatting mountains and bothies with a man called Mike who has just finished all the Corbetts (these are mountains a step down from Munros - over 762 m and under 914.4 m, with a descent of at least 152 m on all sides). Midges hum around us as the coil that Mike has lit burns to nothing. I know tick ranges are on the up in warming weather, but are there more midges because of climate change? Or less because it is dry and hot? Like early snowdrops or late-departing swallows, understanding these patterns seems to be an act of prognostication. It might not be the monstrous creatures or Divine comets of a sixteenth-century manuscript, but we too try to read the signs and work out what to do.

Whiling away time, I wander through the village, and on the way up to the otter hide, I see the school group holed up cosily in the Rùm Bunkhouse. These eight-year-olds will face more of the challenges of the future effects of biodiversity loss and climate change than I will, or their parents or teachers. In the face of such a future it's not always easy to know how to respond, whether to crumble in despair, plough on regardless, or to let hope prevail. But if we are going to inspire action to save this enchanted, entangled world, it must involve children like these. The problem of future thinking is at the heart of much debate over climate action. The rallying cry of Greta Thunberg and of the extensive following she has inspired is that the futures of young people today are most impacted by actions of older generations.[35]

As we face what climate change and environmental destruction means, at both ends of the timescale, past and future, we need to think about big shifts that have been shaping our world and will continue to do so. Yet it remains hard to think with deep time, to imagine futures we will never see or experience. Anthropologist Vincent Ialenti has argued that we must all become deep-time reckoners to face the challenges of the world around us.[36] What we think about the future shapes our sense of duty or obligation to act, but frustratingly, it seems that more scientific knowledge about the damaged futures we are creating doesn't necessarily translate into more action. The number of scientific papers on climate change has increased around six-fold in the last decade, but CO_2 emissions and temperatures have also continued to rise.[37]

So perhaps it's not a question just of knowledge but how we turn what we know into what we should do. The cynic in me says that we tend to care more about things that feel directly relevant. When snow disappears from the Alps for the ski season, it arguably hits home in Europe more acutely than news of floods in Pakistan. There's a greater sharpness to the Anthropocene threat when we see it devastate things close to us, but we need to think beyond immediate experience and the present moment. At the heart this is about ethics and how we can perceive the future as a moral, ethical, human concern, as a risk that we should care about.

At least at a general or abstract level, most people do care about the future, but that still doesn't always help us to decide what we do now, how long into the future we should think, or who or what we account for. Undoubtedly the gambles we are prepared to take now will matter. Perhaps we will be able to engineer our way out of things and negative emission technologies will come good, or perhaps that's like selling the blankets before pawning the jewels, as philosopher Henry Shue put it.[38] Perhaps we will be able to fly to the moon or Mars or to as-yet-undiscovered mirror planets for Earth when we exhaust ours. Personally, if it was a trip with Elon Musk that was the price, I would rather stay Earthbound.

On an individual level the questions about the future consequences of our actions can be even trickier. Like quite a lot of people, I feel eco-anxiety. I try to limit my use of cars and flying if I can; I switched my accounts, where I could, to green banks such as Triodos; I use a refill shop if I can find one. Maybe that's all irrelevant, or maybe it's just virtue-signalling from my position of privilege. It's also easy to lose the will to act as an individual when what we need is action at the corporate and political level, and when companies everywhere are complicit in greenwashing. According to the capitalist ontologies that dominate our world, land, biodiversity, organisms and resources are all part of a system of natural capital.[39] But this is often a flawed approach, giving us the impression that damaging impacts can always be solved with some form of tit-for-tat exchange.[40] Doing volunteer work for the Wildlife Trust, I have seen this first-hand. Going through planning applications, often relating to HS2 (the high-speed rail line designed to connect the West Midlands to London), every proposal justifies its build in environmental terms, with reference to the UK's biodiversity net gain metric. As I chatted with the biodiversity officer however, she explained that while the numbers often looked good on the metric, often no consideration had actually been given to the exact number and combination of wildflower and grasses suitable for a particular location and its soil.

Creating an ethical guide for the Anthropocene is tricky if we don't know when we have passed tipping points or how we even contribute to them. But even in the face of uncertainty and frustration at political inaction, I think individuals do matter. Not because if I refuse to drive ten minutes this will save the world. No one can be perfect, and for reasons of money, resources, time and position, we all have to make compromises with what we can and can't do in the face of climate change. But as individuals, the imperfect attention and kindness we display to each other and the world, multiplied a million times over, are important. Plenty of research shows that what we do as individuals makes a difference because it underscores what we care about and how we might work together in communities.

Maybe having empathy for Guirdil or the midges or the machair dunes is where we can start to build this hope. Evidence suggests that if we feel a sense of responsibility to future generations it promotes personal action, and this often transcends income level, political leaning, race, gender or background, all those things that so radically divide us now.[41] At heart, I guess I would be a virtue ethicist. Hoping we can all strive to do better. To care more about human others and non-human worlds. There's no magical answer, no switch we can flick to enact the large-scale change that so many activists and concerned environmentalists – me included – might want to see and to get people to act. In this battle, I firmly believe that aesthetics, art and the humanities have a central role to play precisely because they invite responses that are questioning and open, an appreciation that we live in an age of uncertainty and instability.

I am of the determined opinion that everyone should read some Ursula Le Guin, fiction or non-fiction, at some point in their life because of her inimitable ability to write about hope and complexity. I think of her musings on utopias and time. When asked by people whether she was going to write about misery and suffering or escapist fantasies in an era of crisis, she said her answer would have to be 'no', because it was an impossible choice between happiness and freedom. I know she was talking about artistic and cultural expression, but her words hit home personally too. It was a choice I felt I had been making again and again over the last decade. Why can't life contain multitudes of possibilities and paths? Le Guin rejected the idea that we should live in 'an either/or situation', where there is only one, seemingly rational, way forward to a utopian future. Le Guin died before Saudi Arabia's city of the future, The Line, was announced, but I am certain she would not have approved of its emphasis on the linear march of progress. The route to utopia she said might have to be 'roundabout or sideways'.[42]

When we dispense with certainties and binaries of the right response or wrong response in the current moment, we may also find that in that gap of not knowing there is a kind of hope. The philosopher Jacques Derrida came up with the concept of undecidability in ethics. Without uncertainty and doubt, there's also no ethical decision-making since a decision 'would simply be the application of a rule, the consequence of a premise, and there would be no problem, there would be no decision'. It also doesn't follow, he argues, that just because we don't know exactly how to act that we should do nothing or 'give up knowledge and consciousness'.[43] Rather, it means that because we live in a messy, complicated, uncertain world, so our manner of engagement with that world cannot be merely rational, empirical and linear but must be creative and capable of holding precariousness and damage. As archaeologists Þóra Pétursdóttir and Tim Flohr Sørensen argue, 'Attempting to respond to this mess we're in makes us hesitate . . . our response must be aesthetic and speculative, allowing also for patience and slowness - a poetic lingering, if you like.'[44] Poetics and ethics go together in feeding hope and allowing us to comprehend complexity in an age of fracture.

It's at least part of the reason I like bothies so much. Not everyone who enters a bothy is an environmentalist, or will care about climate change, global warming and biodiversity loss. But many bothiers have an attentiveness to place, people and environments, and a slow sense of care beyond the individual or just the here and now. They consider the unknown visitor who will come next or what the place will be like in years to come. One visitor to Rùm wrote that he was last here before mobile phones, before the internet, but the place had lived on in his memory for over thirty years until he was able to come back. I remembered words jotted down in the bothy book by Tobi and Gabriel who visited Guirdil a few days before me. They found their experience impossible to describe in words but are planning on coming back.[45] There's the small-scale act of thinking about the future and unseen others by leaving tins, kindling and games for the next visitor or the hope to return. Even though most people are not artists, there's an aesthetic, poetic and sensory engagement with places and problems. And there is also a sense among bothiers of building something for those to come, chipping away together for future generations.

Finding places where we come to know the invisible worlds of non-human others, the different rhythms, and the many deaths and lives of entangled beings is key to future thinking. These don't have to be the same for all of us. For some it might be the bay of Guirdil, for another an urban garden. They don't have to be idylls away from the world. But I like the idea of caring about places where we invest our hopes for the future and nurture our desire to return and to preserve.

Understanding the fragility of places often goes hand in hand with the desire to protect them. Perhaps we do take things for granted, and maybe until it's too late. But it's not too late. Many have hope. I do too. Hope and anxiety don't have to be opposites. They are connected by the sense that we will need to deal with grief and loss and change. Futures are always uncertain, bound up with risk and aspirations, expectation and fear. We have to engage with both, not one or the other. As Le Guin writes, 'neither the either nor the or is a place where people can live'.[46]

As I returned from Rùm, facing an uncertain future myself in the world of academia and my personal life, it was also different from the sensation I had felt in times before Covid, where the future was no future and the weight of depression closed off time in an oppressive present. I wouldn't say bothies rescued me, but somewhere along the way I became resourceful, creative, hopeful, happy in a way I could not have expected. Despite the damage, because of it perhaps, I determined not to waste any more of my time regretting or hiding. In his poem, 'Try to Praise the Mutilated World', Adam Zagajewski tells us to celebrate 'the gentle light that strays and vanishes/ and returns'.[47] It can feel like an oppressive present, too, when it comes to climate change, but I prefer to choose hope in these small spaces that can create a way to go forward together.

I pause and I ponder a poem scrawled in a bothy book. I read it first in the A. K. Bell Library on a warm but cloudy July afternoon as forests in Siberia burned and towns in Germany recovered from devastating floods. And all that in the middle of a pandemic which may well have resulted from us pushing too deep into wild places, so viruses were able to jump species. It's Gary Snyder's moving plea to future thinking.

In the next century
or the one beyond that,
they say,
are valleys, pastures,
we can meet there in peace
if we make it.

To climb these coming crests
one word to you, to
you and your children:

stay together
learn the flowers
go light[48]

EPILOGUE

Sketch from Cadderlie bothy book taken on a return trip in 2023.

All over the walls of Uags bothy on the Applecross peninsula there are hooks. They appealed to me in ways I could not quite understand at the time. A place to hang food safely, a stand for a headlamp, a way not just to string up clothes but to mark out the little corners for each person in the bothy, a signal that someone is home when a coat is slung over the rack in the entrance, an act of generosity to an unknown user from those who maintain the space. Small acts of dwelling and care in the wild.

It was the last bothy I visited before finishing this book, a special place where the sun shone, the sea was cold, the fire was warm, the coffee was good, the whisky even better, and the company joyous.

Over three years on from the first trip, it's hard to imagine how different my life is. I am holed up on the west coast of Scotland. Rain comes down; it's soft, dark rain that's restful and enfolds you in a misty silence. I'm not in a bothy but it's a kind of simple shelter, the old byre of a friend's house. I am not far from Cadderlie, the first bothy I ever visited. There are still rain clouds, mountains and lochs, but everything else is different.

I am at the start of something new. I have left academia, currently untethered and free to make a new path. I have given up my city flat and a permanent home for now, making my way through with the kindness of friends as I seek my own sort of shelter in the world. Whatever that might look like.

The world is changed too. Covid has come and not gone, temperatures have continued to increase, animals gone extinct. There is war and conflict that has brought terror to people's lives in ways which we cannot imagine.

These are horrors we often want to escape from, and perhaps that's the apparent lure of the hut in the wilderness. Yet for me these places do not represent a withdrawal from the world, rather a space to reflect and understand what matters to me, to us. When I started this book, I believed I was running away, but maybe it's running towards a different future.

I think I loved the hooks because they are so domestic

and mundane in a wild place. They represent an act of attentiveness, of consideration, of setting things aside for a moment and pausing but of not forgetting. Your coat still hangs there; you will put it on once more and return from the remote shelter to the world.

One of my favourite finds in a bothy book is an entry by a small boy, Callum. He has noted and underlined his important statement as 'Callum's rule', drawn a lovely little bothy and then written: 'I like the hut.'

I like the hut too, Callum.

Extract from Camasunary bothy book held in the Perth & Kinross Archive, A. K. Bell Library.

ACKNOWLEDGEMENTS

Like any good bothy book, this work has been a collaborative effort woven out of conversations and exchanges in person and on the page. For everyone who has come on journeys with me, whether striding next to me or accompanying me vicariously, you have been joyous companions.

As it was the visitor books that ignited my interest, I am grateful to every person who has ever written an entry, shared a poem or drawn a picture whilst they have whiled away a few hours in a bothy, waiting for their socks to dry or their food to cook. And I also thank those who have looked after the fragile volumes, rescued them from these buildings, and catalogued them in archives or libraries along with other papers, photographs or records. If not in a bothy, I was rarely happier than when I was sitting at the desks in the archive of the University of Dundee, flicking through boxes in the A. K. Bell Library in Perth, sitting in the National Library of Scotland gazing at Arthur's Seat or consulting mining records in Llyfrgell Genedlaethol Cymru / National Library of Wales.

Historians, writers, archaeologists, photographers, artists, walkers, hikers and bothiers have given generously of their time to speak to me about their work, their experiences and their lives. Lesley McFadyen, Alec Finlay, Nicholas J. R. White, Elizabeth Campbell, Calum Wallis, Lesley Young, Simon Birch, Geoff Allan, Julia Laite, Paria Goodarzi, Alex Boyd, Rachel Hunt, all my Birkbeck students, amongst others. Organisations that look after bothies, landscapes and environments - the MBA, Trees for Life and Bothy Project - have not only allowed me and others to get to these stunning locations but spoken to me about their endeavours and their work. The University of Edinburgh gave me precious writing space during a fellowship at IASH and a beautiful room overlooking the Meadows, and Bath Spa University stimulated so many thoughts on ethics, art and anthropology during my MA there. The Scottish Poetry Library hosted me and others for an afternoon of thought-provoking conversation.

I am indebted to readers who are more eagle-eyed than I - Mum, Dad, Jan, Carla, Ed, Sarah, Mette, Hannah, Lyndal, Nick, Caroline, Alison, Simone, Jenny, Alan, Debbie, Dan, Julia, Alison, Alasdair, Mary, Mel, Allie, Róisín, Denise, Katie, Fearn, Jana, Lynn - who offered critiquing encouragement, read endless drafts and chapters and who have saved me from lengthy critiques on hiking blogs. This would be a poorer book without your input, as it would without the incisive work by editors Jo Thompson and Sam Harding, Eve Hutchings and all the fantastic team at William Collins.

My agent Imogen Morrell believed in this from the start and has kept believing ever since. If not for Anna Parker, we might never have met.

And in keeping with the book, heartfelt thanks also to every coffee shop, bus, car, train, field, platform, spare room or empty desk where I have written or edited. People and places have been generous to me.

Finally, I am grateful to the bothies and those who maintain them, for their sleeping platforms, their hooks and their fireplaces, their fairy lights and their rough walls, grateful for the bothy mice, the stags, the rain, the sun, and the stars. Thank you to all the places of simple shelter.

ENDNOTES

Prologue

1 **the history of summer shielings** *Oxford English Dictionary*, s.v. 'bothy, n., sense 1.a', September 2023. https://doi.org/10.1093/OED/3660705809; 'Bothy *n., v.*'; *Oxford English Dictionary*, s.v. 'booth, n., sense 1.a', September 2023. https://doi.org/10.1093/OED/6490614196; *Dictionary of the Scots Language*. 2004. Scottish Language Dictionaries Ltd. http://www.dsl.ac.uk/entry/snd/bothy

2 **the herds for summertime pasture** John Lightfoot, *Flora Scotica: or, A Systematic Arrangement, in the Linnaean Method, of the Native Plants of Scotland and the Hebrides* (London: B. White, 1777).

3 **its first official project** 'MBA History', *Mountain Bothies Website*: https://www.mountainbothies.org.uk/about-the-mba/mba-history/

4 **drew up some rules** *Mountain Bothies Association Journal*, No. 1, January 1966.

5 **enjoyment of outdoor adventures** Denis Mollison, 'Obituaries: Bernard and Betty Heath, couple dedicated to

maintaining bothies', *Scotsman*, 17 May 2022. https://www.scotsman.com/news/people/obituaries-bernard-and-betty-heath-couple-dedicated-to-maintaining-bothies-3695511

6 **disappointment of some traditionalists** Geoff Allan, *The Scottish Bothy Bible: The complete guide to Scotland's bothies and how to reach them* (Bath: Wild Things Publishing, 2017).

One: Cadderlie

1 **rather grim walls** 'The Horrible Bothy', Monica Shaw, 25 February 2021, Eat Sleep Wild, https://eatsleepwild.com/the-horrible-bothy-grwyne-fawr-brecon-beacons/

2 **stay until the morning** Steven McKenzie, 'My fright night in "haunted bothy" at Luibeilt Lodge', BBC News, 24 December 2021, https://www.bbc.co.uk/news/uk-scotland-highlands-islands-59698147

3 **we never stop pretending** Jonathan Gottschall, *The Storytelling Animal: How Stories Make Us Human* (New York: Houghton Mifflin Harcourt, 2021), p. 7.

4 **sense where there seems to be little** Ivor F. Goodson and Scherto R. Gill, 'The Narrative Turn in Social Research', *Counterpoints* 386 (2011), pp. 17–33. http://www.jstor.org/stable/42981362

5 **chronicle called the *Annals of Saint Gall*** Hayden White, 'The Value of Narrativity in the Representation of Reality' in *The Content of the Form* (Baltimore: John Hopkins University Press, 1987), pp. 1–25.

6 **we can't quite grasp in its totality** Timothy Morton, *Hyperobjects: Philosophy and Ecology After the End of the World* (Minneapolis: University of Minnesota Press, 2013).

7 **individuals as well as cultures** Slavoj Žižek, *Living in the End Times* (London and New York: Verso, 2010), p. 328.

8 **on the Isle of Lismore** John Francis Campbell, *Popular Tales*

of the West Highlands Orally Collected, vol. 4 (London: Alexander Gardner, 1893), p. 224.

9 **a fate that followed her** The Ulster Cycle, also known as the Red Branch Cycle, is a medieval collection of Irish legends set mostly at the court of King Conchobar mac Nessa. Telling of a more distant Irish past in the first century BCE, the oldest surviving manuscript is the *Lebor na hUidre/The Book of the Dun Cow*, dating to before 1106, held by the Royal Irish Academy: https://www.ria.ie/library/catalogues/special-collections/medieval-and-early-modern-manuscripts/lebor-na-huidre-book. For a modern translation of the tales, see Randy Lee Eickhoff's renditions published by Macmillan.

10 **the Pass of Brander in 1308** See the notes from the *Ordnance Survey Name Books*: 'Argyll OS Name Books, 1868–1878', Argyll volume 52, OS1/2/52/25. Available online at https://scotlandsplaces.gov.uk/digital-volumes/ordnance-survey-name-books/argyll-os-name-books-1868-1878/argyll-volume-52/24

11 **sanctuary built by Duncan MacDougall** Edmund Chisholm-Batten, *The Charters of the Priory of Beauly: With Notices of the Priories of Pluscardine and Ardchattan and of the Family of the Founder, John Byset* (London: Houlston & Sons for the Grampian Club, 1877), p. 147.

12 **devoted only to God** 'Ardchattan Priory, Loch Etive, Argyll PA37 1RQ', *Historic Environment Scotland*. https://www.historicenvironment.scot/visit-a-place/places/ardchattan-priory/history/

13 **along the west coast** Mhairi Ross, '"Between the Burn and the Turning Sea": The Story of Cadderlie', *Historic Argyll* 16 (2011), pp. 35–42. On Campbell smuggling there is also Charles Hunter, *Smuggling in West Argyll & Lochaber before 1745: From the archives at Ardchattan Priory* (Oban: C. Hunter, 2004).

14 **huts are halls** William Wordsworth, 'Composed in the Glen of Loch Etive' (1831) in *The Poetical Works of William Wordsworth*, vol. III (Boston: Little, Brown and Company, 1859), p. 230.

15 **a free and careless life** *Journals Of Dorothy Wordsworth*, vol. II, edited by William Knight (London: Macmillan Co, 1897), p. 44.

16 **for journeying shepherds and artists** Ross, '"Between the Burn and the Turning Sea"', pp. 41–2.

17 **IUCN Red List** S. Fordham, S. L. Fowler, R. P. Coelho, K. Goldman, & M. P. Francis (2016). *Squalus acanthias*. The IUCN Red List of Threatened Species 2016: e.T91209505A2898271. http://dx.doi.org/10.2305/IUCN.UK.2016-1.RLTS.T91209505A2898271.en

18 **water stacked above them** Natalie Hicks, Tim Brand and the MASTS community, 'Loch Etive MASTS Case Study Workshop Report', (2016), pp. 1–2. Available online at https://www.masts.ac.uk/media/36494/loch-etive-workshop-report_final-report.pdf

19 **large swathes across the UK** On the Loch Etive Woods, a Designated Special Area of Conservation (SAC), see the entry on the Joint Nature Conservation Committee website: https://sac.jncc.gov.uk/site/UK0012750 and the Woodland Trust entry for Cadderlie, https://www.woodlandtrust.org.uk/visiting-woods/woods/cadderlie/. Temperate rainforest used to be common in Britain and Guy Shrubsole mapped the extent of these lost woodlands. Guy Shrubsole, *The Lost Rainforests of Britain* (London: William Collins, 2022).

20 **those of human existence** David Stephenson and Jon Merritt, 'Argyll and the Islands: A Landscape Fashioned by Geology', Field Guide for *Scottish National Heritage* (2011). Available online at https://www.nature.scot/doc/landscape-fashioned-geology-argyll-and-islands

21 **charcoal mounds** There's been an active quarry here for decades, providing work for hundreds of men in the early 1900s. The quarry is now owned by the Breedon Group. For

some information see the Ardchattan Priory archive website: http://ardchattan.wikidot.com/bonawe-quarry

22 **bread over the table** *The Supper at Emmaus*, Rembrandt Harmenszoon van Rijn (1606–69), *ca.* 1628, oil on wood panel, 39 x 42 cm. Now in the Musée Jacquemart-André in Paris.

23 **sparking a Romantic revival** Dafydd Moore (ed.), *The International Companion to James Macpherson* and *The Poems of Ossian* (Glasgow: Scottish Literature International, 2017). The National Library of Scotland has a digital archive of Ossian editions. https://digital.nls.uk/early-gaelic-book-collections/archive/76750236

24 **the Battle of Lora** James Macpherson, *The battle of Lora. A poem. With some fragments written in the Erse, or Irish language, by Ossian, the son of Fingal.* Translated into English verse by Mr Derrick (London: T. Gardner, 1762).

25 **on the banks** 'Ossian Awakening the Spirits on the Banks of the Lora with the Sound of his Harp', François Pascal Simon Gérard (1770–1837), *ca.* 1801. Oil on canvas, 184.5 x 194.5 cm. The original is now in the Kunsthalle, Hamburg.

26 **Smith in 1871** R. Angus Smith, *Loch Etive and The Sons of Uisnach* (London: Macmillan, 1879).

27 **150 horse-power** *Scotsman*, 17 April 1885.

28 **narrate their world** Bob Munro, 'The Bothy Ballads: The Social Context and Meaning of the Farm Servants' Songs of North-Eastern Scotland', *History Workshop Journal* 3 (1977), pp. 184–93. For more on the history of bothy ballads and for some examples, see these online articles: Greg Dawson Allen, 'Bothy Ballads', *The Northeast Folklore Archive*, available online at http://www.nefa.net/archive/songmusicdance/bothy/index.htm and 'Bothy Ballads', *Scots Language Centre*, available online at https://www.scotslanguage.com/Scots_Song_uid65/Types_of_Scots_Song_uid131/Bothy_Ballads_uid3315

29 **open-air past times** For a bit about the history, see the

biographical note on the catalogue pages for University of Dundee archives. https://archives.dundee.ac.uk/ru-298-1/. The DURC is still very active and you can check out their website: https://sportsunion.dundee.ac.uk/rucksack-club/

30 **archive at the University of Dundee** Bothy songbook, University of Dundee Archive RU 298/5/1.

31 **Omar Khayyám in his entries** Entry for 24 September 1948, Visitor Books - Corrour Bothy, Cairngorms, 'Volume 10.' June 1948-June 1950, University of Dundee Archive RU 298/4/1/9.

32 **sojourn in fair Corrour** Entry for July 1928, Visitor Books - Corrour Bothy, Cairngorms, 'Volume 1', June 1928-September 1929, University of Dundee Archive RU 298/4/1/1.

33 **Cheerio my public** Entry for May 1939, Visitor Books - Corrour Bothy, Cairngorms, 'Volume 8', September 1938-August 1940, University of Dundee Archive RU 298/4/1/6.

34 **dancing across the page in joy** Entry for August 1929, Visitor Books - Corrour Bothy, Cairngorms, 'Volume 1', June 1928-September 1929, University of Dundee Archive RU 298/4/1/1.

35 **'proletarian revolution' of hillwalking** Dave Brown and Ian Mitchell, *Mountain Days & Bothy Nights* (Edinburgh: Luath Press, reprint 2001), p. 1.

36 **in modern songs** William Butler Yeats penned and published his version of Deirdre's legend (1907) but also completed the unfinished manuscript for a play written by John Millington Synge (1909), *Deirdre of the Sorrows.* Novels range from the 1923 work *Deirdre* by James Stephens to *The Swan Maiden* (2009) by Jules Watson. Songs about her include the album *A Celtic Tale: The Legend of Deirdre* (1996), written by Mychael and Jeff Danna, and the song 'Of the Sorrows' by Leslie Hudson.

37 **the Burn at Deirdre's Garden** Amy Jeffs, *Storyland: A New Mythology of Britain* (London: Hachette, 2021), chapter 12; Ross, '"Between the Burn and the Turning Sea"', pp. 35-6.

38 **old mythologies** W. B. Yeats, 'A Coat' (1912).

39 **to relive our experience** His words provide the title of the article written by Mhairi Ross as well as an article on the 'Walk of the Week: Cadderlie bothy, Argyll and Bute' by Geoff Allan for *The Times*, 4 November 2021.

40 **just empty backdrops** Tim Ingold, 'The Temporality of the Landscape', *World Archaeology* 25.2 (1993), pp. 152–74.

41 **emigrate across the Atlantic** Tom Devine, *The Scottish Clearances: A History of the Dispossessed 1600 to 1900* (London: Allen Lane, 2018).

42 **Wolfcrag** https://treesforlife.org.uk/into-the-forest/trees-plants-animals/mammals/wolf/

43 **what is still the same** Keith H. Basso, *Wisdom Sits in Places: Landscape and Language Among the Western Apache* (Albuquerque: University of New Mexico Press, 1996), p. 16.

44 **the land as a living place** Information about Sam Lee's work can be found on his website, http://samleesong.co.uk/

45 **in the UK** Jente Ottenburghs, 'Turtle doves under threat', British Ornithologists' Union, 6 April 2023. https://bou.org.uk/blog-jo-turtle-doves-under-threat/

46 **from our vocabularies** Robert Macfarlane and Jackie Morris, *The Lost Words* (London: Penguin, 2017).

47 **come back** Yōko Ogawa, *The Memory Police*, (trans.) Stephen Snyder (London: Penguin Random House, 2019).

48 **new normal** Masashi Soga and Kevin J. Gaston, 'Shifting baseline syndrome: causes, consequences, and implications', *Frontiers in Ecology and the Environment 16* (2018), pp. 220–30. https://doi.org/10.1002/fee.1794

49 **here's to the next time** Entry for 24 May 1940, Visitor Books – Corrour Bothy, Cairngorms, 'Volume 9', August 1940–September 1940, University of Dundee Archive RU 298/4/1/7.

50 **what stories we tell** Ursula K. Heise, *Imagining Extinction: The Cultural Meanings of Endangered Species* (Chicago and London: University of Chicago Press, 2016), p. 5.

51 **telling tales** Michel Serres with Bruno Latour, *Conversations on Science, Culture and Time*, trans. Roxanne Lapidus (Ann Arbor: University of Michigan Press, 1995) p. 50.

52 **sound lives in her** P. Ovidius Naso, Metamorphoses, Book 3, Lines 396–99. (My translation).

53 **healers of ills** Bothy songbook, University of Dundee Archive RU 298/5/1.

Two: Corrour

1 **the previous year** Entries for 21 August 1940, Visitor Books – Corrour Bothy, Cairngorms, 'Volume 8', September 1938–August 1940, University of Dundee Archive RU 298/4/1/6.

2 **Here's hoping it will continue** Entries for 24–26 June 1939, Visitor Books – Corrour Bothy, Cairngorms, 'Volume 9', August 1940–September 1940, University of Dundee Archive RU 298/4/1/7.

3 **Protestants fled persecution** 'The Huguenot refuge', Musée Protestant, https://museeprotestant.org/en/notice/the-huguenot-refuge/

4 **National Trust for Scotland** 'Estate Management', Cairngorms National Park, https://cairngorms.co.uk/working-together/land-management/estate-management/

5 **on the table** Entries for 28 August 1931, Visitor Books – Corrour Bothy, Cairngorms, 'Volume 3', April 1931–June 1932, University of Dundee Archive RU 298/4/1/3.

6 ***drù* and *drùthaidh*** Adam Watson, *The Place Names of Upper Deeside*, compiled by Elizabeth Allan (Rothersthorpe: Paragon Publishing, 2014), p. 98; Ralph Storer, *Corrour Bothy: A Refuge in the Wilderness* (Edinburgh: Luath Press, 2020), p. 2.

7 **meaning 'forbidding or gloomy'** Seton Gordon, *Highways and Byways in the Central Highlands* (London: MacMillan & Co., 1948), p. 308. See for example the Ordnance Survey,

six-inch first edition, 1843–82 for Inverness-shire (Mainland), Sheet LXXXIX (Survey date: 1866–69, Publication date: 1869–72). Available online at https://maps.nls.uk/view/74427110

8 **dun-coloured corrie** Storer, *Corrour Bothy*, p. 7.

9 **look out for poachers** Storer, *Corrour Bothy*, p. 35–6.

10 **deer forest in Scotland** Robert A. Lambert, *Contested Mountains: Nature, Development and Environment in the Cairngorms Region of Scotland 1880–1980* (Cambridge: The White Horse Press, 2001), p. 69.

11 **'haven of rest' for climbers** Storer, *Corrour Bothy*, p. 40. The verse on the opening page of the first book opens with the line, 'O, haven of rest, may thy walls be blest'. Visitor Books - Corrour Bothy, Cairngorms, 'Volume 1', June 1928–September 1929, University of Dundee Archive RU 298/4/1/1.

12 **boulder strewn track** Entries for 28 September 1948, Visitor Books - Corrour Bothy, Cairngorms, 'Volume 10', June 1948–June 1950, University of Dundee Archive RU 298/4/1/9.

13 **down they rushed** Entry for 3 October 1931, Visitor Books - Corrour Bothy, Cairngorms, 'Volume 3', April 1931–June 1932, University of Dundee Archive RU 298/4/1/3.

14 **out of time** Entry for 19 August 1928, Visitor Books - Corrour Bothy, Cairngorms, 'Volume 1', June 1928–September 1929, University of Dundee Archive RU 298/4/1/1. The poem is 'The Last Journey', the epilogue from *The Testament of John Davidson* (London: Grant Richards, 1908).

15 **escaped into the mountains** '"KNAPSACKERY", on the Surrey Hills. The Growth of a New Habit or Rather the Revival of an Old One', 6 September 1930, *The Sphere*. See also Rose Staveley-Wadham, 'Hiking in the 1930s – Exploring the 'Phenomenon of Post-War Youth', *The British Newspaper Archive Blog* 1 June 2021. https://blog.britishnewspaperarchive.co.uk/2021/06/01/hiking-in-the-1930s/

16 **venturing into the outdoors** Simon Robert Thompson, 'The

Fashioning of a New World: Youth Culture and the Origins of the Mass Outdoor Movement in Interwar Britain', unpublished DPhil thesis, King's College London (2018), pp. 20–3.

17 **on his 21st birthday in June 1930** Entry for 22 June 1930, Visitor Books - Corrour Bothy, Cairngorms, 'Volume 2', September 1929–April 1931, University of Dundee Archive RU 298/4/1/2.

18 **side of cheesy** Storer, *Corrour Bothy*, p. 208. See for example his entry for 13 and 16–17 July 1931, Visitor Books - Corrour Bothy, Cairngorms, 'Volume 3', April 1931–June 1932, University of Dundee Archive RU 298/4/1/3.

19 **'soot, grime and smoke' of Glasgow** Entry for July 1931, Visitor Books - Corrour Bothy, Cairngorms, 'Volume 3', April 1931–June 1932, University of Dundee Archive RU 298/4/1/3.

20 **across the Dee** Entry for 29 September 1935, Visitor Books - Corrour Bothy, Cairngorms, 'Volume 6', July 1935–June 1937, University of Dundee Archive RU 298/4/1/11.

21 **trail after the war** Entry for 3 January 1952, Visitor Books - Corrour Bothy, Cairngorms, 'Volume 12', November 1951 - January 1953', University of Dundee Archive RU 298/4/1/11.

22 **a visit to the Cairngorms** Entry for 2 October 1938, Visitor Books - Corrour Bothy, Cairngorms, 'Volume 8', September 1938–August 1940, University of Dundee Archive RU 298/4/1/6.

23 **mountains in the distance** Entry for June 1939, Visitor Books - Corrour Bothy, Cairngorms, 'Volume 8', September 1938–August 1940, University of Dundee Archive RU 298/4/1/6.

24 **Time marches on** Entries for August and September 1939, Visitor Books - Corrour Bothy, Cairngorms, 'Volume 8', September 1938–August 1940, University of Dundee Archive RU 298/4/1/6.

25 **lunch in the sun** Entry for 29 April 2020, Greensykes bothy book, consulted in situ.

26 **higher into the mountains** On the Luibeg burn in spate like

this see *Seton Gordon's Cairngorms: An Anthology*, compiled by Hamish Watson (Dunbeath: Whittles Publishing, 2010), p. 42.

27 **up to 10 km** 'Amphibians: The Cairngorms' tenacious natives', Cairngorms Connect, https://cairngormsconnect.org.uk/news/8/37/Amphibians-The-Cairngorms-tenacious-natives

28 **paradise for frogs** Storer, *Corrour Bothy*, p. 35.

29 **claimed it** Alec Finlay, *Gathering. A Place Aware Guide to The Cairngorms* (Zürich: Hauser & Wirth, 2018).

30 **summer shielings** P. J. Dixon and S. T. Green, 'Mar Lodge Estate Grampian: An Archaeological Survey', *Afforestable Land Survey RCAHMS* (1995).

31 **close to the fire** Entries for 1–2 January 1937, Visitor Books - Corrour Bothy, Cairngorms, 'Volume 6', July 1935–June 1937, University of Dundee Archive RU 298/4/1/4.

32 **Cairngorm climbers** James Carron, 'Shelter Stone', *Secret Scotland*, 9 June 2022, https://secretscotland829724255.wordpress.com/2022/06/09/shelter-stone. The 'Shelter Stone' books are in the National Library of Scotland archives, Cairngorms Club Acc.11538/35 - Shelter Stone Book 1963–1969.

33 **instead of in my tent** Entries for July 1937, Visitor Books - Corrour Bothy, Cairngorms, 'Volume 7', June 1937–August 1938, University of Dundee Archive RU 298/4/1/6.

34 **one at rest** Roda Rani Konadhode, Dheeraj Pelluru, and Priyattam J. Shiromani, 'Unihemispheric Sleep: An Enigma for Current Models of Sleep-Wake Regulation, *Sleep*, 39.3 (2016), pp. 491–4, https://doi.org/10.5665/sleep.5508

35 **tamer euphemism** C. McNeish, *The Munros: Scotland's Highest Mountains* (Broxburn: Lomond Books, 1998), p. 125.

36 **blackness at the other** On the Grey Man see Affleck Gray, *The Big Grey Man of Ben MacDhui* (Moffat: Lochar Publishing, 1989). For Scroggie's account, see Sydney Scroggie, *The Cairngorms: Scene & Unseen* (Scottish Mountaineering Press, reprint, 2021), p. 46.

37 **came to tea** Entry for 2 January 1937, Visitor Books - Corrour Bothy, Cairngorms, 'Volume 6', July 1935–June 1937, University of Dundee Archive RU 298/4/1/4 and entry for 25 June, Visitor Book May 1958–April 1959, University of Dundee Archive RU 298/4/1/15.

38 **those who roam** Entry for 25 August 1928, Visitor Books - Corrour Bothy, Cairngorms, 'Volume 1', June 1928–September 1929, University of Dundee Archive RU 298/4/1/1.

39 **patterns of settlement** Rachel Hunt, 'Huts, bothies and buildings out-of-doors: an exploration of the practice, heritage and culture of "out-dwellings" in rural Scotland', unpublished PhD thesis, University of Glasgow (2016).

40 **against the code of bothies** James Carron, *Highland Hermit: The Remarkable Life of James McRory Smith* (Amenta Publishing, 2010).

41 **protected from the Devil** Kat Hill, *Baptism, Brotherhood, and Belief in Reformation Germany: Anabaptism and Lutheranism, 1525–1585* (Oxford: Oxford University Press, 2015), p. 101.

42 **through the window** Gray, *The Big Grey Man*, pp. 35–7.

43 **enjoying the bothy** Entry for 1 January 1937 Visitor Books - Corrour Bothy, Cairngorms, 'Volume 6', July 1935–June 1937, University of Dundee Archive RU 298/4/1/4..

44 **been made homeless** Entry for 31 July 2022–1 August 2022, Guirdil bothy book, consulted in situ.

45 **contemplative monks** Robert Macfarlane, *The Wild Places* (London: Granta, 2007), pp. 1–3.

46 **and rid of you, I swear** Edna St. Vincent Millay, 'I Only Know That Every Hour With You' (1920).

47 **aside the theft** 'Home is So Sad', From *Collected Poems* by Philip Larkin. Copyright © 1988, 2003 by the Estate of Philip Larkin.

48 **refugees and hostile regimes** David Jenkins and Kimberley Brownlee, 'What a Home Does', *Law and Philosophy 41* (2022), pp. 441–68.

49 **to sense, imagine and think** Martha Nussbaum, *Women and Human Development: The Capabilities Approach* (Cambridge: Cambridge University Press, 2000).

50 **encounter with a stranger** Jessica Bruder, *Nomadland: Surviving America in the Twenty-First Century* (New York and London: W. W. Norton, 2017), foreword.

51 **Two of the Musketeers** Entry for 22 September 1936, Visitor Books - Corrour Bothy, Cairngorms, 'Volume 6', July 1935–June 1937, University of Dundee Archive RU 298/4/1/4.

52 **those who were inexperienced** Craig Williams, 'The worst mountain disaster in British history', BBC News, 20 November 2021.

53 **the unheeding snows** *Seton Gordon's Cairngorms*, p. 47.

54 **filled the air** Entry for 21 September 1940, Visitor Books - Corrour Bothy, Cairngorms, 'Volume 9', August 1940–September 1940, University of Dundee Archive RU 298/4/1/7.

55 **we are not dead** Entry for 3 January 1952, Visitor Books - Corrour Bothy, Cairngorms, 'Volume 12', November 1951-January 1953, University of Dundee Archive RU 298/4/1/11.

56 **revolutionary manifestos** Victor Turner, 'Liminal to Liminoid, in Play, Flow, Ritual: An Essay in Comparative Symbology', in Victor Turner, *From Ritual to Theatre: The Human Seriousness of Play* (New York: Performing Arts Journal Publication, 1982), p. 54–5.

Three: Greensykes

1 **Thanks much like** Entry for 9–11 October 2020, Greensykes bothy book, consulted in situ.

2 **way of living** On Aristotle see Richard Kraut, 'Aristotle's Ethics', *The Stanford Encyclopedia of Philosophy* (Fall 2022 Edition), Edward N. Zalta & Uri Nodelman (eds.), https://plato.stanford.edu/archives/fall2022/entries/aristotle-ethics/. For debates on meanings of the good life see Edward F. Fischer, *The*

Good Life: Aspiration, Dignity, and the Anthropology of Wellbeing (Stanford: Stanford University Press, 2014); Karen Lykke Syse and Martin Lee Mueller (eds.), *Sustainable Consumption and the Good Life, Interdisciplinary Perspectives* (Abingdon and New York: Routledge, 2015).

3 **unprecedented rates** Karen Lykke Syse and Martin Lee Mueller, 'Introduction', in Syse and Mueller, *Sustainable Consumption*, pp. 1–6.

4 **acted too late** Italo Calvino, 'The Petrol Pump', *Numbers in the Dark and Other Stories*, (trans.) Tim Parks (London: Jonathan Cape, 1995).

5 **working as shepherds** Historical notes from the Greensykes history binder, consulted in situ in the bothy.

6 **weary traveller** Report on history of Greensykes written by Kenneth Irving, consulted in situ in the bothy.

7 **the simple as skilful** Rachel Hunt, 'Huts, bothies and buildings out-of-doors: an exploration of the practice, heritage and culture of "out-dwellings" in rural Scotland', unpublished PhD thesis, University of Glasgow (2016), pp. 214–20.

8 **in the morning** Entry for 28 February 2021, Greensykes bothy book, consulted in situ.

9 **loaves of bread** Entry on back cover, Visitor Books - Corrour Bothy, Cairngorms, 'Volume 8', September 1938–August 1940, University of Dundee Archive RU 298/4/1/6.

10 **too modern** Daniel B. Lee, *Old Order Mennonites: Rituals, Beliefs, and Community* (Lanham: Burnham, 2000).

11 **even the 1960s** Murdo MacLeod, 'Bothy culture: a tour of the Highlands' sustainable sanctuaries', *Guardian*, 5 November 2021.

12 **essay on the subject** Thomas E. Hill (1983), 'Ideals of Human Excellence and Preserving Natural Environments', in Ronald D. Sandler and Philip Cafaro (eds.), *Environmental Virtue Ethics* (Lanham: Rowman and Littlefield, 2005), pp. 211–24; Rosalind Hursthouse, 'Environmental Virtue Ethics', in Rebecca L. Walker

and Philip J. Ivanhoe (eds.), *Working Virtue* (Oxford: Oxford University Press, 2007), pp. 154–71.

13 **green thinking** On sustainability and its history see Paul Warde, *The Invention of Sustainability: Nature and Destiny, c.1500–1870* (Cambridge: Cambridge University Press, 2018).

14 **rosy horizon** Thomas Hylland Eriksen, 'Afterword: Beyond the paradox of the big, bad wolf', in Syse and Mueller, *Sustainable Consumption*, pp. 244–56.

15 **reorientate our ideas** Jason Hickel, *Less is More: How Degrowth Will Save the World* (London: Penguin, 2020).

16 **through the fields** Mary Oliver, 'The Summer Day' (1990).

17 **heating options** George Monbiot, 'My burning shame: I fitted my house with three wood-burning stoves', *Guardian*, 27 December 2022.

18 **pig on the tracks** Ursula K. Le Guin, 'A Non-Euclidean View of California as a Cold Place to Be' (1982), in her *Dancing at the Edge of the World: Thoughts on Words, Women, Places* (New York: Grove Press, 1989). Reprinted in the Spring 2010 issue of Fifth Estate), p. 6.

19 **those lives possible** On the potential of huts and hutting culture see also Lesley Riddoch, *Huts: A Place Beyond* (Edinburgh: Luath Press, 2020).

20 **all we have** Eriksen, 'Afterword', p. 246.

21 **place has been lost** Kate Rigby, 'Ecstatic Dwelling: Perspectives on Place in European Romanticism', *Angelaki: Journal of the Theoretical Humanities,* 9.2 (2004), pp.117–42.

22 **spent outdoors** Entries for 2019–21 in the Greensykes bothy book, consulted in situ.

23 **southern Scotland** https://www.samyeling.org/

24 **one year** *Gregorian Chant* (Album), Monks Of The Abbey Of Notre Dame (2016).

25 **day of little tasks** Wendy Cope, 'The Orange', published 1992 Faber & Faber.

Four: Secret Howff

1 **buzz around the experience** As well as Allan's book and many blogs there is also, for example, Phoebe Smith, *The Book of the Bothy* (Kendal: Cicerone Press, 2015).

2 **online blogs** See, for an example of more traditional attitudes, George T. Mortimer, *Bothy Culture* (A Media Underground Publication, 2013).

3 **the guardian, the witness, and the excluded** Anne Dufourmantelle, *In Defense of Secrets* (New York: Fordham University Press, 2021).

4 **owning trusts** 'How the Farquharson family became the custodians of Invercauld Estate', https://www.invercauld.estate/history-of-the-estate

5 **had to be replaced** 'The History of the "Secret" Howff', document consulted in situ in the howff. See also the account by Ashie Brebner, *Beyond the Secret Howff* (Edinburgh: Luath Press, 2017), pp. 27–38.

6 **away to 'howff'** 'howff, n.'. *Oxford English Dictionary*, Oxford University Press, July 2023, https://doi.org/10.1093/OED/5456131002; 'Howf n.1, v.'. Dictionary of the Scots Language. 2004. Scottish Language Dictionaries Ltd. 2023, http://www.dsl.ac.uk/entry/snd/howf_n1_v

7 **half-heard instructions** Patrick Baker, *The Unremembered Places: Exploring Scotland's Wild Histories* (Edinburgh: Birlinn, 2020), pp. 10–18.

8 **Olifab Boys** 'The Howff Project, April 2017', report consulted situ in the howff.

9 **one vast deer forest** William Pembroke Fetridge, *The American Travellers' Guides: Hand-books for Travellers in Europe and the East, vol 1.* (New York, Harper & Brothers Publishers, 1878), p. 138.

10 **paying visitors** https://www.invercauld.estate/country-sports/

11 **nothing has come of it** https://www.geograph.org.uk/photo/4206608

12 **with the self** Dufourmantelle, *In Defense of Secrets*.

13 **in the same way** Jacques Derrida, *Archive Fever: A Freudian Impression*, (trans.) Eric Prenowitz (Chicago: University of Chicago Press, 1996), p. 18.

14 **part of the club** Entry for 16 August 2018, Secret Howff book, consulted in situ.

15 **sources we use** On silences in archives and archival power see for example David Thomas and Michael Moss, *Archival Silences: Missing, Lost And, Uncreated Archives* (Abingdon and New York: Routledge, 2021); Marisa J. Fuentes, *Dispossessed Lives: Enslaved Women, Violence, and the Archive* (Philadelphia: University of Pennsylvania Press, 2016).

16 **othered and suspended** David Sobel, *Children's Special Places: Exploring the Role of Forts, Dens, and Bush Houses in Middle Childhood* (Detroit: Wayne State University Press, 2002).

17 **another world** Entries for 24 October, 1 January 2018 and July 2022, Secret Howff book, consulted in situ.

18 **land beyond unknown** https://www.loc.gov/collections/discovery-and-exploration/articles-and-essays/recognizing-and-naming-america/

19 **enchanted places** 1635 Blaeu Map Guiana, Venezuela, and El Dorado https://zh.wikipedia.org/wiki/File:1635_Blaeu_Map_Guiana,_Venezuela,_and_El_Dorado_-_Geographicus_-_Guiana-blaeu-1635.jpg

20 **winding paths** Melinda Alliker Rabb, *Satire and Secrecy in English Literature from 1650 to 1750* (New York: Palgrave Macmillan, 2007), pp. 21–45.

21 **summer staycation** https://www.cntraveller.com/gallery/bothies-in-scotland

22 **bothy code** https://www.mountainbothies.org.uk/bothies/bothy-code/

23 ***Bothy Bible*** https://kearvaigpipeclub.co.uk/

24 **what in fact is** Ursula K. Le Guin, 'A Non-Euclidean View of California as a Cold Place to Be' (1982, Reprinted in the Spring 2010 issue of *Fifth Estate*), p. 3.

25 **wants and needs** Kate Rigby, 'Ecstatic Dwelling: Perspectives on Place in European Romanticism', *Angelaki: Journal of the Theoretical Humanities*, 9.2 (2004), p. 137.

26 **stuck in the ring** 'The Prometheus Story', National Park Service, https://www.nps.gov/grba/learn/historyculture/the-prometheus-story.htm

27 **antipathy between the two animals** William Eamon, *Science and the Secrets of Nature: Books of Secrets in Medieval and Early Modern Culture* (Princeton, Princeton University Press, 1996), pp. 15–16, 213–14.

28 **rare and exotic** Leonard Dubkin, *The Natural History of a Yard* (Chicago: Henry Regnery, 1955), p. 6; see also Dubkin, *My Secret Places: One Man's Love Affair with Nature in the City* (New York: David McKay, 1972).

29 **even under threat** Toni Lyn Morelli *et al.*, 'Climate-change refugia: biodiversity in the slow lane', *Frontiers in Ecology and the Environment* 18.5 (2020), pp. 228–34.

Five: Sweeney's

1 **township of men** Alec Finlay, *Sweeney on Eigg* (Scottish Borders: Corbel Stone Press, 2014).

2 **million years ago** http://isleofeigg.org/enjoy-eigg/geology-archaeology/.

3 **that does the same** On the history of Bothy Project see https://www.bothyproject.com/about/ and https://www.bothyproject.com/programme/shelters/. For Khan's work see Lloyd Khan, *Home Work: Handbuilt Shelter* (Bolinas: Shelter Publications, 2004).

4 **North Cascades** John Suiter, *Poets on the Peaks: Gary Snyder, Philip Whalen & Jack Kerouac in the North Cascade* (Berkeley: Couterpoint, 2002); Edward Thomas, 'The Shieling' (1917).

5 **all to myself** Henry David Thoreau, *Walden, or, Life in the Woods* (Boston: Ticknor and Fields, 1854), pp. 141–2.

6 **modern psyche** Dan Richards, *Outpost: A Journey to the Wild Ends of the Earth* (Edinburgh: Canongate, 2019), Introduction.

7 **at the sea** Kathleen Jamie, 'Flight' (2014). https://www.bothyproject.com/blog/kathleen-jamie/

8 **went mad** Seamus Heaney, *Sweeney Astray: A Version from the Irish* – a version of the Irish poem *Buile Shuibhne* (London: Faber, 1983), Introduction.

9 **Donnan's cave** Heaney, *Sweeney Astray*.

10 **mad journey** Alec Finlay, 'Sweeney's Bothy, Bothan Shuibhne' (2013). https://alecfinlayblog.blogspot.com/2013_05_11_archive.html

11 **in a tree** On the design and building of Sweeney's, see also James Crawford, 'A View with a Room: Sweeney's Bothy, Eigg 2014', in Alexander McCall Smith, Alistair Moffat, James Crawford, James Robertson and Kathleen Jamie, *Who Built Scotland: A history of the nation in twenty-five buildings* (Edinburgh: Historic Environment Scotland), pp. 299–313.

12 **Ludwig Wittgenstein** https://www.fondazioneprada.org/project/machines-a-penser/?lang=en; see Finlay's essay in the publication that accompanied the exhibition: Alec Finlay, 'HUTOPIA', *Machines à penser*, ed. Dieter Roelstraete (Fondazione Prada, 2018), pp. 257–322.

13 **commanding library** For Calum Wallis's work see https://calumwallisart.com/

14 Kaddy Benyon: Self Directed Residency, 2016, https://www.bothyproject.com/blog/kaddy-benyon-island-of-the-big-women/

15 **great inner solitude** Rainer Maria Rilke, *Letters to a Young Poet*, (trans.) M. D. Herter Norton (Revised edition, New York:

Norton & Company, 1954; originally published in German in 1929), p. 45.

16 **from 2003** Entry from April 2003, Camasunary bothy book, March–October 2003, A. K. Bell Library, Perth, ACC13/43, Box 2.

17 **wood smoke** Entry for 3 August 1973, Maol-bhuidhe bothy book 1970–1973, A. K. Bell Library, Perth, ACC13/43, Box 2.

18 **sprawling illustrations** Visitor Book – Corrour Bothy, May 1996–September 1996, University of Dundee Archive RU 298/4/1/179.

19 **pen or pencil** Entry for 16–17 April, 1938, Visitor Books – Corrour Bothy, Cairngorms , 'Volume 7,' June 1937–August 1938, University of Dundee Archive RU 298/4/1/3.

20 **to be art** Rick Rubin, *The Creative Act: A Way of Being* (Edinburgh: Canongate, 2023).

21 **makes an appearance** Nicholas J. R. White, *Black Dots* (Another Place Press, 2018).

22 **inspiration here** Alice Strang, *Winifred Nicholson in Scotland* (National Galleries of Scotland: Edinburgh, 2003), p. 9.

23 **Bring my lover** Kathleen Raine, 'Love Spell' (1952).

24 **of the sea** Kathleen Raine, 'The Marriage of Psyche' (1952).

25 **hope to be wanted** Kathleen Raine, *Autobiographies* (Coracle Press, 2009) p. 319.

26 **Love Spell** Strang, Winifred Nicholson, pp. 36–7.

27 **fire soot** Strang, Winifred Nicholson, p. 23.

28 **bay off Laig** Strang, *Winifred Nicholson*, pp. 47–8, 51.

29 **of the blest** Strang, *Winifred Nicholson*, pp. 50, 56–7.

30 **to write** Quoted in Robert Macfarlane, *The Wild Places* (London: Granta, 2007), Chapter 3.

31 **duties and care** Strang, *Winifred Nicholson*, p. 56.

32 **insular conversation** *Oxford English Dictionary*, s.v. 'insular, adj., sense 4.a', September 2023. https://doi.org/10.1093/OED/2386810703; Samuel Johnson, *A Journey to the Western*

Islands of Scotland (1st edition, Glasgow: Richard Griffin & Co., 1775), p. 260.

33 **paid off** For the story of Eigg and the buyout, see Camille Dressler, *Eigg: The Story of an Island* (Edinburgh: Birlinn, 2014, new edition).

34 **its people** https://www.communitylandscotland.org.uk/

35 **in Cleadale** http://www.spanglefish.com/eigghistorysociety/index.asp?pageid=346760

36 **and tourism** Podcast 3 – 'A stag on the porch, a vole in the wall', Bothy Project, Neighbourhood Residency podcasts 2021, https://www.bothyproject.com/residencies/neighbourhood-2/

37 **like writing** Fliss Fraser talking about her time. See Sandra Dick,'Humble bothies help locals to make life-changing decisions', *Herald*, 2 December 2022. https://www.heraldscotland.com/news/23168984.humble-bothies-help-locals-make-life-changing-decisions/

38 **Queen of Moidart** 'HEBRIDES: H9. Papadil (Small Isles, Rùm)', Papar Project,http://www.paparproject.org.uk/hebrides9.html and https://kaddybenyon.com/2016/11/06/island-of-the-big-women/

39 **transform them** Rilke, *Letters to a Young Poet*, p. 69.

40 **has become!** Nan Shepherd, *The Living Mountain* (first published 1977, this edition Edinburgh: Canongate, 2014), p. 42.

Six: Maol-Buidhe

1 **meant to move** Torbjørn Ekelund,*In Praise of Paths:Walking Through Time and Nature* (Vancouver: Greystone Books, 202), 'The Beginning'.

2 **densities in Europe** 'Lochaber, Skye and Wester Ross: Key statistics, November 2019', *Highlands and Islands Enterprise* https://www.hie.co.uk/media/6368/lochaber-plusskyeplusandpluswesterplusrosspluskeyplusstatisticsplus2019-1.pdf

3 **feet and an active mind** Henry David Thoreau, 'Walking', in *The Natural History Essays* (Salt Lake City: Peregrine Smith Books, 1980), pp. 93–136; Rebecca Solnit, *Wanderlust: A History of Walking* (London: Granta, reprint 2022).

4 **Karakoram range** Sean Kelly, 'Out with the Boys & Girls again – KMC in the 70s', Karabiner Mountaineering Club, https://www.karabiner.org/articles/viewer.php?aid=3110; John Allen, 'In Memoriam: Brian Ripley, 1943-–1968', *Alpine Journal* (1969), pp. 393–4.

5 **RIP Whisky II** Entry for 20 February 1970, Maol-bhuidhe Bothy Book, 1970–73, A. K. Bell Library, Perth, ACC13/43, Box 2.

6 **Hinchliffe in 1983** Denis Brook and Phil Hinchcliffe, *North to the Cape: A Trek from Fort William to Cape Wrath* (Kendal: Cicerone Press, 1999).

7 **layers of legend** David Lintern, 'Scotland's thunder road: Seeking history and humanity on the trail to Cape Wrath', *National Geographic*, 6 September 2022. For a recent account of walking the trail, see Alex Roddie, *The Farthest Shore: Seeking solitude and nature on the Cape Wrath Trail in winter* (Sheffield: Vertebrate Publishing, 2021).

8 **bin Rashid Al Maktoum** https://www.aberdeenlive.news/news/scottish-news/billionaire-world-leader-who-owns-8697151

9 **she is fierce** William Shakespeare, *A Midsummer Night's Dream*, Act 3, Scene 2.

10 **countless hikers** Sir Hugh T. Munro, *Munro's Tables and Other Tales of Lower Hills*, revised and edited by Derek A. Bearhop (Scottish Mountaineering Trust, 1997).

11 **human mind** Robert Macfarlane, *Mountains of the Mind: A History of a Fascination* (London: Granta, 20th anniversary edition, 2023), p. 15.

12 **yet a world,/ Immensity** Nan Shepherd, 'Summit of Corrie Etchachan' from *In the Cairngorms* (Edinburgh: The Moray Press, 1934).

13 **cracks of the mountain** Nan Shepherd, *The Living Mountain* (first published 1977, this edition Edinburgh: Canongate, 2014) pp. 41–6. See also Kerri Andrews, *Wanderers: A History of Women Walking* (London: Reaktion Books, 2020), pp. 177–204.

14 **Hamish and co** Entry for 2 January 1974, Maol-bhuidhe Bothy Book, 1970–1973, A. K. Bell Library, Perth, ACC13/43, Box 2.

15 **transformation, and fulfilment** Solnit, *Wanderlust*, pp. 45–63.

16 **shieling sites** 'Case Study: Transhumance and Shielings', *ScARF National Framework*, https://scarf.scot/national/scarf-modern-panel-report/modern-case-studies/case-study-transhumance-and-shielings/

17 **harsher months** History of Maol-bhuidhe, information board consulted in situ in the bothy.

18 **hardship and hope** Peter Wessel Zapffe, 'The Road', translation Ceciel Verheij and Jan van Boeckel, *Open Air Philosophy*. https://openairphilosophy.org/the-road/. Original publication in Norwegian: Peter Wessel Zapffe, *Veien. Barske glæder og andre temaer fra et liv under åpen himmel* (1952).

19 **recover her skin** https://old.visitfaroeislands.com/en/be-inspired/in-depth-articles/legend-of-kopakonan-(seal-woman)/

20 **for employment** History of Maol-bhuidhe, information board consulted in situ in the bothy.

21 **from their homes** Georg Braun and Frans Hogenberg, *Civitates orbis terrarum*, 6 vols. (Cologne, 1575–1618); Joan Blaeu, *Atlas Maior*, 11 vols. (Amsterdam, 1662–1672).

22 **far from our homes** On Felix Fabri see Kathryne Beebe, *Pilgrim & Preacher: The Audiences and Observant Spirituality of Friar Felix Fabri* (1437/8–1502) (Oxford: Oxford University Press); Judith Schalansky, *Pocket Atlas of Remote Islands: Fifty Islands I Have Not Visited and Never Will*, (trans.) Christine Lo (London: Penguin, 2010).

23 **into inaccessible landscapes** https://www.pathsforall.org.uk/blog-post/alec-finlay-on-proxy-walks; Alec Finlay, *a far-off*

land, artwork, publication, for Macmillan Cancer Support (*Morning Star*, 2017). See also Alec Finlay, 'the poet limps in words as a balance for worlds', in Louise Kenward (ed.), *Moving Mountains: Writing Nature Through Illness and Disability* (London: Footnote Press, 2023).

24 **often told** See, for example, Paul Readman, 'Walking and Environmentalism in the Career of James Bryce: Mountaineer, Scholar, Statesman, 1838–1922', in Chad Bryant, Arthur Burns and Paul Readman (eds.), *Walking Histories, 1800–1914* (London: Palgrave Macmillan, 2016), pp. 287–318.

25 **legally protected right** https://hansard.parliament.uk/Commons/1884-10-29/debates/c5ff915a-588e-449b-934c-5606e55199cc/AccessToMountains(Scotland)Bill

26 **making it through** Robert A. Lambert, *Contested Mountains: Nature, Development and Environment in the Cairngorms Region of Scotland 1880–1980* (Cambridge: The White Horse Press, 2001), pp. 60–74; Ben Mayfield, 'Access to the countryside: the tragedy of the house of commons', Legal Studies 37.2 (2017), pp. 343–62.

27 **radical** Nick Hayes, *The Book of Trespass: Crossing the Lines that Divide Us* (London: Bloomsbury, 2020).

28 **across its land** Ruaridh Nicoll, 'Break down barriers to our right to roam', *Observer* 3 December 2006; Jamie Mann, 'Call for legal action against Scots estate wrongly restricting public access', *The National*, 19 September 2021.

29 **staying and going** https://www.lawscot.org.uk/members/journal/issues/vol-52-issue-05/access-or-excess/

30 **the sky** Entry for June 1930, Visitor Books – Corrour Bothy, Cairngorms, 'Volume 2', September 1929–April 1931, University of Dundee Archive RU 298/4/1/2; Gerald Gould, 'Wander-thirst' (1906).

31 **cut across it** Hartmut Rosa, *Social Acceleration: A New Theory of Modernity* (New York: Columbia University Press, 2015), p. 99.

Seven: Kearvaig

1 **Polish coast and Russia** Robert Macfarlane, *The Old Ways: A Journey on Foot* (London: Penguin, 2013), '5- Water - South'.

2 **English, *wroth*** Bronze and amber brooch, possibly eighth century, found at Loch Glashan, Scotland, https://collections.glasgowmuseums.com/mwebcgi/mweb?request=record;id=148587;type=101; 'Cape Wrath Wild Land Area', *NatureScot Description of Wild Land Area* (2015), p. 2.

3 **fall from grace** William Cronon, 'The Trouble with Wilderness: Or, Getting Back to the Wrong Nature', in *Uncommon Ground: Rethinking the Human Place in Nature* (London: W.W. Norton, 1995), pp. 69–91, On wilderness and philosophy see also John O'Neill, *Markets, Deliberation and Environment* (London: Routledge, 2007), Part 3: 'Bringing environmentalism in from the wilderness', pp. 115–44.

4 **wild land qualities** 'Cape Wrath Wild Land Area', *NatureScot,* p. 5.

5 **grassland and clifftops** Alex Boyd, 'Tir an Lairm/Land of the Military', https://portfolio-jvnijbz.format.com/tir-an-airm-land-of-the-army

6 **remain within the landscape** Peter Latz, 'Landschafts Park Duisburg-Nord: The metamorphosis of an industrial site', in Niall Kirkwood (ed.), *Manufactured Site Rethinking the Post-Industrial Landscape* (Abingdon: Taylor & Francis, 2001), pp. 150–61. See also Caitlin DeSilvey, 'A Positive Passivity: Entropy and ecology in the ruins', in Torgeir Rinke Bangstad and Þóra Pétursdóttir (eds.), *Heritage Ecologies* (Abingdon: Taylor & Francis, 2021).

7 **65 per cent since 2000** 'Cape Wrath SPA - Site Condition Monitoring of cliff nesting seabirds 2017', *Scottish Natural Heritage* Research Report No. 1064. For details on the SAC status: https://sac.jncc.gov.uk/site/UK0030108. Entry in Kearvaig bothy book for June 2023, consulted in situ.

8 **60 overnight** Tom Dunlop, 'HMS *Sutherland* conducts night firing at Cape Wrath range', UK Defence Journal, 16 October 2019, https://ukdefencejournal.org.uk/hms-sutherland-conducts-night-firing-at-cape-wrath-range/

9 **for the habitats** 'Cape Wrath SSSI/SAC – Site Condition Monitoring of coastal features 2015', Scottish Natural Heritage Research Report No. 1066.

10 **waste and wilderness** Peter Galison, 'Waste-Wilderness: A Conversation between Peter Galison and Smudge Studio', *Discard Studies*, 26 March 2016, https://discardstudies.com/2014/03/26/waste-wilderness-a-conversation-between-peter-galison-and-smudge-studio/. See also Rodney Harrison, 'Heritage as future-making practices', in Rodney Harrison, Caitlin DeSilvey, *et al.*, *Heritage Futures: Comparative Approaches to Natural and Cultural Heritage Practices* (London: UCL Press, 2020), pp. 20–50.

11 **vision for the future** DeSilvey, 'A Positive Passivity', p. 303.

12 **nineteenth century** 'Kearvaig', *Canmore*, https://canmore.org.uk/site/272934/kearvaig

13 **existed before** Tom Devine, *The Scottish Clearances: A History of the Dispossessed 1600 to 1900* (London:Allen Lane, 2018), pp. 226–31.

14 **Duke of Sutherland** See the notes from the Ordnance Survey name books: 'Sutherland OS Name Books, 1871–1875', Sutherland, volume 16 OS1/33/16/8. Available online at https://scotlandsplaces.gov.uk/digital-volumes/ordnance-survey-name-books/sutherland-os-name-books-1871-1875/sutherland-volume-16/8

15 **recent renovations** 'Kearvaig memories', MBA website, https://www.mountainbothies.org.uk/about-the-mba/archive/kearvaig-memories/

16 **ca. 1744** Alexander Bryce, *A Map of the North Coast of Britain, from Row Stoir of Assynt, to Wick in Caithness: By a*

Geometrical Survey with the Harbours, Rocks, & an Account of the Tides in the Pentland Firth, done at the Philosophical Society at Edinburgh / R. Cooper sculpt. (Edinburgh; s.n., 1744), National Library of Scotland. See online at https://maps.nls.uk/scotland/rec/168. On Bryce see Richard B. Sher, 'Bryce, Alexander (bap. 1713, d. 1786)', *Oxford Dictionary of National Biography* (2004). For the history of mapping see Alastair Mitchell, *The Immeasurable Wilds: Travellers to the Far North of Scotland, 1600–1900* (Dunbeath: Whittles Publishing, 2022).

17 **an end to this book** 'Strath-Navernia. Cathenesiae Nova Descriptio' and the maps 'Strath-navernia, Strath-navern / Auct. Timotheo Pont.; and 'Cathenesia / Auct. Timotheo Pont.', Blaeu Atlas of Scotland, 1654, Volume V of Joan Blaeu's *Atlas novus*, translations of Latin by Ian Cunningham (Amsterdam: Blaeu, 1654), pp. 117–21, National Library of Scotland. See online at https://maps.nls.uk/atlas/blaeu/browse/84 and https://maps.nls.uk/atlas/blaeu/browse/972

18 **vastness of the ocean** Timothy Pont, '[Eddrachilles; Northwest Sutherland; Loch Shin] - Pont 3 (front)' and '[Ben Hee to Faraid head, Northwest Sutherland] – Pont 3 (back)', [ca. 1583–96], National Library of Scotland Adv.MS.70.2.9 (Pont 3 and 3v). See online at https://maps.nls.uk/counties/rec/258 and https://maps.nls.uk/rec/259

19 **epiphany and violence** Seamus Heaney, 'North' published 1975 Faber & Faber.

20 **land can be found** Blaeu Atlas of Scotland, 1654, p. 120.

21 **avoid Cape Wrath** Bryce, *A Map of the North Coast*.

22 **not be saved** 'Margaret's Story', *Guardian*, 18 December 2002.

23 **sun and wind** Blaeu Atlas of Scotland, 1654, p. 120.

24 **Jon Krakauer's book** Jon Krakauer, *Into the Wild* (New York: Villard, 1996).

25 **lighted by burning men** 'The Want of Peace' by Wendell Berry from *New Collected Poems*. © Counterpoint Press, 2012.

26 **wild systems** Gary Snyder, 'The Etiquette of Freedom', in *The Practice of the Wild* (San Francisco: North Point Press, 1990), pp. 14–15.

27 **below on the earth** Blaeu Atlas of Scotland, 1654, p. 118. See the reference in Samuel Butler, *Hudibras* (published in three parts 1663, 1664 and 1678), Part II, Canto III, lines 894–99.

28 **was banished** Blaeu Atlas of Scotland, 1654, p. 118.

29 **wound down** See https://www.highlifehighland.com/north-coast-visitor-centre/museum/dounreay-exhibition/ and Linda M. Ross, 'Dounreay: Creating the Nuclear North', *Scottish Historical Review*, Volume C, 1: No. 252 (2021), pp. 82–108.

30 **a 'ghost-town'** Select Committee on Scottish Affairs Written Evidence, Appendix 9: Memorandum submitted by David R. Craig BSc MSc CChem MRSC, 13 January 2004, https://publications.parliament.uk/pa/cm200405/cmselect/cmscotaf/259/259we12.htm

31 **hadn't gone away** Ross, 'Dounreay', p. 101.

32 **dark ecology** Richard Misrach and Kate Orff, *Petrochemical America* (New York: Aperture Foundation, 2012); Timothy Morton, *Dark Ecology: For a Logic of Future Coexistence* (New York: Columbia UP, 2016).

33 **co-becoming** Morton, *Dark Ecology*, Chapter: 'Ending before the beginning'; Morton, *The Ecological Thought* (Cambridge MA: Harvard UP, 2010), pp. 16–17; https://www.darkecology.net/about

34 **crashing seas** Ross, 'Dounreay', p. 83.

Eight: Penrhos Isaf

1 **Theatr Clwyd** Matthew Knight, 'A golden introduction: Prehistoric gold in Britain's auriferous regions', National Museums Scotland blog, 9 May 2018, https://blog.nms.ac.uk/2018/05/09/a-golden-introduction-prehistoric-gold-in-britains-

auriferous-regions-2450-800-bc/; the Mold Gold Cape, British Museum, Museum number 1836,0902.1 https://www.britishmuseum.org/collection/object/H_1836-0902-1

2 **El Dorado in Wales?** Cuttings from the *Daily Mail*, 10 October 1930 and the *Evening Standard*, 9 October 1930, National Library of Wales Archive, O. P. Hughes Collection of Merionethshire Gold Mining Records, Folder 9.

3 **arched windows** https://cadw.gov.wales/visit/places-to-visit/cymer-abbey; William Wordsworth, 'Lines Composed a Few Miles above Tintern Abbey, On Revisiting the Banks of the Wye during a Tour' (13 July 1798).

4 **mine in Cwymstwyth** David Henry Williams, *The Welsh Cistercians: Written to Commemorate the Centenary of the Death of Stephen William Williams (1837–1899) (The Father of Cistercian Archaeology in Wales)* (Leominster: Gracewing, 2001), p. 269.

5 **name of reform** Allison Stielau, 'The Dolgellau Chalice and Paten', Object Narrative, in *Conversations: An Online Journal of the Center for the Study of Material and Visual Cultures of Religion* (2014), doi:10.22332/con.obj.2014.21

6 **wind and stone** Edward Thomas, 'The Shieling' (1916).

7 **have been discovered** Information taken from reports written by local MBA members, sent to the author. Tony Blackburn, 'Bothy Archives: Morris Evans and Pen Rhos Isaf' and 'Pen Rhos Isaf – a Welsh bothy history'.

8 **£4 million** Tom Scotson, 'Country plot is real little gold mine', *MailOnline* 23 September 2022, https://www.dailymail.co.uk/news/article-11242601/Welsh-forest-estate-river-ponds-sale-3-75million.html

9 **beneath the mountains** Arthur Talbot Vanderbilt, *Gold, Not Only in Wales but also in Great Britain and Ireland* (London: Swann Sonnenschein & Co., 1888), pp. 14–15.

10 **Mawddach** https://www.nationaltrust.org.uk/visit/wales/

dolaucothi/history-of-dolaucothi and John Glover, 'View of the river with mountains in the distance. Group of people panning for gold on the banks of the river'. Undated (1790s). Now in the National Museum Wales. See also Tim Colman, 'Gold in Britain: past, present and future', *British Geological Survey* (2010).

11 **galena (lead ore)** Arthur Dean, 'Notice respecting the Discovery of Gold Ores in Merioneth', *Report of the Fourteenth Meeting of the British Association for the Advancement of Science Held at York in September 1844* (London: John Murray, 1844), p, 54; Colman, 'Gold'.

12 **red gold** John Calvert, *The Gold Rocks of Great Britain and Ireland* (London: Chapman and Hall, 1853); Professor A. C. Ramsay, 'On the Geology of the Gold-Bearing District of Merionethshire, North Wales', *Quarterly Journal of the Geological Society* 10 (1854), pp. 242–7.

13 **in the world** Information taken from the boards around the Gwynfynydd gold-mine trails.

14 **venture ceased** For reports on the mid-century activity see 'Commissioners' report: The Gold Reef of Merioneth', Merioneth Gold Mining Inquiry, Folder sent to Professor Louis after the inquiry, 7–9 October 1930, O. P. Hughes Collection of Merionethshire Gold Mining Records, Folder 1; Ian Rutherford, *Welsh Gold: The story of Gwynfynydd Gold Mine* (Dolgellau: Gwynfynydd Gold Mine Ltd., 1993); Professor Henry Louis, *Report of Professor Henry Louis as to the possibilities of developing the production of gold and other minerals in Merionethshire* (London: H. M. Stationery Office, 1930) in National Library of Wales Archive, O. P. Hughes Collection of Merionethshire Gold Mining Records, Folder 6; 'Welsh gold', Clogau, https://www.clogau.co.uk/pages/history-of-welsh-gold

15 **unimaginable wealth** Norena Shopland, *The Welsh Gold King: The Life of William Pritchard Morgan* (Barnsley: Pen & Sword, 2022).

16 **mills or shafts** Tony Blackburn, 'Pen Rhos Isaf – a Welsh bothy history'.

17 **fitting birthday present** Entry for 25 to 27 October 1983, Penrhos Isaf bothy book 1982-1988, A. K. Bell Library, Perth, ACC13/43, Box 2.

18 **not compare** 'Royal Heritage',Clogau, https://www.clogau.co.uk/pages/royal-heritage.

19 **earth formed** 'The Geology of the Dolgellau Gold-Belt', *Geology Wales*,http://www.geologywales.co.uk/dgb/;University of Bristol. 'Where does all Earth's gold come from? Precious metals the result of meteorite bombardment, rock analysis finds.' *ScienceDaily*, 9 September 2011. www.sciencedaily.com/releases/2011/09/110907132044.htm.

20 **sun god** Molly H. Bassett, *The Fate of Earthly Things: Aztec Gods and God-Bodies* (Austin: University of Texas Press, 2015) p. 113; 'Materials of Work', *Aztec Art*, https://aztecart2017.ace.fordham.edu/exhibits/show/serpent-labret-with-articulate/materials.

21 **of its production** Val Plumwood, 'Shadow Places and the Politics of Dwelling', *Australian Humanities Review* 44 (2008), pp. 139–50.

22 **appalling conditions** For examples of the extensive literature on past and contemporary exploitation of land and people see Andrew Shaler, 'Indigenous peoples and the California gold rush: labour, violence and contention in the formation of a settler colonial state', *Postcolonial Studies* 23 (2020), Issue 1: New Directions in Settler Colonial Studies, pp. 79–98; Moitsadi Moeti, 'The Origins of Forced Labor in the Witwatersrand', *Phylon*, 47.4 (1986), pp. 276–84; Mauricio Angelo, 'Persistence of slave labor exposes lawlessness of Amazon gold mines', *Mongabay*, 4 March 2011. https://news.mongabay.com/2021/03/persistence-of-slave-labor-exposes-lawlessness-of-amazon-gold-mines/; Justin McCurry, 'Japan and South Korea in row

over mines that used forced labour', *The Guardian*, 19 February 2022. For an interesting account of the gold rush see Kathryn Taylor Morse, *The Nature of Gold: An Environmental History of the Klondike Gold Rush* (Washington: University of Washington Press, 2009).

23 **dead, eerie** 'Environmental Impacts of Gold Mining', *Earthworks*, https://earthworks.org/issues/environmental-impacts-of-gold-mining/; 'Stop mining for new gold, say Oxford researchers', *Smith School of Enterprise and Environment University of Oxford*, 20th December 2022, https://www.smithschool.ox.ac.uk/news/stop-mining-new-gold-say-oxford-researchers.

24 **countryside** 'Report of the Controller of the Department for the Development of Mineral Resources in the United Kingdom', presented to Parliament (London: H. M. Stationery Office, 1918), p. 5, in National Library of Wales Archive, O. P. Hughes Collection of Merionethshire Gold Mining Records, Folder 11.

25 **lost to the nation** Cutting from the *Cambrian Daily*, 7 November 1934, National Library of Wales Archive, O. P. Hughes Collection of Merionethshire Gold Mining Records, Folder 9; Kristof Haneca, Sjoerd van Daalen and Hans Beeckman, 'Timber for the trenches: a new perspective on archaeological wood from First World War trenches in Flanders Fields', *Antiquity* 92.366 (2018), pp. 1619–39; 'Merioneth Gold Mining Inquiry, October 7–9, 1930, Verbatim Report', p. 6, National Library of Wales Archive, O. P. Hughes Collection of Merionethshire Gold Mining Records, Folder 1.

26 **Alba Mineral Resources website** *Abandoned mines and the water environment* (Bristol: Environment Agency, 2008). For the Alba Minerals website, see albamineralresources.com/project/gwynfynydd-gold-mine-wales/

27 **with water** 'Report of the Controller of the Department for the Development of Mineral Resources', pp. 22, 41–2.

28 **non-coal operations** *Abandoned mines and the water environment*, p. 15.

29 **and flooding** Adam P. Jarvis and Paul L. Younger, 'Broadening the scope of mine water environmental impact assessment: a UK perspective', *Environmental Impact Assessment Review* 20.1 (2000), pp. 85-96. https://doi.org/10.1016/S0195-9255(99)00032-3

30 **our lives** *Metal Mine: Strategy for Wales, Environment Agency Wales* (2022). More generally on this, see Cal Flyn, *Islands of Abandonment: Life in the Post-Human Landscape* (London: William Collins, 2021).

31 **this at risk** See *Metal Mine: Strategy for Wales*. Lesley McFadyen, 'Dead Isle – Endangered heritage ecologies', online talk for Council of British Archaeology, April 2023. https://www.archaeologyuk.org/get-involved/events-and-activities/event-calendar/this-is-archaeology-dead-isle-endangered-heritage-ecologies.html

32 **abandonment** See, for example, https://www.obsidianurbexphotography.com/other/cavern-of-lost-souls-abandoned-car-cave-wales/

33 **in Llanfacreth** Blackburn, 'Pen Rhos Isaf – a Welsh bothy history'

34 **in Wales** 'An Introduction to Welsh Woodlands, woodland biodiversity and Ancient woodlands', *Coed Cymru, Welsh woodlands and timber*. https://coed.cymru/images/user/IAR%20Ancient%20Woodlands.pdf

35 **area that week** Entry for 20 April 1984, Penrhos Isaf bothy book 1982–1988, A. K. Bell Library, Perth, ACC13/43, Box 2.

36 **and Africa** 'Africa's Growing Graphite Mining Potential', S&P Global Market Intelligence, 26 December 2022. https://spglobal.com/marketintelligence/en/news-insights/research/africa-s-growing-graphite-mining-potential

37 **and silent skies** David Farrier, *Footprints: In Search of Future Fossils* (London: 4th Estate, 2020).

38 **we did before** https://www.trashfreetrails.org/

Nine: Peanmeanach

1 **both meaning point** Alan Macniven, *The Vikings in Islay: The Place of Names in Hebridean Settlement History* (Edinburgh: Birlinn, 2015).

2 **in the 1970s** Peter Stewart-Sandeman, *Ardnish – A Potted History*, p. 15. Available online at https://www.ardnish.org/ardnish-potted-history-v3-170119-final.pdf. See also Sandeman's Linked-In profile https://www.linkedin.com/in/peter-stewart-sandeman-07a6ab17/?originalSubdomain=uk

3 **coming by** John Clare, 'Trespass' (1836/37).

4 **spike in population soon subsided** *Ardnish – A Potted History*, p. 26.

5 **no children left to teach** Alison Campsie, 'The Highland bothy that tells the story of an abandoned place and its people', *Scotsman*, 4 April 2021. https://www.scotsman.com/heritage-and-retro/heritage/the-highland-bothy-that-tells-the-story-of-an-abandoned-place-and-its-people-3188402;James Crawford, 'Peanmeanach, Ardnish Peninsula', in *Wild History: Journeys into Lost Scotland* (Edinburgh: Birlinn, 2023), pp. 263–9.

6 **building on Ardnish** Entry for Peanmeanach, 'Correspondence relating to surveys and conditions of bothies, organised in alphabetical order, D-Z, 1965-1975', A. K. Bell Library, Perth, ACC13/43, Box 4.

7 **these islands' centre** David Gange, *The Frayed Atlantic Edge: A Historian's Journey from Shetland to the Channel* (London: William Collins, 2019), p. 293.

8 **back to 8000 BCE** Highland Historic Environment Record, https://her.highland.gov.uk/monument/MHG3987

9 **1,500 years ago** Canmore: National Record of the Historic Environment, https://canmore.org.uk/site/22509/eilean-nan-gobhar-sound-of-arisaig

10 **Norse system of land rents** *Ardnish - A Potted History*, pp. 9–10.

11 **property of a businessman** Rev. A. Macdonald, *The Clan Donald*, vol. 3 (Northern Counties Publishing Company, 1909), p. 277.

12 **MBA shelter** Entry for Peanmeanach, 'Correspondence relating to surveys', A. K. Bell Library, Perth, ACC13/43, Box 4.

13 **An Sgùrr** https://her.highland.gov.uk/monument/MHG17342

14 **could not be trusted** Entries for Grulin, 'Correspondence relating to surveys', A. K. Bell Library, Perth, ACC13/43, Box 4.

15 **1.7 million hectares** Severin Carrell, 'Report calls for reform of 'unhealthy' land ownership in Scotland', *Guardian*, 20 March 2019; see https://whoownsscotland.org.uk/media/uploads/docs/20230630_map.pdf

16 **code of responsibility** Bob Smith, 'Ardnish Estate to end free use of Peanmeanach bothy due to visitor numbers', 19 February 2020, *Grough: The Inside View of the Outdoor World*. Available online at https://www.grough.co.uk/magazine/2020/02/19/ardnish-estate-to-end-free-use-of-peanmeanach-bothy-due-to-visitor-numbers

17 **piled in for parties** Ellie Forbes and Kathleen Speirs, 'Scots bothy owners forced to lock up after surge in Covidiot partygoers trashing beauty spots', 1 April 2021, *Daily Record*. Available online at: https://www.dailyrecord.co.uk/news/scottish-news/scots-bothy-owners-forced-lock-23834847

18 **shut its doors** https://www.mountainbothies.org.uk/2021/03/an-cladach-bothy-no-longer-maintained-by-mba/

19 **fucked up dickhead** Entry for 2000, Tunskeen bothy book, 1999–2000, A. K. Bell Library, Perth, ACC13/43, Box 2.

20 **rubbish in the woods** Simon Robert Thompson, 'The

Fashioning of a New World: Youth Culture and the Origins of the Mass Outdoor Movement in Interwar Britain', unpublished DPhil thesis, King's College London (2018), p. 15.

21 **lived in towns** Access to Mountains Bill. House of Commons Debate 15 May 1908, vol. 188, cc.1439–1523. Order for Second Reading. Mr Trevelyan's comments, c. 1439.

22 **crowds round the Lakes** See, for example, Andrew Forgrave, '"Shocking" scenes on Snowdon as massive queues of walkers ignore Covid-19 curbs', 27 September 2020, *Daily Post*, https://www.dailypost.co.uk/news/local-news/shocking-scenes-snowdon-massive-queues-19005683

23 ***Financial Times* piece** Gemma Bowes, '10 of the coolest holiday rentals in Scotland', *Guardian*, 1 May 2021, https://www.theguardian.com/travel/2021/may/01/10-coolest-holiday-rentals-scotland-cabins-castles-bothies; Tom Robbins, 'In the Highlands, a lonely bothy begins a new life', *Financial Times*, 27 March 2022.

24 **responsibility for** Val Plumwood, 'Shadow Places and the Politics of Dwelling', *Australian Humanities Review* 44 (2008).

25 **cornets playing** Access to Mountains Bill, House of Commons Debate, 15 May 1908 vol 188, cc.1439–1523. Order for Second Reading. Mr Lane-Fox's comments, cc. 1452–3.

26 **woven into their lives** https://www.righttoroam.org.uk/

27 **who is land for** Andy Wightman, *The Poor Had No Lawyers: Who Owns Scotland (and How They Got It)* (Edinburgh: Birlinn, 2015, new edition).

28 **meadow to mines** John Gurney, *Brave community: The Digger Movement in the English Revolution* (Manchester: Manchester Unviersity Press, 2013), especially chapter 5. On land ownership see also Guy Shrubsole, 'Who Owns St George's Hill, Birthplace of the Diggers?', 10 September 2017, *Who Owns England*, https://whoownsengland.org/2017/09/10/who-owns-st-georges-hill-birth place-of-the-diggers/. For the Peasants' War see Peter Blickle, *The*

Revolution of 1525: The German Peasants' War from a New Perspective (Baltimore: John Hopkins University Press, 1985).

29 **large private estates** See, for example, Nick Hayes, *The Book of Trespass: Crossing the Lines that Divide Us* (London: Bloomsbury, 2020).

30 **only be degradation** Garrett Hardin, 'The Tragedy of the Commons', *Science* New Series, Vol. 162, No. 3859 (1968), pp. 1243–8.

31 **privatisation** Milton Friedman, *Capitalism and Freedom (40th Anniversary Edition)* (Chicago: University of Chicago Press, 2002).

32 **collective sustainability** Elinor Ostrom, *Governing the Commons: The Evolution of Institutions for Collective Action* (Cambridge: Cambridge University Press, 1990).

33 **more sustainable** Lynn Crowe and Paul Reid, 'The increasing commercialization of countryside recreation facilities: the case of Scottish mountain bothies', *Managing Leisure* 4.3 (1998), pp. 204–12.

34 **nested responsibility** Jay Walljasper, 'Elinor Ostrom's 8 Principles for Managing A Commons', 2 October 2011, *On the Commons*, https://www.onthecommons.org/magazine/elinor-ostroms-8-principles-managing-commmons

35 **operate in communities** Aldo Leopold, 'The Land Ethic', in *The Sand County Almanac* (Oxford: Oxford University Press, 1949).

Ten: Papa Westray

1 **cow bells** Harriet Lyon and Alexandra Walsham, 'Introduction: Early Modern Nostalgia: Memory, Temporality and Emotion', in Lyon and Walsham (eds.), *Nostalgia in the Early Modern World: Memory, Temporality, and Emotion* (Martelsham: Boydell & Brewer, 2022), pp. 1–2.

2 **past and present** Svetlana Boym, *The Future of Nostalgia* (New York: Basic Books, 2008).

3 **modernity post-1789** Peter Fritzsche, 'Specters of History: On Nostalgia, Exile, and Modernity', *American Historical Review,* 106.5 (2001), pp. 1587–618.

4 **sea routes** David Gange, *The Frayed Atlantic Edge: A Historian's Journey from Shetland to the Channel* (London: William Collins, 2019), pp. 116–17. See also Papar Project, http://www.paparproject.org.uk/hebrides9.html

5 **whole country** Jocelyn Rendall, *A Jar of Seed-Corn: Portrait of an Island Farm* (Orcadian Ltd., 2002), p. 4.

6 **around the world** Mure Dickie, 'Scientists look to seaweed-eating Scottish sheep to tackle climate change', *Financial Times*, 24 December 2021, https://www.ft.com/content/3df345ad-e14e-4f61-b3cb-d2db370f6af7; https://www.orkney.com/life/live/economy

7 **Shetland and beyond** 'ORKNEY: O2. Papa Westray', Papar Project, http://www.paparproject.org.uk/orkney2.html

8 **and tails** Willem Janszoon Blaeu and Joan Blaeu, *Orcadum et Schetlandiae Insularum accuratissima descriptio* (Amsterdam: Blaeu, 1654), National Library of Scotland. See online at https://maps.nls.uk/view/00000495

9 **family in 1967** Rendall, *A Jar of Seed-Corn*, pp. 8–15, 45, 85.

10 **church is visible** Murdoch MacKenzie, *North west coast of Orkney* (London: Printed for the Author, in the year MDCCL. [1750], National Library of Scotland. See online at https://maps.nls.uk/view/85449283

11 **few stools** Information board in the Bothy Museum, consulted in situ.

12 **the idea that images were timeless** John Berger, *Ways of Seeing* (London: BBC and Penguin Books, 1972), p. 18.

13 **modern world** Vanessa Ogle, 'Time, Temporality and the History of Capitalism', *Past & Present*, 243 (2019), pp. 312–27;

E. P. Thompson, 'Time, Work-Discipline, and Industrial Capitalism', *Past and Present*, 38 (1967), pp. 56–97.

14 **standing still** Entry for July 2022, Guirdil bothy book, consulted in situ.

15 **saving' time** Pierre Bourdieu, 'The attitude of the Algerian peasant toward time', in Julian Pitt-Rivers (ed.), *Mediterranean Countrymen: Essays in the Social Anthropology of the Mediterranean*, (Paris: Mouton & Co., 1963), pp. 55–72.

16 **prairies of America** Michael Bunce, 'Reproducing Rural Idylls', in Paul Cloke (ed.), *Country Visions* (Harlow: Pearson Educational Limited, 2003), pp. 14–30.

17 **eye is a myth** John Urry and Jonas Larsen, *The Tourist Gaze 3.0* (London: Sage Publications, 2011), p. 1.

18 **state of filth** Greg Dawson Allen, 'Bothy Ballads', *North East Folklore Archive*, http://www.nefa.net/archive/songmusicdance/bothy/index.htm#

19 **radical rupture** Bruno Latour, *We Have Never Been Modern* (Cambridge, MA: Harvard University Press, 1993), p. 48; Rachel Hunt, 'Huts, bothies and buildings out-of-doors: an exploration of the practice, heritage and culture of "out-dwellings" in rural Scotland', unpublished PhD thesis, University of Glasgow (2016), p. 193; Lynn Hunt, *Measuring Time, Making History* (Budapest: Central European University Press, 2008), p. 47.

20 **places of labour** Rebecca Smith, *Rural: The Lives of the Working-Class Countryside* (London: William Collins, 2023), pp. 4–5.

21 **fell into disuse** Keir Strickland, 'Landscapes of change: archaeologies of the Rousay Clearances', Talking Humanities | Oct 6, 2015 | Being Human festival, Features, Republished, https://talkinghumanities.blogs.sas.ac.uk/2015/10/06/landscapes-of-change-archaeologies-of-the-rousay-clearances/; Robert Oliphant Pringle, 'On the Agriculture of the Islands of Orkney', *Transactions of the Highland and Agricultural*

Society of Scotland, Fourth Series, Vol. VI (Edinburgh, 1874), pp. 35–39; Rendall, *A Jar of Seed-Corn*, pp. 25–31.

22 **calling sea birds** George Mackay Brown, *An Orkney Tapestry*, edited by Linden Bicket and Kirsteen McCue (Edinburgh: Birlinn, 2021; first published 1969).

23 **cows and sheep grazing on the grass** 'Papa Westray, Knap Of Howar', Canmore National Record of the Historic Environment, https://canmore.org.uk/site/2848/papa-westray-knap-of-howar

24 **in the age of turbo capitalism** Andreas Huyssen, 'Nostalgia for Ruins', *Grey Room* 23 (2006), p. 10.

25 **in hedgerows,** Fritzsche, 'Specters of History', p. 1611.

26 **enrage them the more** Reverend George Low, *Fauna Orcadensis: or, The Natural History of the Quadrupeds, Birds, Reptiles, and Fishes, of Orkney and Shetland* (Edinburgh: George Ramsay and Company, 1813), pp. 119–20.

27 **sea and sky** Rendall, *A Jar of Seed-Corn*, p. 25.

28 **oval patch** William Lewin, *The Birds of Great Britain, systematically arranged, accurately engraved, and painted from nature* (London: John Johnson, 1800), p. 46 and plate 223.

29 **on her nest** Jeremy Gaskell, *Who Killed the Great Auk?* (Oxford: Oxford University Press, 2000), pp. 11–12.

30 **mid 1840s** Low, Fauna Orcadensis, p. 107; Gaskell, *Who Killed the Great Auk?*

31 **unrepeatable and irreversible time** Boym, *The Future of Nostalgia*, p. 13.

32 **century BCE** See Ovid's version of the tale, Publius Ovidius Naso, *Metamorphoses* translated by Brookes (Boston, Cornhill Publishing Co. 1922); Stephen Moss, 'Weatherwatch: the "halcyon days" of December hark back to the kingfisher', *Guardian*, 12 December 2017. See the Seventh Idyll of Theocritus, https://www.theoi.com/Text/TheocritusIdylls2.html#7

33 **gone pastoral** Boym, *The Future of Nostalgia*, p. 136; Cal Flyn, *Islands of Abandonment: Life in the Post-Human Landscape* (London: William Collins, 2021).
34 **declining rapidly** Northern Ireland Priority Species https://www.habitas.org.uk/priority/species.asp?item=100022#
35 **fractures as irreversible** Glenn A. Albrecht, *Earth Emotions: New Words for a New World* (Ithaca and London: Cornell University Press, 2019); Paul Bogard (ed.), *Solastalgia: An Anthology of Emotion in a Disappearing World* (Charlottesville: University of Virginia Press, 2023).
36 **amid this fear** Malachy Tallack, 'What We Talk About When We Talk About Solastalgia', in Kathleen Jamie, *Antlers of Water: Writing on the Nature and Environment of Scotland* (Edinburgh: Canongate, 2021, paperback), pp. 143–55.
37 **human and non-human** Anna Lowenhaupt Tsing, *The Mushroom at the End of the World: On the Possibility of Life in Capitalist Ruins* (Princeton and Oxford: Princeton University Press, 2015), pp. 19–20.
38 **not reasonable** Albert Camus, *The Myth of Sisyphus and Other Essays*, translated by Justin O'Brien (New York: Vintage Books, 1991). Translation originally published by Alfred A. Knopf, 1955. Originally published in France as *Le Mythe de Sisyphe* by Librairie Gallimard, 1942.
39 **thing mourned** Judith Schalansky, *An Inventory of Losses*, translated by Jackie Smith (London: MacLehose Press, 2020).
40 **hills are rebuilt** Entry for 29 April 1985, Penrhos Isaf bothy book 1982–1988, A. K. Bell Library, Perth, ACC13/43, Box 2.

Eleven: Athnamulloch

1 **Dundreggan estate** 'The Trees for Life Caledonian Forest Story', Trees for Life https://treesforlife.org.uk/about-us/

narrative/; George Monbiot, *Feral: Rewilding the land, sea and human life* (London: Penguin, 2013), pp. 108–11.

2 **disappeared from the UK** Monbiot, *Feral*, p. 112; Roger Morgan-Grenville, *Across a Waking Land: A 1,000-Mile Walk Through a British Spring* (London: Icon Books, 2023), chapter 10: 'Forests and Farm Clusters'.

3 **contested pasts and futures** See for example: Johan T. du Toit, Nathalie Pettorelli, and Sarah M. Durant (eds.), *Rewilding* (Cambridge: Cambridge University Press, 2019); Paul Jepson and Cain Blythe, *Rewilding: The Radical New Science of Ecological Recovery: The Illustrated Edition* (Cambridge, Mass.; MIT Press, 2022), particularly chapter 7.

4 **women in London** Joanna Bourke, *Birkbeck: 200 Years of Radical Learning for Working People* (Oxford: Oxford University Press, 2022).

5 **to Morvich** See the Ordnance Survey, one-inch to the mile, Scotland, first edition, 1856-1891, Sheet 72 - Clunie, Surveyed: *ca.* 1871 to 1874, Published: 1880. Available online at https://maps.nls.uk/view/74490415

6 **shooting and stalking** Susan Swarbrick, 'Glen Affric: Ancient forests, elusive beasts and a fleeing prince', *Herald*, 26 July 2020. https://www.heraldscotland.com/news/18604873.glen-affric-ancient-forests-elusive-beasts-fleeing-prince/.

7 **volunteers and visits** 'The Trees for Life Caledonian Forest Story', Trees for Life, https://treesforlife.org.uk/about-us/narrative/. There is also debate about the extent of the pines in Caledonian Forest and what should be done. See Christopher Smout, 'The History and the Myth of Scots Pine', Scottish Forestry Trust, https://www.scottishforestrytrust.org.uk/userfiles/file/projects/p13-243%20inaugural%20rsfs%20annual%20lecture/scots%20pine.pdf

8 **10 per square km** 'Deer and People', John Muir Trust, 2

August 2021. https://www.johnmuirtrust.org/resources/943-deer-management-faq-july-2021#q13

9 **rare species** 'Dundreggan', Trees for Life, https://treesforlife.org.uk/dundreggan/

10 **some legends** 'Aspen mythology and folklore', Trees for Life, https://treesforlife.org.uk/into-the-forest/trees-plants-animals/trees/aspen/aspen-mythology-and-folklore/; Anne Elliott, 'Aspen in myth and culture', in Peter Cosgrove and Andy Amphlett (eds.), *The Biodiversity and Management of Aspen Woodlands: Proceedings of a one-day conference held in Kingussie, Scotland*, on 25th May 2001, pp. 81–4.

11 **landscapes of the past** Alan Watson Featherstone, 'The Trees for Life Aspen Project', in *The Biodiversity and Management of Aspen Woodlands*, pp. 69–73.

12 **scent and sound** Alec Finlay, 'I was a humandwolf', *MAP Magazine*, March 2019, https://mapmagazine.co.uk/i-was-a-humandwolf

13 **language and place names** Lee Raye, *The Atlas of Early Modern Wildlife: Britain and Ireland between the Middle Ages and the Industrial Revolution* (London: Pelagic Publishing, 2023), pp. 44–7.

14 **the wild** Monbiot, *Feral*, pp. 118–31; 'Wolf reintroduction & conservation', *Rewilding Britain*, https://www.rewildingbritain.org.uk/reintroductions-key-species/key-species/eurasian-wolf; Hannah Devlin, 'Britain is not ready for reintroduction of lynx and wolves, says Ray Mears', *Guardian*, 8 June 2023.

15 **back to the Highlands** 'Lynx to Scotland', *Trees for Life,* https://treesforlife.org.uk/about-us/lynx-to-scotland/

16 **wolves or lynx** Severin Carrell, 'Wildcats released in Scottish Highlands in effort to prevent extinction in UK', *Guardian*, 13 October 2023.

17 **part of the glen** John Alexander Harvie-Brown and Thomas E. Buckley, *A Fauna of the Moray Basin*, Volume 1 (Edinburgh: D. Douglas, 1895), pp. 162–3.

18 **symptom of a problem** Guy Shrubsole, 'Using bracken maps as a guide for regenerating rainforest', *Lost Rainforests of Britain*, 3 February 2022, https://lostrainforestsofbritain.org/2022/02/03/using-bracken-maps-as-a-guide-for-regenerating-rainforest/

19 **folk of the region** http://www.glenmoriston.org.uk/Glenmoriston/Miscellaneous/Places%20Of%20Interest/

20 **turned to dust** 'The Story of the Fiddlers of Tomnahurich' told by Ruairidh Maclean, *Map of Stories*. https://mapofstories.scot/the-story-of-the-fiddlers-of-tomnahurich-english/

21 **draconian measures** Tom Devine, 'The rise and fall of illicit whisky making in Northern Scotland, *c.* 1780–1840', *The Scottish Historical Review* 54 (158), pp. 155–77; Charles Maclean and Daniel MacCannell, (eds.) *Scotland's Secret History: The Illicit Distilling and Smuggling of Whisky* (Edinburgh: Birlinn, 2017).

22 **yellow arc** James Kirkwood, *This map of Scotland, constructed and engraved from the best authorities...* (Edinburgh: J. Kirkwood & Sons, and London: W. Faden, 1804), National Library of Scotland. See online at https://maps.nls.uk/view/74400666

23 **bootleggers** Highland Archive Centre Facebook post with images of L/INV/SC/42/15/12, https://www.facebook.com/highlandarchives/posts/1861704863957410/.

24 **isolated places** 'Case Study: Archaeologies of tax evasion – illicit whisky distilling' and 'Case Study: Transhumance and Shielings', *ScARF National Framework*, https://scarf.scot/national/scarf-modern-panel-report/modern-case-studies/case-study-archaeologies-of-tax-evasion-illicit-whisky-distilling/ and https://scarf.scot/national/scarf-modern-panel-report/modern-case-studies/case-study-transhumance-and-shielings/

25 **thirteenth centuries** AOC Archaeology Group, Appendix 7.1 Gazetteer for BHLARAIDH WIND FARM EXTENSION,

26 **site for burial** 'Corrimony', *Canmore*, https://canmore.org.uk/site/12256/corrimony

27 **still was set up** 'Prince Charlie's Cave, Ceannacroc, Glenmoriston', Am Baile – Highland History and Culture, https://www.ambaile.org.uk/asset/10605/

28 **wildlife and landscapes** Fraser MacDonald, 'Wild Beasts', *London Review of Books*, vol. 43, no. 18, 23 September 2021, https://www.lrb.co.uk/the-paper/v43/n18/fraser-macdonald/diary

29 **Tayvallich Initiative** https://www.highlandsrewilding.co.uk/blog/memorandum-of-understanding

30 **below ground** Alan Watson Featherstone, 'Fantastic fungi', Alan's Blog, Miscellaneous: 21 January 2017. https://alanwatsonfeatherstone.com/fantastic-fungi/

31 **domestication and order** Anna Tsing, 'Unruly Edges: Mushrooms as Companion Species: For Donna Haraway', *Environmental Humanities* (2012) 1 (1), pp. 141–54.

Twelve: Guirdil

1 **near the island** Edward Daniel Clarke, *The Life and Remains of Edward Daniel Clarke, LL D, Professor of Mineralogy*, by William Otter, 2 volumes, vol. I (George Cowie and Co.: London, 1825), p. 322.

2 **much higher** Kathryn Goodenough and Tom Bradwell, *Rum and the Small Isles: A Landscape Fashioned Geology* (Perth: Scottish Natural Heritage, 2004).

3 **isostatic uplift** Goodenough and Bradwell, *Rum and the Small Isles*, pp. 28–9.

4 **other bothies** 'Rum, Guirdil', Canmore, https://canmore.org.uk/site/11019/rum-guirdil

5 **forced off the island** https://coast.scot/stories/the-rum-clearances/

6 **uncertain date** 'Rum, Glen Shellesder', Canmore, https://canmore.org.uk/site/11001/rum-glen-shellesder

7 **settlement in Scotland** https://www.isleofrum.com/amazing-rum/isle-of-rum-timeline/

8 **offered us a landing place** Clarke, *The Life and Remains of Edward Daniel Clarke*, p. 321.

9 **natives term one of their villages** *Ibid.*, pp. 321–3.

10 **substitute for flint uplift** Goodenough and Bradwell, *Rum and the Small Isles*, p. 30.

11 **were submerged uplift** Ibid., p. 2.

12 **end of the century** Michael Oppenheimer *et al.*, 'Sea Level Rise and Implications for Low-Lying Islands, Coasts and Communities', in: Hans-Otto Pörtner, Debra C. Roberts *et al.* (eds.), *IPCC Special Report on the Ocean and Cryosphere in a Changing Climate* (Cambridge and New York: Cambridge University Press, 2019), pp. 321–445. https://doi.org/10.1017/9781009157964.006; G Durand *et al.*, 'Sea-Level Rise: From Global Perspectives to Local Service', *Frontiers in Marine Science* 8 (2021). https://doi: 10.3389/fmars.2021.709595

13 **waves at 1.5° C** https://picturing.climatecentral.org/location/55.8596311,-4.2898974

14 **a given** Damian Carrington, 'Rapid ice melt in west Antarctica now inevitable, research shows', *Guardian*, 23 October 2023.

15 **will be devastating** https://www.bas.ac.uk/data/our-data/publication/sea-level-rise-2/

16 **will be underwater** Lines (57° 59' N, 7° 16'W), https://niittyvirta.com/lines-57-59-n-7-16w/

17 **to these rises** Land Use Consultants (2011). 'An assessment of the impacts of climate change on Scottish landscapes and their contribution to quality of life: Phase 1 – Final report'. *Scottish Natural Heritage Commissioned Report* No. 488.

18 **for ever below tides** Robert Duck, *This Shrinking Land: Climate Change and Britain's Coasts* (Dundee: Dundee

University Press), pp. 14–18, 77–78; Jim Dwyer and Josh Haner, 'Saving Scotland's Heritage From the Rising Seas', *New York Times*, 25 September 2018. https://www.nytimes.com/interactive/2018/09/25/climate/scotland-orkney-islands-sea-level.html. See also Matthew Green, *Shadowlands: A Journey Through Lost Britain* (London: Faber, 2022).

19 **extinguishing its biodiversity** Natalie Hicks, Tim Brand and the MASTS community, 'Loch Etive MASTS Case Study Workshop Report', https://www.masts.ac.uk/media/36494/loch-etive-workshop-report_final-report.pdf

20 **winter of 1983–4** Mike Rivington and Mike Spencer, 'Snow Cover and Climate Change on Cairngorm Mountain: A report for the Cairngorms National Park Authority', *The James Hutton Institute* and *SURC*, 20 April 2020.

21 **blue drips from the heavens** Albrecht Dürer, 'Dream Vision', 1525. Watercolour on paper, 30 x 43 cm. Kunsthistorisches Museum, Vienna.

22 **on his face** Dennis Rixon, *The Small Isles: Canna, Rum, Eigg and Muck* (Edinburgh: Birlinn, 2011, reprinted from 2001), p. 22.

23 **calving earlier** https://rumdeer.bio.ed.ac.uk/

24 **to be seen** Thor Hanson, *Hurricane Lizards and Plastic Squid: The Fraught and Fascinating Biology of Climate Change* (London: Icon, 2021).

25 **underway on Rùm since 1958** NatureScot Rum NNR - Management Planning documents, 'The Story of Rum National Nature Reserve', https://www.nature.scot/doc/rum-nnr-management-planning-documents.

26 **wooded** 'Forest n.'. Dictionary of the Scots Language. 2004. Scottish Language Dictionaries Ltd. Accessed 19 Nov 2023. http://www.dsl.ac.uk/entry/snd/forest. For the name see 'HEBRIDES: H9. Papadil (Small Isles, Rùm)', Papar Project, http://www.paparproject.org.uk/hebrides9.html.

27 **medieval sporting preserve** Rixon, *The Small Isles*, p. 99–102.

28 **British Isles** https://map.lostrainforestsofbritain.org/

29 **fragile ecosystems** Emily Sanders, 'Machair landscapes threatened as sea levels rise', RSPB, 7 April 2014, https://community.rspb.org.uk/ourwork/b/climatechange/posts/machair-landscapes-threatened-as-sea-levels-rise

30 **the Rùm Cuillin** Goodenough and Bradwell, *Rum and the Small Isles*, p. 17.

31 **in the UK** On at-risk species in the UK, see Sophie Pavelle, *Forget Me Not: Finding the Forgotten Species of Climate-change Britain* (London: Bloomsbury, 2022). On the dormouse see: https://www.zsl.org/what-we-do/species/hazel-dormouse

32 **forms of life** Deborah Bird and Thom van Dooren (eds.), *Unloved Others: Death of the Disregarded in the Time of Extinctions* (Australian Humanities Review 50. Canberra: ANU E-Press, 2011).

33 **dismissal of spirituality** On Weber see Sung Ho Kim, 'Max Weber', *The Stanford Encyclopedia of Philosophy* (Winter 2022 Edition), Edward N Zalta & Uri Nodelman (eds.). https://plato.stanford.edu/archives/win2022/entries/weber/

34 **edges of the truth** Katherine Rundell, *The Golden Mole and Other Vanishing Treasure* (London: Faber, 2023, paperback).

35 **older generations** John Norton, 'Future Generations in Environmental Ethics', in Stephen M. Gardiner and Allen Thompson (eds.), *The Oxford Handbook of Environmental Ethics* (Oxford: Oxford University Press, 2017), pp. 344–54.

36 **world around us** Vincent Ialenti, *Deep Time Reckoning: How Future Thinking Can Help Earth Now* (Cambridge, Mass.: MIT Press, 2020).

37 **continued to rise** Reto Knutti, 'Closing the Knowledge-Action Gap in Climate Change', *One Earth* 1.1 (2019), pp. 21–3. https://doi.org/10.1016/j.oneear.2019.09.001

38 **Henry Shue put it** Henry Shue 'Climate Dreaming: Negative

Emissions, Risk Transfer, and Irreversibility', *Journal of Human Rights and Environment*. 8.2 (2017), pp. 203–16.

39 **natural capital** Dieter Helm, *Natural Capital: Valuing Our Planet*, (New Haven: Yale University Press, 2015).

40 **tit-for-tat exchange** Sian Sullivan and Mike Hannis, 'Nets and frames, losses and gains: Value struggles in engagements with biodiversity offsetting policy in England', *Ecosystem Services* 15 (2015), pp. 162–73.

41 **divide us now** Stylianos Syropoulos and Ezra Markowitz, 'Taking responsibility for future generations promotes personal action on climate change', LSE blog, 23 August 2021. https://blogs.lse.ac.uk/businessreview/2021/08/23/taking-responsibility-for-future-generations-promotes-personal-action-on-climate-change/

42 **roundabout or sideways** Ursula K. Le Guin, 'A Non-Euclidean View of California as a Cold Place to Be' (1982, Reprinted in the Spring 2010 issue of *Fifth Estate*), p. 19.

43 **knowledge and consciousness** Jacques Derrida, 'Hospitality, justice and responsibility. A dialogue with Jacques Derrida', in Richard Kearney, and Mark Dooley (eds.), *Questioning ethics: Contemporary debates in philosophy*, (London and New York: Routledge, 1999), pp. 65–83.

44 **if you like** Þóra Pétursdóttir and Tim Flohr Sørensen, 'Archaeological encounters: Ethics and aesthetics under the mark of the Anthropocene', *Archaeological Dialogues* 30.1 (2023), pp. 50–67.

45 **planning on coming back** Entries for 17 August 2022.

46 **where people can live** Le Guin, 'Non-Euclidean View', p. 19.

47 **and returns** Adam Zagajewski, 'Try to Praise the Mutilated World' (2002).

48 **go light** Gary Snyder, 'For the Children' (1969); Entry for 8–9 May 1985, Penrhos Isaf bothy book 1982–1988, A. K. Bell Library, Perth, ACC13/43, Box 2.